Studies in Economic Ethics and Philosophy

Series Editor
Peter Koslowski

Editorial Board
F. Neil Brady
James M. Buchanan
Richard De George
Jon Elster
Amitai Etzioni
Gérard Gäfgen
Serge-Christophe Kolm
Michael S. McPherson
Yuichi Shionoya
Philippe Van Parijs

Springer

Berlin
Heidelberg
New York
Barcelona
Hong Kong
London
Milan
Paris
Singapore
Tokyo

Peter Koslowski (Ed.)

Contemporary Economic Ethics and Business Ethics

With 14 Figures
and 1 Table

 Springer

174.4
C761

Prof. Dr. Dr. h.c. Peter Koslowski
Centre for Ethical Economy and Business Culture
The Hannover Institute of Philosophical Research
Gerberstr. 26
D-30169 Hannover
Germany
E-mail: P. Koslowski@fiph.uni-hannover.de

Cau

Printed with the support of the Fritz Thyssen Stiftung Köln

ISBN 3-540-66665-6 Springer-Verlag Berlin Heidelberg New York

Cataloging-in-Publication Data applied for
Die Deutsche Bibliothek – CIP-Einheitsaufnahme
Contemporary economic ethics and business ethics / Peter Koslowski (ed.). – Berlin; Heidelberg; New York; Barcelona; Hong Kong; London; Milan; Paris; Singapore; Tokyo: Springer, 2000
  (Studies in economic ethics and philosophy)
  ISBN 3-540-66665-6

This work is subject to copyright. All rights are reserved, whether the whole or part of the material is concerned, specifically the rights of translation, reprinting, reuse of illustrations, recitation, broadcasting, reproduction on microfilm or in any other way, and storage in data banks. Duplication of this publication or parts thereof is permitted only under the provisions of the German Copyright Law of September 9, 1965, in its current version, and permission for use must always be obtained from Springer-Verlag. Violations are liable for prosecution under the German Copyright Law.

© Springer-Verlag Berlin · Heidelberg 2000
Printed in Germany

The use of general descriptive names, registered names, trademarks, etc. in this publication does not imply, even in the absence of a specific statement, that such names are exempt from the relevant protective laws and regulations and therefore free for general use.

Hardcover Design: Erich Kirchner, Heidelberg

SPIN 10724761   42/2202-5 4 3 2 1 0 – Printed on acid-free paper

Preface

In the discussion on economic ethics and business ethics, the Continental European scholars have mainly looked to the American approaches for inspiration. This volume attempts to introduce the German and European approaches to economic ethics and business ethics to the English-speaking scholars. The collection of original essays in this book demonstrates that the approaches to economic ethics and business ethics in Continental Europe and those in America differ considerably but that they also share the interest in turning business ethics into a subject relevant and useful for business practice as well as for the philosophical debate on ethics.

The volume at hand publishes the proceedings of the conference "Historism as a Challenge to Economic Ethics and Philosophy", held at Marienrode near Hannover, Germany, on 2-4 November 1997. The conference formed Section II of Part C of the conferences "Economics and Ethics in the Historical School. Achievements and Present Relevance" organized by the Centre for Ethical Economy and Business Culture - Centrum für Ethische Ökonomie und Wirtschaftskultur, The Hannover Institute of Philosophical Research - Forschungsinstitut für Philosophie Hannover, Hannover, Germany, with the support of the Fritz Thyssen Stiftung Köln, Germany.

A special word of gratitude is due the Fritz Thyssen Stiftung whose financial support made this conference possible.

Hannover, October 1999   Peter Koslowski

University Libraries
Carnegie Mellon University
Pittsburgh PA 15213-3890

Contents

CONTENTS

Chapter 4

Chapter 5

Part B

Business Ethics

Chapter 6

Chapter 7

Chapter 8

CONTENTS

Chapter 9

Chapter 10

Chapter 11

Part A

Ethics and Economic Ethics

Chapter 1

The Theory of Ethical Economy
as a Cultural, Ethical, and Historical Economics:
Economic Ethics and the Historist Challenge

PETER KOSLOWSKI

I.   Economics as a Cultural Science and as Understanding Sociology
II.   Economics as a Historical Science
III.   The A Priori Character of the Rationality Principle
IV.   Beyond A Priori Rationality

The merger of two disciplines always implies that the synergetic effect works both ways. Both disciplines take over concepts of the other discipline and gain by the merger of their own concepts with those concepts they take over from the other side. In the case of the merger of ethics and economics the same process is effective. Ethical economy implies as well the use of ethical concepts in economic analysis as the use of economic tools or economic concepts in philosophical ethics. The second interdisciplinary transfer from economics into ethical theory has not attracted so much scholarly attention yet although there are still many synergetic effects to be won in this transfer. It will however not be in the centre of this paper.

The approach of ethical economy is an economic theory of ethics as well as an ethical theory of economics.[1] It is not only an ethical theory of economics, but it will have also effects on an economic theory of ethics. By these synergetic effects of economics on ethical theory is not meant that ethics can be reduced to economics, a position taken by some scholars. Karl

---

1   Cf. PETER KOSLOWSKI: *Prinzipien der Ethischen Ökonomie*, Tübingen (Mohr Siebeck) 2nd edition 1994.

Homann, e. g., seems to assume that economics becomes a kind of a super-theory of action that also takes over ethics completely.[2]

In the following paper, the ethical theory of the economy, of business ethics in the normative sense and the ethical analysis of economic action in the positive sense will be investigated. Ethical economy, or the ethical analysis of economics, has a twofold meaning and direction, a normative and a positive one, the normative direction of the theory of business ethics on the one hand and the positive or hermeneutical side of an analysis and understanding interpretation of the culture and the spirit of the economy. The spirit of the economy is here taken in the Hegelian sense of the objective self-description and institutional self-definition of the economic institutions.

Since historism is first a theory of the culture and objective spirit of a society and of a historical epoch it can serve as an essential supplier of analytical tools and concepts for the positive cultural analysis of the economy, for a positive theory of ethical economy as the analysis of the given ethos and culture of an economy before any questions of normative ethics are considered.

I. Economics as a Cultural Science and as Understanding Sociology

Ludwig von Mises as one of the main thinkers of the Austrian School and Alfred Schütz, one of the main proponents of *Verstehende Soziologie*, understanding sociology, have called economics the most developed branch of understanding sociology.[3] For them, economics is the most advanced branch of the understanding sociology. It is the principle of understanding

---

2 Cf. KARL HOMANN, FRANZ BLOME-DREES: *Wirtschafts- und Unternehmens-ethik*, Göttingen (Vandenhoeck & Ruprecht) 1992.

3 L. VON MISES: "Soziologie und Geschichte. Epilog zum Mehodenstreit in der Nationalökonomie", *Archiv für Sozialwissenschaften und Sozialpolitik*, 61 (1929), pp. 465-512, and A. SCHÜTZ: *Der sinnhafte Aufbau der sozialen Welt. Eine Einleitung in die verstehende Soziologie* (1932), Frankfurt am Main (Suhrkamp) 1971, pp. 342ff.

sociology to understand actions by the subsumption of a subjective context of purpose and meaning under an objective context of meaning and purpose.[4]

One of the central objective contexts of meaning in modern societies is the objective context of meaning formed by the economy. The definition of the social context of meaning and the definitions of the situations of choice and behaviour and of the behavioural expectations or role expectations are much better defined and more precise in the economy than in other systems or spheres of culture. The role expectations of the entrepreneurs and the consumers concerning the rationality of their behaviour in the system of culture of the economy are very well defined. Finding out about the success of behaviour and actions in this sphere of culture is easier than in other systems of culture since the economic calculation of the prices is better defined than other measures of success within institutions in the other spheres of culture.

Since it is rational to presuppose that in economic action economic and locally maximising rationality determines the pursuit of goals by the individuals, the pursuit of goals can be understood more easily and more univocally in the economy than other social action or other action in the other systems of culture of society. The thesis that economics is the most advanced branch of understanding sociology is justified by the fact that the understanding social science of the most calculable sphere of culture or subsystem of society, the economy, is also the most calculable and most univocal part of the social sciences. We can understand rational, economically self-interested action best of all kinds of action – better than for example action that is more diffuse in its rationality and its means-ends-relationships and that is directed not on by formal rationality and economic calculation according to market success but aims at the realisation of cultural and material goals, material here in the sense of Max Weber's and Max Scheler's theory of value rationality as opposed to *Zweckrationalität*.

It is obvious that the understanding of human action cannot be restricted to the understanding of economic motives and strategies of profit and utility maximisation although we would like it to be that way. Since economic goals and the actions stemming from the pursuit of these goals and motives are the easiest to understand the social sciences would like all human motives to be as easily understood as them. If we want to understand human

---

4   Cf. SCHÜTZ, *ibid.*, p. 340.

action more deeply we must, however, also understand the other goals and contexts of meaning that determine human action. We must understand determinants like the moral and cultural ones.

The difference between Neo-classical and Austrian economics on the one hand and Historist and cultural economics on the other hand is the difference in the scope of motives, the degree to which they include the extra-economic determinants within economic analysis. The Historical School of economics views economics not only as a logic of choice between means for given ends but also as an analysis to the ends and as a theory of the interdependence of ends and means.

Schmoller gives an instructive example for the extension of economic analysis into the explanation of those factors which Neo-classical and Austrian economics take for given, namely the formation of preferences and the elasticities of demand. He describes that the reactions to increases in the price of sugar were different in England and in Germany at his time. Whereas in England an increase in price leads to a drop of demand, in Germany this not does happen. Economics according to Schmoller has the task to explain and understand the different reactions to these fluctuations of prices. It has to give an explanation for the differences of price elasticities of demand. It can not take them as given.[5]

In contrast, Ludwig von Mises, the proponent of the Austrian School states that price elasticities are given. They are historical data, historical facts that are not to be further questioned and explained by economics. The economist must take the elasticities of demand as historical data.

II. Economics as a Historical Science

This example demonstrates the difference between the Historical School and the Neo-classical and Austrian School of economics. Neo-classical economics takes as data the features of the economy that have arisen historically - the institutional framework, the general attitudes and customs of

---

5 Cf. for Schmoller P. KOSLOWSKI: "Ethical Economy as Synthesis of Economic and Ethical Theory", in: P. KOSLOWSKI (Ed.): *Ethics in Economics, Business, and Economic Policy*, Berlin, Heidelberg, New York (Springer) 1992, pp. 15-56 (= Studies in Economic Ethics and Philosophy, Vol. 1).

the consumers and the goals of economic actions. It confines itself to the logic of rational choice for the maximisation of profit or utility under the given historical circumstances.

The Historical School that discovered institutionalism, on the other hand, takes the institutional framework and the culture and ethics of the economy as historically formed and as culturally formable, as a variable that has to be explained by cultural analysis and cultural reasons.

The difference between the Austrian and the Historical School can be traced to the historical situation in which they were developed, not so much to political differences but to the historical situation. The Historical School intended economics and the human sciences not only to be a tool to realise rationality under a given cultural framework. Rather it thought economics to have the task to support the creation of an economic culture that furthers economic and social progress, the wealth of a nation and its social policy. For this reasons it supported the creation of a single market in 19th century Germany whereas the Austrian School being in a supra-national state did not consider it to be the task of economics to secure economic progress within the nation state.

It was intentional that, in the Historical School, the culture forming the environment of the economy was not taken as given but as a variable that should become also the object of economic policy as cultural policy. This is evident in the main theoretical work on the theory of the human sciences and, so to say, critique of historical reason in Wilhelm Dilthey's *Introduction into the Study of Society and History*. Dilthey demands interestingly enough and in contrast to the present hermeneutical theory that seems to have lost this perspective on economics that it is not only the task of the human sciences to understand cultures, to enter by empathy (*Einfühlung*) into different cultures, but that the human sciences also have the task to shape culture, to render culture the object of politics and policy. The human sciences are at the same time a theory of culture and a theory of cultural policy. Dilthey explicitly acclaims Schmoller's attempt to merge the endeavours of the cultural sciences and those of the economic sciences. This merger is the scholarly achievement of Schmoller's approach. It is also clear that the development of the human sciences (*Geisteswissenschaften*) and of the historical, ethical and cultural approach to economics is closely connected.

The Historical School is a theory of economics that aims at a more extensive control of the economy and of economic development than the Aus-

7

trian and Neo-classical theory of economics because it aims also at a theory and politics of culture and of the ethics of the economy. It attempts to render the cultural habits and the ethical beliefs and norms to be able of being shaped by discourse and reflection. It is a very modern concept of the Historical School that it renders something controllable that hitherto had been considered as given.

The Historical School aims as a cultural foundation of economic policy, it aims at the cultural presuppositions of economic policy and of the policy of the economic order (*Ordnungspolitik*). One can see the influence of this idea of the cultural foundations of the economic order in the theory of the social market economy of Alfred Müller-Armarck[6] and Ludwig Erhard, particularly in Erhard's idea of a *formierte Gesellschaft*, an integrated society where the theory of the economic order and economic policy is in harmony with its culture and its cultural policy, social policy and other fields of policy.

On the other hand, the Austrian and Neo-classical theories of economics take the cultural and historical "environment" as given. This cultural environment is not the object of economic science. It is not a clear and easy task to translate these differences in economic theory into political categories. The Austrian School is in some sense much more conservative than the Historical School, because it takes the whole cultural and social framework as given. After the dominant presentation of this debate between the Austrian and the Historical School in economics since the 1950es and due to Hayek's influence to many economists it seems the other way around. The Austrian School apppears to be liberal and the Historical School to be reactionary. This qualification does not correspond to the actual situation in the 19th century. The Historical School supported the German economic unification under Prussian leadership in contrast to the Austrian School that did not share the emphasis on the national single market. One may dislike Prussia, but it is a matter of fact that Prussia was rather the revolutionary power

---

6   Cf. P. KOSLOWSKI: "The Social Market Economy: Social Equilibrium of Capitalism and Consideration of the Totality of the Economic Order. Notes on Müller-Armack", in: P. KOSLOWSKI (Ed.): *The Social Market Economy. Theory and Ethics of the Economic Order*, Berlin, Heidelberg, New York (Springer) 1998, pp. 73-95 (= Studies in Economic Ethics and Philosophy, Vol. 17).

disturbing the whole order in Europe. One cannot qualify it as conservative in the sense of traditionalist.

III. The A Priori Character of the Rationality Principle

Mises and the Austrian School have succeeded in excluding all cultural and ethical determinants of economic actions from economics by equating human action with rational action. It is a very interesting move by Mises to define human action as a priori and always rational. Where human action appears to be irrational it does so only since we do not know or understand from outside the goals for which the person acting "irrationally" chooses his or her means.

Mises's apriorism follows from the insight that economic laws are laws of choice and action and not laws of motion and reaction. The economy principle is a law that determines the logic of the human's preference of one course of action to another. It is not a law which describes the effects that external events have on human behaviour and make it react to their stimuli. Just the same way as the rules of the logical syllogism determine the way theoretical conclusions are drawn the economic laws of rationality determine the rules of the practical syllogism. They determine the conclusions to be drawn from the perception of the ends-means-situation. When the premises of the practical syllogism, of the end and of the means that are available, are formulated, the economy principle demands that as a conclusion from these premises the maximum-minimum-solution be chosen. It is to be emphasised that the solution of the rational act is chosen and not determined by the reality outside of the actor.

The economy principle is an a priori principle of the logic of choice and action in the sense that all conscious acts of choice must follow the economy principle just as all acts of thinking must follow the logical principle of non-contradiction. Both principles, the economy principle and the principle of non-contradiction are, however, not always realised in human decisions and acts of thinking. Neither complete economising nor strict logical drawing of conclusions is realised in all human actions and thoughts.

Mises is right in his emphasis on the mental and a priori nature of the economy principle. He is, however, mistaken in his equation on human action with completely rational or economising action. Mises contends:

9

PETER KOSLOWSKI

"Human action is necessarily and always rational. The term 'rational action' is therefore pleonastic and must be rejected as such."[7] Not in every
action, however, the full extend of rationality is realised although there is
no action that does not at least partially follow the economy principle. It is
likely that Mises considered it to be necessary to equate action and rational
action in order to avoid the possible objection that the economy principle
can not be a priori since it is not applicable and not true for all actions.

The experience that acting persons do not always follow the rationality
principle is not a refutation of the general and a priori validity of this principle. Popper makes the objection against the a priori character of the economy principle that the rationality principle is not an empirically or psycho-
logically testable proposition since it always refers to the situations and
objectives as they are perceived by the acting person.[8] But we as outsiders
of a person's mind are not able to recognise from the outside how an agent
has perceived his or her situation of decision-making since we are not able
to take over his view of the situation completely. The rationality principle is
not empirically testable. But it is according to Popper not an a priori principle either, since it is not always applicable. People do not always behave
rational. Popper concludes from this observations that an a priori principle
that is not always true is either wrong or not a priori. The rationality principle is therefore, Popper contends, an indispensable principle but a principle of very weak content. It includes just a minimum principle. We adapt
our action to the situations, as we subjectively perceive them.

Two objections must be raised against this critique. First the rationality-
principle is not refutable by an external observer. It is not decidable from
the outside whether an agent has acted rationally, since the rationality principle in its weak form is not able of being falsified. The acting person might
always have had good reasons to act like he or she did. The rationality
principle can therefore be true a priori but we cannot be certain about its
universal and a priori validity. Secondly, it is not necessary that an a priori
principle is always completely fulfilled. Popper's definition of apriority as
strict necessity is not convincing. Not all a priori principles are always

---

7   L. VON MISES: *Human Action. A Treatise on Economics*, New Haven (Yale
    University Press) 1949, p. 18.
8   K. POPPER: "La rationalité et le statut du principe de rationalité", in: J. RUEFF,
    E. M. CLAASSEN (Eds.): *Les fondements philosophiques des systèmes écono-
    miques*, Paris (Payot) 1967, pp. 142-150.

10

adhered to, even the rules of logic are not always followed although they are valid and do not loose their a priori character by the fact that human do not always adhere to them. As Wittgenstein says: "That logic is a priori stems from the fact that nothing *can* be thought illogically."[9] From this proposition of Wittgenstein it does not follow however that everything is always thought logically. Nothing can be thought without logic and not everything is thought logically. It is impossible to act without rationality but not all causes of action are rational.

Since logic and rationality are not discrete but continuous qualities the a priori character of the logic of thinking and of the logic of action is not refuted by the fact that there are degrees of logic and of rationality in thinking and in actin. The fact that people do not always act rationally does not yield the conclusion that the economy principle is not a priori valid for conscious decisions and actions. Especially it is not intelligible to an external observer how the situation of decision had been perceived by the agent ex ante. How had the agent's decision calculus been adapted to the situation as perceived by him? How had the relationship between means, ends, and effects been anticipated by him? Since there exist degrees of being logic there are also degrees of rationality. Lesser degrees of logic in the individuals' thinking are not to be considered as a refutation of the validity of logic. To quote again Wittgenstein: "One did have a rough idea that there must be a law of least action before one knew, what its exact content was. Here as always the a priori certain turns out to be something nearly logical."[10] Just as logical rules of thinking do not guarantee the drawing of correct conclusions the a priori character of the rationality principle in decision-making does not guarantee the rationality of decisions and actions. "The logical rules like the rationality principle demonstrate how little is reached by the fact that the problems are solved".[11]

---

9   L. WITTGENSTEIN: *Tractatus logico-philosophicus* (1921), Frankfurt am Main (Suhrkamp) 14th edition 1979, p. 76, proposition 5.473.

10 *Ibid.*, p. 105, proposition 6. 3211.

11 *Ibid.*, Preface.

IV. Beyond A Priori Rationality

The formal and a priori character of logic and of the rationality principle make sure that the true problems start, where the formal ones are solved. That the true problems start where the formal ones are solved describes the situation in which the discussion of economic ethics and of economics in general finds itself. Economic theory cannot restrict itself to solve the formal problems of choice only. It must also give a theory of the genesis of the culture of the economy in which the rational choices are made. To give an example: the habits and culture of sugar consumption cannot only be parameters for the entrepreneur who wants to invest in sugar, since he wants to know what causes these parameters to be as they are. He wants them to become variables of an economic explanation. The economist can say that sugar is a superior good in Germany but not in England. This is a further description of what has been described empirically before. What it is that makes sugar a superior good in 19th century Germany is not explained by saying that it is a superior good.

Economics must strive to find out more about the sociology of consumption, about what causes sugar to be a superior good in Germany but not in England, which classes of consumers demand sugar, which cultural values, which history of sugar consumption and so on, determine the differences of elasticities of demand for it. Since society and culture are historical, a cultural analysis always implies also a historical analysis. That is the reason why the Historical School has put so much emphasis on historical studies. It was not because they were historians but because they were convinced that the cultural determinants can only be understood, when they are understood as historically shaped determinants.

This is also the reason for the historical orientation of German education in the 19th century. Wilhelm von Humboldt said that the military personal must study former wars and strategies as a case-study for future tasks. History was considered to be the case-study for present problems or for learning and practising the solution of case-study problems. Going back in history is not a waste of time. One can also argue that the historical case-study method has clear advantages over the American case-study method. When you study historical cases you are forced to do a very important operation of intellectual transfer. The study of the historical case you study is necessarily transferred to present cases, a transfer that is not induced to the same extent in the study of a case of the present age. When one studies a present case one is not forced to make the transfer. The student might be tempted to think all cases are like the case studied. The main problem for the case-study method is not only to solve the present case but also to enable the student to make the transfer from the case studied in the classroom to the other cases that are different from the one made in the class room.

Culture and society are of historical nature. History is most historical in society, more so then in nature. It is very often overlooked that nature also has a history. Present biological science emphasises even more than Darwin did that there is also a history of nature and that this changes the status of Darwinism as a purely analytic theory.

Ethical economy in the sense of a positive and cultural analysis develops the theory of an understanding economics (*Verstehende Wirtschaftswissenschaft*) that aims at understanding the economic culture and develops methods for doing so. The main method of understanding is the hermeneutical one developed by Dilthey, Bollnow, Spranger and also by Gadamer[12]. In the new interest in Gadamer's contribution, it is somehow overlooked how much he stand in the tradition of the Historical School of the human and social sciences, particularly of Dilthey and Spranger. Dilthey and Spranger are closer to the social sciences and to economics than most of today's hermeneutics, which concentrates too much on the hermeneutics of texts. For the older theory of the human sciences texts are only one object to be analysed by the cultural sciences.

The method of understanding follows the circle of cultural expression. This circle of cultural expression is described by the sequence of an experiencing of a cultural context (*Erleben, Erlebnis*) by an author, by expressing this experiences in a symbolic medium by the author, and by the reception of an author's expression by a recipient. The recipient tries to understand this expression of an experience and thus closes the circle of understanding

---

12 In Gadamer there is however a reduction of the *Geisteswissenschaften* to a hermeneutics of text that is not characteristic for the older tradition of the *Geisteswissenschaften* that is more orientated towards the unity of the social, cultural, and human sciences.

between the first experiencing by the author and the re-experiencing by the recipient.[13]

Ethical economy as a cultural theory of the economy does not face a problem of relativism since a culture is always relative to others, to time, place and to other cultures. An absolute culture or the idea of an absolute culture is impossible and where a culture claims to exist as an absolute culture one can be sure that nationalism or fundamentalism is present. Culture is always necessarily relative to the spirit of a time (*Zeitgeist*) and to a population - be it a nation or a supranational entity. In the 19th century, the idea of the *Volksgeist* referred to the nation. Today it might be more the spirit of certain groups of nations.

It is the task of economics as an ethical and cultural theory to understand the style and objective spirit of an economy in a certain epoch and population. It must analyse the unifying and differentiating features of a culture that are economically relevant in the culture of consumption and in the culture of production. Since the nations of the West form an integrated culture of consumption and production the spirit of this economic culture is not national anymore but supranational.

The research into the *Zeitgeist* and into economic culture is highly developed in marketing and consumer behaviour research that is relevant for the cultural understanding of the economy and the positive theory of management. The foundations of such a theory and its methodology have been laid in the Historical School of Economics and the human sciences (*Geisteswissenschaften*).

The culture of a society has not only a positive side of being given as an order or a way of life and as an interpretation of human existence. Eduard Spranger distinguished culture as *Lebensordnung* and *Daseinsdeutung*, as a way of life and as an interpretation of human existence.[14] A culture has also the normative side of being an order of obligation, of an ought to be, of duty and law. The customs and habits of a culture become also partly the law of a society.

---

13 Cf. EDUARD SPRANGER: "W. Dilthey, Gedächtnisrede", in: E. SPRANGER: *Vom pädagogischen Genius. Lebensbilder und Grundgedanken großer Erzieher*, Heidelberg (Quelle & Meyer) 1965, p. 210.

14 EDUARD SPRANGER: *Kulturfragen der Gegenwart*, Heidelberg (Quelle & Meyer) 1953.

The law is in turn complemented by the morality and morals of conscience. The codification of culture and law and the "spontaneity" of ethics reflect the twofold nature of law that is at the same time an order of willingness (*Wollensordnung*) and an order of ought and obligation (*Sollensordnung*). This double character of the law as *Wollensordnung* and *Sollensordnung* makes it necessary to analyse law and normative ethics together. The complete separation of law and ethics is artificial. Law and ethics are not identical since the realm of that which is ethically demanded transcends that which is legally demanded. The two are not disjunct but partially identical.

Normative ethical economy must be developed in a close interaction and exchange with civil law or the law of economic exchange. The law in itself also shows the double nature of positive and moral content quite similar to that of ethical economy, which is also an economic ethics in the normative sense and a cultural economics in the positive sense. The law has the aspect of norming those relationships and matters that could also be different as it is effected in the sphere of industrial norms by norms like DIN, ISO. These norms are normative but not moral norms. At the same time, the law shows the moral dimension of basic laws of human rights etc. that are not only legally and contingently but also morally and intrinsically obliging.

The norms of business ethics as the practical ethos and morality of business cannot be in contradiction to the laws of economics and vice versa. Tensions and contradictions can of course arise temporarily and then they must be overcome. Business ethics must be a critique of existing economic law where it contradicts basic moral norms of business. Business ethics must however also learn from the experience and expertise of the law and of the law scholars. In addition to the discipline of law and economics, a triad of law, ethics and economics should be developed in which, in the economic theory of law, not only the efficiency principle is applied to the law but also the principles of ethics and efficiency together are used for finding the right legislation and jurisdiction.

Due to its historical and cultural orientation, the Historical School of economics has first recognised the close relationship between law and economics. Schmoller's yearbook was named "Yearbook for Economics and Legislation".

16 - 36

A13
D11 D72   Chapter 2

Moral Motives and Political Mechanisms[*]

ALAN HAMLIN

I.   Introduction
II.   Moral Desires
III.   Moral Behaviour
IV.   Political Mechanisms
V.   Voting and Representation
VI.   Overview

I. Introduction

    In this essay, I will attempt to sketch out some of the consequences for the study of political institutions that follow from taking both rationality and morality as constitutive features of individual agents. This represents a departure from more standard lines of economic analysis which typically focus on rationality as the central characteristic of individual agency, and then address questions concerning morality either in terms of the aggregation of individual utilities (in the generally utilitarian tradition), or in terms of principles that might be agreed by rational agents (in the generally contractarian tradition). These standard economic approaches draw a stark divide between motivation and justification. Policies, or institutions, may be *justified* by their moral properties, but these moral properties can play no

---

[*] The discussion presented here draws heavily on recent joint work with Geoffrey Brennan, and I am happy to acknowledge his major and continuing contribution. I am also pleased to acknowledge helpful comments made at the Fifth Annual SEEP Conference on Economic Ethics and Philosophy, Marienrode, 2-4 November 1997.

direct role in *motivating* the individuals concerned either with choosing the policies/institutions or with living under them. This aspect of economic analysis is both a strength and a weakness. A strength because it focuses attention on what might generally be called the compliance problem; that is, the issue of structuring the environment so as to ensure that agents will comply with justified institutions and rules, without simply assuming compliant motivation. This strength is shown most clearly in the various applications of 'invisible hand' theorems which serve to show that even self-interested individuals can be led to produce socially efficient outcomes. A weakness because, in focusing on invisible hand mechanisms, there is a tendency to overlook other mechanisms that may be of considerable value. This weakness is, I believe, particularly significant in the context of the economic analysis of political institutions.

In recent times economists and political theorists have become very familiar with the idea of studying democratic politics from an essentially economic viewpoint: conceptualising political process as the interaction between rational individuals in a manner that draws heavily on the analysis of interactions in the market place. This move towards rational actor political theory (RAPT) reflects what might be called the 'public choice critique' of the more traditional analysis of government in economics, as well as the analytic power of the rational choice model. Traditional policy analysis in economics was built on a characterisation of government as a benevolent despot: government was assumed to want outcomes that served the public interest (the benevolence assumption); and to be powerful enough to take whatever action was required to achieve those outcomes (the despot assumption). The public choice critique, by contrast, emphasised self-interested motivations amongst politicians and bureaucrats, and the principal-agent structure of democratic government[1]. On this view, politicians are agents appointed to serve the citizenry at large; but political agents, like agents in other areas of economics, should be assumed to be motivated to pursue their own ends. This view stresses the need to restrict and channel the power of politicians to guard against the abuse of their power. In short, the public choice critique replaces the benevolent despot with *homo economicus*.

---

1   For clear statements of the principal agent approach see ROBERT BARRO (1973), BARRY WEINGAST (1984).

ALAN HAMLIN

The constitution, and the political institutions that the constitution supports, are then seen as the outcome of an implicit and incomplete contract
between the citizenry and the set of political agents. This constitutional
contract attempts to structure political life so as to bring the private ambitions of political agents in line with the interests of the citizenry by the use
of a range of institutional and procedural devices - most obviously, competitive elections. Political institutions attempt to ensure that the political
process acts as an invisible hand mechanism in a manner that mirrors the
operation of idealised markets. Given the emphasis on standard economic
rationality - taken to be both instrumental in structure and broadly self-
interested in content - it is inevitable that this analysis of political institutions has focused largely on their incentive properties.

While I believe that the public choice critique and the economic approach to political institutions has made a major contribution to both economics and politics, I also believe that it is flawed, and that the basic flaw
lies in the application of the assumption of self-interested motivation in the
area of politics. It is clear that in many areas of economics there has been a
steady expansion in the set of motivations that are accepted as the basis for
analysis. In public choice and RAPT, however, there seems to be a strong
desire to differentiate the economic approach to politics from more traditional 'compliance theories' of political behaviour by insisting on relatively
narrow conceptions of self-interest. For example, Mueller defines the public
choice approach to politics in terms of the assumption that "man is an egoistic, rational, utility maximiser"[2]. Whether we characterise individuals as
narrowly 'egoistic' or as more broadly self-interested in attempting to
maximise their own concept of "welfare as they conceive it, whether they
be selfish, altruistic, loyal, spiteful or masochistic"[3] the economic approach
to motivation almost always stops short of any explicit consideration of
morality itself as a motivator.

I should immediately stress that I do not wish to replace the *homo
economicus* assumption of (broad) self-interest with the opposite *homo
heroicus* assumption of universal morality. I do not want to resurrect the
benevolent despot, or introduce the benevolent citizen. Rather, I seek to
build an analysis of democratic political institutions on the basis of the more
moderate assumption that individuals have both broadly self-interested de-

---

2   DENNIS MUELLER (1989, p. 2).
3   GARY BECKER (1993, p. 385).

18

sires and what might be termed a 'moral desire'; that is, a desire to act as morality requires. Agents are still taken to be rational, and so this work should be seen as lying within the analytic tradition of RAPT. But rationality is not the same thing as the pursuit of (narrow or broad) self-interest. It is this further broadening of the range of basic desires to include the desire to act as morality requires that implies a departure from the emerging RAPT and public choice orthodoxy[4]. In terms of the distinction between motivation and justification, the basic idea to be explored here is to allow those arguments that have justificatory force to also have at least some motivational force - that is, to steer a course between the two extremes offered by the complete separation of justification from motivation, and the complete identification of justification with motivation

In fleshing out this line of thought, I will begin by saying a little more about the structure and nature of the morality I assume, and about the impact of this morality on behaviour. This discussion will then allow the identification of a range of political mechanisms which includes, but is not restricted to, the set of incentive mechanisms. This range of political mechanisms in turn invites an alternative analyses of particular political institutions which complement and extend the analysis that derives from the more traditional RAPT model.

II. Moral Desires

I will formulate the relevant basic motivational assumptions as simply as is possible. I assume that, among the desires (the basic motivational triggers) that agents have, the desire to behave morally is one. Importantly, however, the desire to act, as morality requires will be only one desire among many, and will not be privileged relative to other (more self-interested) desires[5]. Given this structure of desires, agents are assumed to

---

4   For other recent attempts to inject morality into a public choice framework see
    SERGE-CHRISTOPHE KOLM (1996) and BRUNO FREY (1997).
5   DAVID SCHMIDTZ (1995) provides a detailed argument to support the view that
    self-interested and moral considerations can fit together in an account of rational

ALAN HAMLIN

be rational in the traditional Humean sense (but see below) - roughly, they
behave so as to maximise the satisfaction of their desires given their beliefs
- including their beliefs about morality. It is important to note that the line
of argument sketched here does not attempt to reduce morality to rationality
in the manner of David Gauthier (1986), or to reduce rationality to morality. Rather, morality and rationality are seen as two distinct but equally
fundamental aspects of an individual's character - with rationality imposing
a structural relationship on the individual's desires, beliefs and actions,
while morality provides at least some substantive content to the individual's
desires and beliefs[6].

The simple existence of this moral desire provides for the possibility of
moral action, but the fact that it is just one desire among many implies that
moral action will not always occur. Moral considerations will weigh with
our typical individual, but may easily be outweighed by more self-
interested considerations in specific cases.

The existence of the moral desire also allows the possibility of effective
moral argument. In a world populated exclusively by *homo economicus*,
moral argument is useless. Individuals of that type are simply immune to all
forms of preaching or moral suasion. They can not recognise the relevant
normative categories and, even if they could recognise them, could not
grant them reason-giving status. But our more moral individuals can both
recognise and value moral argument - without invariably acting on it.

As with other desires (or preferences) there is no reason why all agents
will exhibit the desire to behave morally to the same extent, or assess its
detailed content in exactly the same way. Some people will be more im-
pelled by moral considerations than will others, and detailed beliefs about
what morality requires in specific situations may also differ to some degree
from person to person. In short, we should expect some moral heterogeneity.

One question that arises immediately is whether such moral motivations
will really matter in any practical setting. It might seem obvious that the
motivations of individual agents will matter for the operation of political or
other social institutions, but there are at least some grounds for doubting

---

human motivation. See also MICHAEL SMITH (1994), GEOFFREY BRENNAN and
ALAN HAMLIN (1995b), JEAN HAMPTON (1997), MICHAEL SLOTE (1997).

6   Compare this with the discussion of the "rational" and the "reasonable" in JOHN
RAWLS (1993, pp. 48-54).

this. In fact, there are several distinct reasons why morality might not matter - I will mention just two[7]. One possibility is that there is just insufficient agreement as to the substantive content of morality for moral motivations to have any systematic impact on political or social outcomes. Beliefs about what morality requires might be so diverse that there is nothing resembling moral consensus. In that case morality could not underpin widespread political compliance, and might simply add a sort of 'statistical noise' to self-interested behaviour in the social and political spheres. The second possibility is that even if there is a consensus of moral beliefs, the moral desire is simply too weak to have any major influence on behaviour. This is probably the view taken by many economists and other enthusiasts for *homo economicus*. On this view, morality may be a part of an individual's decision making calculus, but it is rarely a decisive part - only where interests and morality pull in the same direction is morality apparently effectual, and even here the appearance is deceptive.

I explicitly reject both of these possibilities. I deny that there is inadequate consensus in moral beliefs to make morality a source of systematic behaviour. I accept that the fine-grained detail of moral belief will be subject to variation from person to person, but I believe that there is sufficient agreement on basic elements of 'common sense morality' - on the coarse-grained structure of morality - to ground the idea of a shared morality[8]. And I note that the situation with respect to moral desires is not very different from the situation with respect to more self-interested desires and preferences. In the case of preferences the economist relies on a shared, coarse-grained structure of preferences (more of a good is preferred to less, the principle of diminishing marginal utility, and so on), rather than any unanimity at the level of the fine-grained detail (the marginal rate of substitution between any two goods, for example), and there seems to be good reason for extending this treatment of self-interested desires to moral desires.

I also reject the idea that moral desires have insufficient weight to be effective. At least, I reject this idea as an *a priori* and all embracing view of the relationship between moral and self-interested desires. The question of

---

7   Other possibilities are discussed in GEOFFREY BRENNAN and ALAN HAMLIN (forthcoming).

8   For discussion of the structure of such a shared morality and the process by which we improve our value judgements, see JAMES GRIFFIN (1996).

which type of desire is most effective seems to be one that is answerable
only by reference to the particular context of choice - desires that are dormant in one context may be rendered particularly salient in another context.
The strength or relative effectiveness of different desires is not simply an
exogenous matter. It is, at least in part, endogenously influenced by the
circumstances of choice - including the institutional framework within
which the choice is set. It may be, for example, that the context of the market tends to pick out desires of one type while the context of democratic
politics tends to pick out desires of another type. And, indeed, I wish to
argue that this is the case.

A second question that arises immediately concerns the more substantive
content of the moral beliefs that form the core of the shared morality. I
shall not attempt anything like a full account of this shared morality here -
and nor will I need to. All that is required for our discussion of the political
and institutional impact of recognising moral motivations is that such a
shared morality exists, and that it includes a concern for the standard notion
of the 'public interest' which may be defined in terms of the individual
interests of the citizenry as a whole. This is not to commit to any simple
utilitarianism - I have no need to insist on the simple sum of individual
utilities as the relevant measure of the public interest; nor on any specific
definition of individual interests; nor on the moral irrelevance of all non-
welfarist considerations. Rather it is to set up our common morality in a
manner that seems most appropriate for the analysis of democratic political
institutions. Democracy has many dimensions, but two that seem to be fundamental are that democracy involves government *for* the people, as well as
by the people. A common morality that is at least responsive to benefits and
costs *for* the people seems to be a necessary prerequisite for any sensible
account of the more detailed structuring of how democratic institutions
operationalize the idea of government *by* the people.

III. Moral Behaviour

Granted the basic idea of a moral desire, I argue that there are two distinct ways - one direct and the other indirect - in which this moral desire
may become effective, so that moral action results. I also argue that both of

these lines of argument pick out democratic politics as an arena in which moral behaviour can be expected to arise relatively frequently. I will sketch each of these arguments in turn.

The direct argument first. Just as with any other desire, the satisfaction of the desire to act as morality requires will generally carry a cost in terms of other desires forgone. And, just as in the case of other desires, the moral desire will be more likely to be effective (that is, moral action is more likely to result) the lower is that cost. Put crudely: moral behaviour will be subject to a downward sloping demand curve. Moreover, just as with any other desire, different individuals may be expected to display the moral desire with different strengths so that, once again, we should expect a degree of heterogeneity with respect to moral behaviour.

How do these points suggest that moral behaviour may be more common in the political arena than in, say, the market place? One key connection is via the theory of an essential aspect of democratic politics - voting. I shall return to the discussion of voting in slightly more detail in a later section but, for the moment, the point can be made by a simple contrast between the act of voting for an outcome and the act of choosing that same outcome. The act of choice, I assume, carries direct consequences - one outcome is chosen, others are rejected. By contrast, the act of voting for an outcome does not (except in very unlikely circumstances) cause that outcome to come about. Neither can the cost of voting for an outcome be seen as alternative outcomes forgone. The comparable cost of voting is simply alternative possible votes foregone. In this way, voting is almost perfectly inconsequential in that it has no discernible impact on the choice of the associated outcome. This inconsequential nature of voting acts to disengage voting from the voter's particular interests, and this in turn renders the individual's moral desires more salient and, therefore, more likely to be the proximate determinants of voting behaviour. So, on this account, the institution of voting may be seen to pick out moral desires rather than self-interested ones. Voting provides an institutional setting in which moral behaviour may be encouraged.

I do not mean to suggest that all political behaviour is moral and all market (or consequential) behaviour self-interested. The weaker, but still substantial, claim is simply that the detailed institutional structure will influence the way in which rational agents will act, and that the institutional arrangements that we associate with voting and politics more generally may be expected to engage with moral desires more frequently and more

23

strongly than do the institutions of exchange and contract that we associate with the market.

There is a second and more indirect route by which moral behaviour may arise - a route which depends on a rather broader interpretation of Humean rational choice. It is now a common-place in the social sciences and philosophy that directly self-interested calculation may be self defeating in the sense that explicit pursuit of this goal may fail in its own terms[9]. This tells us that a rational and self-interested agent would have good reason to choose a *disposition* other than self-interested calculation, if only such a disposition could be chosen in such a way as to be effective. A *disposition* here may be thought of as a type of mind-set or mode of decision making: a disposition governs the way in which day-to-day decisions are made, at least over some range of decisions.

To be effective a disposition requires both longevity and translucency. Longevity is required of a disposition since a disposition must commit the agent to a mode of decision making for a sequence of decisions - if a new disposition could be chosen for each decision, or dispositions abandoned at will, they could not work to constrain directly rational calculation. In this sense a disposition is to an individual rather like a constitution is to a polity: just as the value of a constitution depends in part on its relative fixity, so to the value of a disposition depends on its holding a status of relative permanence.

Translucency is required of a disposition since many of the benefits of having a particular disposition will depend upon others believing that you have it - a disposition to be trustworthy is most valuable if others recognise it and trust you. An ability to signal your dispositional type in a way that is broadly reliable (and, in particular, not too prone to counterfeiting) will be important.

Since a disposition of this type serves to improve on directly rational calculation,[10] it is not the case that each action taken by an individual operating under such a disposition can itself be termed 'rational'. Definitionally, the action taken will not always be the action, of those actions that are available to the individual that best serves the desires of the individual. But

---

9   See DEREK PARFIT (1984) for a detailed discussion.

10 One could, of course, identify direct rational calculation as a disposition in itself, so that all individuals are dispositional. In which case our comments here only apply to dispositions other than this one.

although the *act* may not be strictly rational, I would suggest that the *actor* is rational in choosing such a disposition, and acting under it, if she can do so. And I am more concerned with rational *actor* theory than with the theory of rational *action* defined more narrowly.

All of this applies with equal force to our more moral agent whose desires include the desire to act, as morality requires. She too may have good reason to adopt a disposition that partially commits future decision making, rather than relying of the direct evaluation of alternative actions at each point in time (even though such direct evaluation will be made relative to the full set of desires including the moral desire). But now this dispositional choice itself may be morally motivated. I identify such rationally chosen, moral dispositions as *virtuous* dispositions. A virtuous individual, then, is someone who has adopted a mind-set of acting as morality requires even when direct calculation using the full set of moral and self-interested desires would not support the choice of that action. But such a virtuous disposition is not to be understood as irrational in itself - it may be the disposition that is most likely to achieve the agents overall desires (both self-interested and moral) in the long-run.[11]

Notice that once the idea of virtuous dispositions is accepted a second-order version of the earlier direct argument for moral behaviour can be re-employed. A virtuous disposition will be more likely to be chosen or maintained the lower is the cost to the individual in terms of particular interests forgone. Again, this will carry implications for the type of virtuous dispositions that are adopted and for the dispositional heterogeneity of the population. Some virtuous dispositions - for example trustworthiness - may be very attractive because the virtue is low-cost in the sense that trustworthiness, like honesty, may also be the best policy even in narrowly self-interested terms. Other virtuous dispositions may carry a much higher price in terms of self-interested opportunities forgone, and so be much rarer in any heterogeneous population.

Once again, I argue that this dispositional route to moral behaviour is likely to be more effective in some institutional settings than in others. Most obviously, virtuous dispositions will be unnecessary wherever direct calculation on the full range of basic desires is not self-defeating. And this is the traditional ground of invisible hand arguments - where the privately rational

---

11 More detailed accounts of the idea of virtue as a disposition are presented in GEOFFREY BRENNAN and ALAN HAMLIN (1995a) and in ALAN HAMLIN (1996).

actions of all individuals leads society as a whole to an outcome that is the best available, in the sense of being Pareto efficient with respect to the underlying desires - moral and self-interested. The idealised free market is such an invisible hand mechanism; and, as I have stressed, much of economic analysis is concerned with the design and operation of invisible hand mechanisms. Where such mechanisms are available, virtuous dispositions will lie relatively dormant, but where such mechanisms are not available - where institutions depend on placing individuals in positions of power, for example - virtuous dispositions may be of considerable importance. Almost by definition, democratic politics provides a setting in which some individuals are placed in positions of power over others and so, once again, we might expect moral desires and, in particular virtuous dispositions to be especially important in politics.

IV. Political Mechanisms

Having sketched an outline of an extended motivational and behavioural model the obvious question is: How does this model of behaviour bear on the appraisal and design of institutions and, in particular, the design of political institutions? An initial response to this question is to point to the fact that the recognition of motivations and dispositions that go beyond directly rational calculation based on self-interest opens up access to a range of institutional mechanisms that can be analysed and employed.

As I have already noted, RAPT and public choice are essentially committed to consider those mechanisms that operate as invisible hands: mechanisms, in other words, that work *via* incentives. Incentive based mechanisms may operate negatively or positively (sticks or carrots), and may work in a number of different ways - perhaps by creating incentives to reveal information, or by incentives to build reputations - but the essential object is always the same: to create a positive correlation between the individual's self-interested motivation and the socially desired action. I do not wish to suggest that incentive mechanisms are unimportant - just that they are not the only, or necessarily the most important, class of mechanisms that are relevant to questions of the design and reform of particular political institutions.[12] I will here identify three further types of mechanism that I believe to be relevant and which can be analysed within our suggested motivational framework even though they will tend to be overlooked by analysts of the more traditional RAPT school.

The first additional type of mechanism is a screening mechanism. The basic idea here is very familiar in other areas of economics, where screening models are commonly employed to analyse situations in which individuals may be sorted according to their type. In labour economics, for example, the idea of screening for particular skills or abilities is a standard part of the discussion of the allocation of individuals to jobs. The difference here is just that a key-defining characteristic that identifies an individuals type is motivational or dispositional in nature. Put most crudely, a screening mechanism might be employed to allocate virtuous individuals to those roles in which virtue is most valuable - where virtue has a comparative advantage.[13] Since the standard RAPT model does not allow of this type of motivational heterogeneity, it simply can not analyse institutions in terms of their motivational screening effects.

A second additional class of mechanism might be termed 'virtue producing mechanisms'. The idea here is that the stock of virtue in society (roughly, the number, or proportion, of individuals who are characterised by a virtuous disposition) is endogenous, and that virtuous dispositions are more likely to be adopted and maintained under some institutional arrangements than others. In this way, some institutional arrangements might be argued to produce (or, more accurately, encourage the production of) virtue, while others might be argued to erode the stock of virtue. Again, standard RAPT cannot recognise such institutional effects since it does not rec-

---

12 Incentive effects are not the only institutional effects recognised in traditional RAPT and public choice. A further type of institutional effect that is recognised and studied in that framework might be termed the 'aggregation' effect; that is, the effects induced by alternative means of aggregating individual actions (or preferences) into collective actions (or values) - most obviously in the social choice theoretic literature and the discussion of alternative voting rules. We discuss this class of effects and other related issues elsewhere, see GEOFFREY BRENNAN and ALAN HAMLIN (1995b, 1996, forthcoming), but I suppress that discussion here.

13 A model of such a motivational screening mechanism is presented in GEOFFREY BRENNAN and ALAN HAMLIN (1995a).

ognise the relevant motivational and dispositional categories, still less their endogeneity.

The third and final class of mechanism to be mentioned here might be termed 'virtue enhancing mechanisms'. The idea here is that some institutions may work to amplify or enhance the impact of whatever stock of virtue there may be in society, even though they do not attempt either to screen virtuous individuals or to encourage the production of virtue. The idea behind this type of mechanism is not as easily seen as the ideas behind the screening and virtue-producing mechanisms, and an example may help to make the point. The example is set in the context of the classic enforcement problem of *quis custodiet ipsos custodes* (who shall guard the guardians). Put briefly, if some individuals - the guardians or enforcers - are to be empowered to enforce the law, what is to prevent them from exploiting their power? The traditional RAPT approach to enforcement often begs the question of how the enforcers should themselves be motivated to enforce the law. In models, which recognise only self-interested behaviour, all enforcement must ultimately be self-enforcement in the sense that, ultimately, the guardians/enforcers must face private incentives to enforce the law. This places limits on the possibilities for credible enforcement. However, in a world in which some, but not all, guardians/enforcers are virtuous, the calculus is crucially different. Enforcement may now be a practicable institutional option simply as a result of the non-zero *probability* that the enforcer will be virtuous, rather than by the provision of self-interested incentives to all enforcers. Essentially, law breaking may be rationally deterred by the probability of virtuous enforcement even when that probability is relatively small; so that even a small proportion of virtuous enforcers may reduce the equilibrium level of law-breaking to zero. It is in this sense that the institution amplifies or enhances the social impact of virtue. Of course, this effect would be strengthened by any means of selecting enforcers disproportionately from the ranks of the virtuous; or by any general increase in the stock of virtue. But even without these aids, the simple existence of some virtuous enforcers may be sufficient to render enforcement credible in circumstances where no self-enforcement mechanism would be available if all individuals were self-interested. In these cases, the existence of (some) individuals with virtuous dispositions may serve to justify an institution of enforcement, and the institution of enforcement will enhance the effect of the existing stock of virtue.

These three additional institutional mechanisms may interact with each other, and with more standard incentive mechanisms, in a variety of ways. One possibility that has occupied the attention of critics of 'economic rationalism' in its self-interested form has been the possibility that reliance on institutions that operate via incentive mechanisms may erode virtue in society. In our vocabulary this claim asserts a negative feedback effect from incentive mechanisms to virtue producing mechanisms. Geoffrey Brennan and I have investigated this claim at a relatively abstract level elsewhere and found that it is by no means necessarily true.[14] The relevant feedback effect can be positive, negative or zero depending on the details of the institutional design. And I suggest that this investigation and its result display a clear merit of the approach advocated here. It allows the explicit investigation of questions of considerable importance to the topic of institutional and constitutional design within a unified framework; a framework that admits a much wider variety of effects than can be accommodated within the mainstream RAPT approach, but which still retains the structure and analytic power associated with rational actor analysis.

V. Voting and Representation

There is still a considerable gulf from the identification of a range of mechanisms that can be studied within the broader motivational and dispositional framework proposed here, to the more practical issues involved in the appraisal and design of workable political institutions. In this section I want to sketch out a particular line of argument that uses this framework to provide a discussion of the most basic and commonplace institutional arrangement of representative democracy: the election of representatives[15].

The standard RAPT analysis of voting in large-scale elections operates on the assumption that voters vote their interests. However, that same RAPT analysis points out that, on this account, voting is almost never rational, so that theoretical predictions of turnout are very low and often zero. The basic idea is simply that, because the probability that any particular

---

14 See GEOFFREY BRENNAN and ALAN HAMLIN (1995a).
15 This section draws on GEOFFREY BRENNAN and ALAN HAMLIN (1998a, 1988b).

ALAN HAMLIN

agent will be decisive is vanishingly small in even close-run elections, no-one could reasonably believe that their vote will be causally effective in bringing about their desired outcome. I have already noted this idea that voting in mass elections is inconsequential; and the idea that, precisely for this reason, voting is a case in which satisfying a desire to act morally will be virtually costless in terms of the consequences of this behaviour for the satisfaction of other desires. And all of this is true whether the objects to be voted on are outcomes, policies or representatives. The move from direct to representative democracy apparently does nothing to overcome the inconsequential nature of voting. And, indeed, the traditional RAPT analysis of voting makes little distinction between voting on policies or on representatives - representatives are seen simply as ciphers for the policies they will pursue.

At the same time, as I have also already noted, the central problem of democratic political process from the RAPT perspective is often identified as a kind of principal-agent problem. But this diagnosis of the central problem of politics clearly presupposes that democracy is representative rather than direct in nature. It would be possible, at least in principle, to avoid the principal-agent problem altogether by the simple expedient of adopting directly democratic procedures. In this way, the RAPT approach to democratic politics often simply assumes that political representation is an unavoidable fact of life - that direct democracy is either too costly to contemplate or in some other way infeasible. Representative democracy is accepted on an (often implicit) argument of the second-best type. Direct democracy forms the relevant ideal case, and representative democracy offers a more practicable means of approximating the outcomes that would be achieved under idealised direct democracy. The principal-agent problem is then seen as the major cost involved in accepting this second-best procedure.

This approach begs obvious questions. If representation is to be viewed as a means of approximating direct democracy at reduced costs, what are the costs involved and how does the move to representation economise on them? If representation is viewed in this way, why is it important that representatives be elected rather than, say, appointed by an appropriate sampling technique?

Against this background we offer a very different account of elective representation: one that offers a first-best argument for representative democracy as being potentially superior to direct democracy, and one that brings together the ideas of non-instrumental voting and the potential

30

screening role of elections. In outline, the argument suggests that representation by means of popular elections may provide a means of selecting more virtuous politicians. This suggestion is scarcely novel,[16] the only novelty we aspire to is the ability to capture this important aspect of political reality within a rational actor framework.

The argument may be sketched as follows. First, as we have seen, the critique of the instrumental account of voting gives rise to an alternative account of rational voting which emphasises expressive considerations.[17] Expressive voting views the act of voting as expressing support for an alternative rather than choosing that alternative, where 'expressing support' might be rendered to mean 'passing favourable comment on'. A point to emphasise here is that expressive voting provides the basis for a model that predicts substantial levels of turnout in large-scale popular elections - even when the election is not expected to be close. Since voting is not motivated by direct consideration of the outcomes, participation is not deterred in the manner that is familiar in more instrumental accounts of rational voting.

Now, the shift from direct to indirect or representative democracy shifts the immediate focus of voters' attention from policies to candidates. Whereas direct democracy calls for voters to comment on policy options, representative democracy calls for voters to comment on potential representatives. It is the characteristics of individual candidates, rather than policies *per se,* that will be uppermost in the voters' minds, so that the domain of relevant considerations under expressive voting is very different from the domain of relevant considerations under instrumental voting[18]. Under the expressive conception of voting, it would be perfectly rational for individual citizens to vote on the basis of a candidate's physical appearance or speaking voice, if those were the characteristics the voter identifies with and wishes to express favourable comment on. But most voters, most of the

---

16 In particular, the suggestion is strongly reminiscent of arguments by Condorcet, Madison and Schumpeter. For further details see GEOFFREY BRENNAN and ALAN HAMLIN (1988b).

17 For a full discussion of the *a priori* argument for expressive voting see GEOFFREY BRENNAN and LOREN LOMASKY (1993).

18 Of course, policy commitments may be included in the set of relevant candidate characteristics, but the manner of their inclusion will not necessarily reflect the expected benefits to the voter, and they will not exhaust the set of relevant characteristics.

time, do not see good looks or accents as central. In expressing electoral comment, I believe, they are more likely to consider the candidates' character and competencies - at least insofar as these can be discerned.

It seems clear that, *ceteris paribus,* candidates with relatively attractive characters will receive more favourable electoral comment - and therefore more votes - than will others. And it is hardly a rash conjecture to think that, again *ceteris paribus,* voters will systematically favour - and therefore vote for - candidates who they believe to be decent, honourable, sincere, morally serious and publicly concerned. In short, candidates they belief to be of a virtuous disposition. Voters are not acting instrumentally in supporting such candidates. Indeed, it is precisely because of the weakness of the instrumental logic that these considerations are salient. My vote for a particular candidate is just an expression of favourable comment. But, of course, in the aggregate, votes do determine the electoral outcome; so that the predictable result of such expressive voting will be a tendency to elect virtuous candidates.

There remains the important question of the strength of the *ceteris paribus* clauses in the above argument. We might all agree that that voters have rational grounds for supporting virtuous candidates, *ceteris paribus*, but still think that this will have no significant impact on electoral behaviour all things considered. I do not think that the *ceteris paribus* clauses are too strong in this case, and I offer two reasons in support of this view. The first simply observes that the powerful idea of rational ignorance - the idea that individuals will lack incentives to collect and process information if that information is not of importance to their effective choices - tends to deflect the force of many other potentially relevant factors. The expressive voting argument is especially salient because it works with the grain of the rational ignorance argument rather than against it. The second reason is simply the idea that the characteristic of a virtuous disposition is, by the very nature of a shared morality, likely to appeal to most, if not all, citizens. Other attributes - looks or accent - might be considered attractive by some voters, and might provide the basis of some votes. However the aggregating effects of majority voting will tend to pick out those characteristics that are widely approved, with other, more idiosyncratic, attractions tending to cancel out.

These various considerations, taken together, provide the basis for a first-best theory of electoral representation. An account that stresses the idea of constructing an assembly in which virtue is over-represented in statistical terms, and also explains how voting is an important part of the way in which such screening may come about. Virtuous individuals are both politically attractive as candidates and politically productive as politicians. Their political attractiveness explains why individuals express support for them, while their political productivity provides the basis for the normative appeal of such a representative structure. This expressive theory of representation sees elections primarily as screening devices which function to create what might be termed a democratically elite assembly - democratic in its mode of selection (and in its mode of internal decision making - not discussed here), but elite in terms of its civic virtue and competence.

Of course, I do not mean to suggest that all elected politicians or officials are angels. All that I claim is that the process of voting, properly understood, will tend to refine and improve the characteristics of the elected assembly relative to the population at large. As Madison claimed, there is good reason to think that representatives will be on average more public-spirited, conscientious and virtuous than those whom they represent.

The libertarian spirit of much public choice and RAPT may not much admire this view of democratic politics. The better democratic politics works, the more the balance between the domain of politics and the domain of the market should shift in favour of politics; and the more that we can rely on politicians to be virtuous, the more we might be inclined to leave them to get on with the business of government free of costly constraints on their discretionary power. But I would not wish to over-exaggerate this line of argument. Rather I would emphasise the fact that good government is likely to require a delicate balance between institutions supporting virtue and laying the foundations for allowing scope for discretionary power, and institutions that guard against the abuse of such discretionary power. RAPT analysis has focused almost entirely on the second of these, I believe that the type of account I have outlined here may be an appropriate route to a more balanced approach.

VI. Overview

Public choice theory and RAPT provides a useful analytic framework for studying democratic institutions - but only up to a point. That point is its view of human motivation. Between the idea that all politicians and voters always look only to their chequebooks, and the equally extreme idea that politicians and voters are all moral heroes seeking only to promote some appropriate concept of the public interest, there is a huge middle ground. I believe that this middle ground can be inhabited with profit and without loss of the rigour associated with the RAPT tradition. I believe that the resulting analysis is capable of yielding results about the way political institutions work that are richer, more plausible and more friendly to traditional political theory than the orthodox public choice alternative.

For a start, the type of analysis that I recommend here provides us with an appropriate analytic vocabulary that can acknowledge a wide range of institutional mechanisms and personal motivations. It also connects RAPT to the traditions of Madison and others who see a political constitution as striking a balance between: the limitation of government powers; the expression of political opinion through processes of deliberation and representation (refining private opinions and selecting the most virtuous for office); and the maintenance of an environment which encourages individuals to participate in political life in an appropriate spirit. While the orthodox RAPT approach to constitutional design easily recognises the first of these three elements, it must fail to provide an account of the remaining two, and of the trade-offs between them.

At a more practical level I would also claim that this framework provides novel perspectives on a number of the most familiar aspects of the traditional liberal constitution. I have sketched above a distinctive analysis of electoral behaviour and a distinctive defence of the representative institutions. In this context, the analysis provides an account of relatively high levels of voter turnout (even when the expected outcome of the election is not close), explains the fact that political competition is as much concerned with the personal characteristics of political leaders as with policies, and argues that representation can act as an important means of selecting or screening politicians so as to improve the performance of the political system relative to the alternative of direct democracy. Similar applications can be made to other topics of institutional and constitutional interest such as the separation of powers, bicameralism, federalism and so on.

But the most important lesson I would like to be taken from this discussion is the most basic one. The possibility that moral motivations matter is one that must be studied in particular institutional contexts. The immediate corollary of this proposition is that, in attempting to model alternative constitutional arrangements, we must allow the possibility of a wide rage of detailed motivations if we are to be sensitive to the variety of direct and indirect effects that institutions may have on social and political outcomes.

References

BARRO, R.: "The Control of Politicians: an Economic Model", *Public Choice,* 14 (1973), pp.19-42.

BECKER, G.: "The Economic Way of Looking at Behavior", *Journal of Political Economy,* 101 (1993), pp. 385-409.

BRENNAN, G., HAMLIN, A. (1995a): "Economizing on Virtue" *Constitutional Political Economy,* 6 (1995), pp. 35-56.

BRENNAN, G., HAMLIN, A. (1995b): "Constitutional Political Economy: The Political Philosophy of Homo Economiçus?", *Journal of Political Philosophy,* 3 (1995), pp. 280-303.

BRENNAN, G., HAMLIN, A.: "Economical Constitutions", *Political Studies,* 44 (1996), pp. 605-619.

BRENNAN, G., HAMLIN, A. (1998a): "Expressive Voting and Electoral Equilibrium", *Public Choice,* 95 (1998), pp. 149-175.

BRENNAN, G., HAMLIN, A. (1998b): "On Political Representation", *British Journal of Political Science,* (1998) forthcoming.

BRENNAN, G., HAMLIN, A.: *Democratic Devices and Desires,* Cambridge (Cambridge University Press) forthcoming.

BRENNAN, G., LOMASKY, L.: *Democracy and Decision,* Cambridge (Cambridge University Press) 1993.

FREY, B.: *Not Just for the Money,* Cheltenham (Edward Elgar) 1997.

GAUTHIER, D.: *Morals By Agreement,* Oxford (Oxford University Press) 1986.

GRIFFIN, J.: *Value Judgements: Improving our Ethical Beliefs,* Oxford (Oxford University Press) 1996.

HAMLIN, A.: "Promoting Integrity and Virtue: The Institutional Dimension", *The Good Society,* 6 (1996), pp. 35-40.

HAMPTON, J.: "The Wisdom of the Egoist: The Moral and Political Implications of Valuing the Self", *Social Philosophy and Policy,* 14 (1997), pp.21-51.

KOLM, S-C.: "Moral Public Choice", *Public Choice,* 87 (1996), pp. 117-141.

MUELLER, D.: *Public Choice II,* Cambridge (Cambridge University Press) 1989.

PARFIT, D.: *Reasons and Persons,* Oxford (Oxford University Press) 1984.

RAWLS, J.: *Political Liberalism,* New York (Columbia University Press) 1993.

SCHMIDTZ, D.: *Rational Choice and Moral Agency,* Princeton (Princeton University Press) 1995.

SLOTE, M.: "The Virtue in Self-Interest", *Social Philosophy and Policy,* 14 (1997), pp. 264-285.

SMITH, M.: *The Moral Problem,* Oxford (Basil Blackwell) 1994.

WEINGAST, B.: "The Congressional-Bureaucratic System: a Principal-Agent Perspective", *Public Choice,* 44 (1984), pp. 147-192.

A13

Chapter 3

Integrative Economic Ethics – Towards a Conception of Socio-Economic Rationality

PETER ULRICH

I. In Search for a Life-Conducive Economics: Integrative Economic Ethics and its Relation to the Historical School of Economics

Economic ethics may be seen as *the other economics:* an economic science which takes its point of departure from the practical questions of overall economic *life*, whereas neo-classical economics only deals with the functional logic of the economic (market) *system*. The latter represents today's mainstream economics; it claims to develop a "pure", i.e. value-free theory explicating nothing else than the logic of interactions between individuals modelled upon the *homo oeconomicus* assumption. The result is the generalised logic of equally advantageous exchange between mutually unconcerned individuals in all spheres of society, in politics as well as in the market.[1] The strictly self-interested and mutually unconcerned individuals as modelled in "pure" economic *system's* theory do not need to know anything about the ethical dimension of human interactions, of course, since that theory pursues the strange ideal of a society that "works" as nothing but a system of well-ordered egoism; this is the "ideal" of a society that does not demand any moral virtues from its citizens so that the only virtue needed is that of maximising private advantage, profit or success.[2]

In contrast, it has always been the common point of departure for classical political economy as well as for later approaches by *dissenting economists* that economic science must not be reduced to pure economic system's logic because it deals with a complex social practice. And this means, that economics has to be *irreducibly* conceived as *social economics*, always depending on a historical context of meanings and values, norms and institutional settings. Social economics is therefore part of "humanities" or, in other words, a cultural science[3] as Max Weber stated more than 90 years ago.[4]

Such a cultural science of social practice can neither be conceptualised context-free nor value-free – quite on the contrary, the historical context of social values forms the very first subject of social economics (or socio-economics). Now, it can deal with that context in two methodologically different ways, namely for theoretical or practical purposes. As a *theoretical* approach, the socio-cultural context is only taken as the "given" frame, which is adequate to *understand* how the economic system works. As a *practical* approach, however, the intention is to *critically reflect* the guiding ideas and normative measures according to which all economic actors have to *legitimate* their "economic" advantage- or profit-seeking and into which the market system has to be *embedded*. And this is the precondition that market economies are *life-conducive* in a double sense: making sense in the light of cultural drafts of the "good life" (Aristotelian dimension of ethics)

---

1   This kind of mutually disinterested (economic) rationality is nothing else than the axiomatics of *methodological individualism* as defined by RAWLS (1971), BUCHANAN (1975), or GAUTHIER (1986).
2   That is obviously the dream of possessive individualism. Cf. MACPHERSON (1962).
3   In this respect, I agree with KOSLOWSKI (1988, pp. 138ff.).
4   Cf. WEBER (1904).

as well as being justifiable from the moral point of view, with regard to the just and solidary living together (Kantian dimension of ethics).

Economic ethics, then, means the philosophical reflection on the normative foundations of *practical socio-economics*.[5] This has to be distinguished from what is called "Socio-Economics" today, an approach that until now only develops its theoretical dimension as defined, yet seems not to be quite clear about its own methodological status. This is an old phenomenon in economics: In the tradition of classical political economy, the theoretical and the practical purpose of knowledge have never been sharply distinguished, which was a result of deeply rooted natural right metaphysics. Thus, what there *is* in the "economic cosmos", represented by the market system of the "natural freedom", may be supposed to be good and normatively right simply because it shares in the inscrutable wisdom of God's creation. Until today, economists have never completely ceased to turn their theoretical explanations or even their "pure" models of the ideal market into normative recommendations, i.e. to extend theoretical to practical economics in a methodologically uncontrolled way; so there is still a branch of the discipline that explicitly defines itself as *normative economics*, although it lacks any philosophically well-founded ethical categories and therefore is nothing more than "pure" moral economics. Sometimes, such a "moral economics" is even declared to be the essence of "modern" economic or business ethics.[6]

Compared with that, the earlier *German historical and ethical school of economics* was much more aware of the normative character of the basic socio-economic questions. But seen from today, it was still deficient in ethical categories: due to the positivistic philosophy of science in the first half of the 20th century, rational arguing on ethical questions was viewed to be impossible. That is why a dilemma between normative dogmatism and decisionism seemed inevitable. Under such methodological conditions, the historical and ethical school of (socio-) economics had no real chance to be established as what was needed than and is needed now, namely economics which do not start from the (impersonal) functional problems of the market

---

5   Cf. ULRICH (1986, pp. 341ff.) for a methodological draft of "practical socio-economics" from a perspective of history of economic thought.

6   In the German debate on economic ethics/business ethics, this position is advocated especially by KARL HOMANN; cf. HOMANN/BLOME-DREES (1992), HOMANN/PIES (1994). For a systematic critique cf. ULRICH (1997, pp. 106ff.).

system but from the human and social problems of life-world. By the way, business ethics is publicly "asked" so much today because our main problems in economic practice no longer relate to the technical questions of how to make the market system more efficient – instead, our main problems more and more relate to the question how we (as mature citizens of a free and democratic society) politically want to design and to arrange the *normative framework* of the market in order to secure that the market forces and the enormous productivity of our economic system still serve the good life and the just living together of people.

But is there any reason why economic ethics should be more promising today than the historical and ethical school has been some decades ago? I think the answer is clearly 'yes', yet it is 'yes' under an essential prerequisite: economic ethics may today be founded as a serious discipline on the level of modern philosophical ethics – or not at all. This seems to be trivial but it is not, since the majority of today's approaches in business ethics are lacking in critical reflection on good reasons for *all* normative presumptions. Instead, they usually stop that reflection at a certain point of the old "metaphysics of the market". Such unfounded *belief* in the market as a guarantor of a well-ordered society may be called *economism*.[7]

II. Critique of Economism: From Corrective Business Ethics to Integrative Economic Ethics

In business ethics as well as in everyday life, economism does not always appear in the form of explicitly normative messages, as it is the case with "normative economics". More often, economism appears in disguise behind the force of the circumstances of market competition that are pretended to be the economic "conditions" of the "possibility" of moral action in business. But why should this type of *Sachzwangargument*, i.e. referring to the empirical "necessities" (of economic self-defending in market competition) or "impossibilities" (of acting morally), be given an unproved *normative* status as a prerequisite of any "possible" business ethics? It would be a naturalistic fallacy to draw normative results from empirical facts, therefore the reference to market conditions makes only sense within an ethical

---

7   Cf. WEISSER (1954).

argumentation as far as the market mechanism itself – and with that the pure economic reasoning and orientation of the actors – is supposed to be normatively justified. Indeed, most of today's business ethics is what I call *corrective business ethics:* it starts with the presumption that market results are "normally" good results in an ethical sense as long as there is workable competition on open markets, so that in theory and practice, business ethics' only task is that of correcting or constraining the economic reasoning in those cases when the market does *not* work in a perfect or at least sufficient way (so-called market failure). But again: what exactly are the *normative* preconditions, which justify a market solution of any problem of social co-ordination or conflict regulation? If business ethics stops critical reflection facing this core problem, it falls into a symptomatic self-contradiction:

– On the one hand, it is presupposed that the empirically "given" market conditions stand beyond the scope of ethical reflection. Thus the market conditions have to be conceived as "ethics-free" facts.

– On the other hand, the "market principle" is given normative meaning since it is supposed that market solutions are ethically right as long as market failure does not exist.[8]

The economistic circle of that kind of half-cut economic ethics which binds the "necessity" of ethics in business to situations of market failure is now obvious: How can we rationally decide that market solutions of a practical social problem are ethically justifiable or that the market "fails" – without any ethical reflection on the normative status of the "market principle" itself?

This is the point of departure for the *integrative economic ethics* approach we have conceptualised in St. Gallen.[9] This approach begins with a critical reflection on the normative foundations of the economic way of thinking (or economic rationality) itself, by means of today's philosophical ethics and without stopping before any suppositions.

---

8 As KOSLOWSKI (1989, p. 351) in earlier times made the (wrong) point: *"Ethik ist bei vollständiger Konkurrenz überflüssig."* ("Ethics is superfluous under complete competition.") The same wrong supposition lies behind the conception of business ethics as a "situational corrective of the profit principle" by STEINMANN/LÖHR (1988, p. 308). There is no such thing as an ethical *principle* of profit (maximization) at all! Cf. to that criticism ULRICH (1997, pp. 397ff., especially 424ff.); for a comprehensive critique of the "market principle" cf. THIELEMANN (1996).

9 For a systematic elaboration of that approach cf. ULRICH (1997, pp. 116ff.).

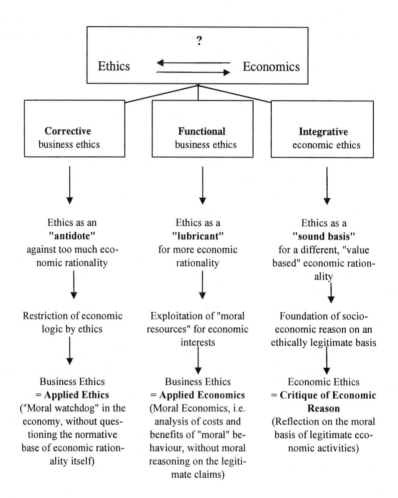

Figure 1: Three approaches to business ethics.

It is different from "applied ethics" as far as this means to bring ethics *into* the economy, which then is misunderstood as a domain that is still free from moral judgements.[10] Instead, the integrative approach intends an ethical critique *of* the economic logic (of the market). This is necessary because normative claims or suppositions are already hidden *within* the "pure" economic logic of the market system. Therefore, the critical light of practical (ethical) reason has to be cast upon economic rationality itself in order to reconstruct it as an ethically valuable *socio-economic rationality*. In other words: integrative economic ethics does not stop at defining moral limits to economic rationality form outside; rather it aims at integrating ethical reason into the guiding idea of (socio-) economic rationality so that the former is no longer the antagonist to the latter but its normative ground. This means that integrative economic ethics works as a fundamental and comprehensive reflection on the normative preconditions of ethically sound and life-conducive ways of rational economic "value-creation".

Three main tasks are recognised and tackled by integrative economic ethics: *first*, the critique of "pure" economic reason and of economism; *second*, the clarification of an ethically integrated idea of socio-economic rationality (as the moral point of view for integrated economic ethics) and of the basic dimensions of a life-conducive economy; and *third*, the determination of the "loci" of moral reasoning and responsibility with respect to economic behaviour and policies in a well-ordered society of equally free citizens, which means that economic ethics turns out to be a piece of political ethics, as we will see. I can only give a rough sketch of these three systematic tasks without treating them exhaustively in the remaining sections.

III. The First Task of Integrative Economic Ethics: The Critique of "Pure" Economic Reason and of Economism

Neo-classical economics is noncognitivistic with regard to moral arguing. It is assumed that morality and rationality are incompatible, i.e. that moral questions cannot be decided upon reason. The result is ethical relativism and scepticism, which is characteristic for the axiomatics of the neo-classical theory. Thus, rationality is limited to strategic rationality.

---

10 For examples of that mistaken "two-worlds conception" of morality and economic rationality which lies behind the approach of business ethics as "applied ethics" and for detailed criticism cf. ULRICH (1997, pp. 97ff.).

Integrative economic ethics does not agree with that; it starts from the insight that modern philosophical ethics very well knows a precise idea of ethical reason: that is the *normative logic of "interhumanity"*.[11] This is not the place to develop the basics of the – indeed *the* (sole and universal) – *moral point of view* of modern philosophical ethics. The point to make here is just to emphasise the fundamental difference between ethical reason (i.e. the normative logic of interhumanity) on the one side and economic rationality on the other. The latter can be understood as the logic of exchange, which is mutually advantageous, as we have seen in the first section. Now, the critique of economic rationality begins with the insight that this logic of mutual exchange based on nothing but self-interest (whose paradigmatic model is market exchange, of course) may give rise to a precise definition of (Pareto-)"efficiency"[12] but is not at all neutral or "value-free" with regard to the interests involved, because the outcomes of such an exchange always depend on the *status-quo* of "given" power relations. In contrast, the normative logic of interhumanity depends on the ethical principle of *moral equality* of all human beings, i.e. that all are beings which earn the same unconditional respect of their human dignity and the same inviolable basic human rights. Thus, moral rights and responsibilities, not power and counterpower (as implied in Pareto economics), become decisive. To put it briefly: Pareto-efficiency has nothing to do with justice!

This is why the *primacy of morality over the logic of the market* is constitutive for all serious economic ethics. The primacy of ethical reason over economic rationality cannot be eliminated by any arguments based upon "pure" economic rationality. However, two types of such argumentations are widespread not only in every-day rhetoric but also common in economic or business ethics:

– The *first* type tries to *avoid* the (uncomfortable) primacy of morality by declaring it "impossible" due to the *force of circumstances*, especially of competition in market situations. In this way, the domain of "permissible" ethical claims regarding economic activities is kept away from the "pure"

---

11 In German, I call it *die normative Logik der Zwischenmenschlichkeit*; cf. ULRICH (1997, pp. 23ff.). Of course, humanity is always "interhumanity" in this sense.

12 This was done by COASE (1960) and especially by BUCHANAN (1977). For detailed criticism cf. THIELEMANN (1996, pp. 40ff.) and ULRICH (1997, pp. 191ff.).

economic interest of (maximum) self-interest or profit, and this means that business ethics stops critical reflection before these decisive "private" purposes! But the strict maximising of any end is on no account a legitimate goal, since by definition it makes the consideration of all conflicting values or aspects literally impossible – and with that the primacy of morality over self-interest. This does not mean that economic interests do not count *morally,* but they only count as *claims* which have to be proved and justified; interests cannot serve as the *criteria* of ethical justification themselves. Thus, "given" interests cannot form or result in any *empirical* "necessities" or "impossibilities" for ethical consideration; rather it is a *normative* question how much abandonment may be demanded from economic actors, keeping in mind that they stand under the force of competitive circumstances in the market. And this question has to be reasonably decided according to the *moral rights* of all those involved, including the economic actors themselves. As these actors have legitimate claims (i.e. moral rights), too, only a restricted measure of self-abandonment can be demanded from them. But a certain measure of self-restriction with regard to private advantage must always be demanded from everybody. That is why the so-called "profit principle", too, is certainly not a "possible" legitimate purpose of a business company. Instead, it is a mere expression of economism.

Now, how much self-restriction may be demanded from the economic actors essentially depends on the *intensity of market competition.* The more competitive the market is, the stronger the force of circumstances works on the actors and the sooner their legitimate claims are touched. Then, the *partiality of the market* for those powerful purposes and interests, which stand behind the anonymous «force of the circumstances», becomes obvious. These are the dominating interests according to the status quo – in a "free" market society usually the "capital" interest of the shareholders. Consequently, to stop ethical criticism before the force of the competitive circumstances is simply bad economic ethics, endangered to fulfil an ideological function for the dominant interests. Contrary to that, the main task of economic ethics today is, at least in my perspective, to make clear that the neoliberal policy of unlimited intensification of market competition is not the solution but a central part of many problems in business and society. That's why a *"vital" policy of restricting the realm of markets and of directing the forces of competition in a life-conducive way* is required to make ethical demands of individual self-restriction reasonable. Integrative economic ethics is aware of that problematic logic of the market economy and intends to fully enlighten the economistic *Sachzwangdenken* and its ideological partiality.

– The *second* type of economism tries to *dissolve* the conflict between ethical and economic rationality by declaring both identical, so that the "market principle" itself seems to be the guarantor of the moral principle, at least under certain preconditions. This forms the background for a normative turn of the economic logic of mutually advantageous exchange toward a pretended *morality of the market*. Now, the market itself is regarded as the moral authority. The resulting "argument" is that ethics in business is *not necessary* as long as market competition works (whereas in the first type of economism, ethics was regarded to be more or less impossible). As a consequence, the idea of an unrestricted "free" market society already seems to meet the requisite of a well-ordered, just society of free citizens.

Due to its metaphysical roots in the natural theology as well as in utilitarianism, neo-classical mainstream economics has to be called a main cause of today's revival of such a confused and economistic world-view. All the more, economic ethics should not stay uncritically *beside* such economic ideology but critically interfere *in* it and enlighten its premodern grounds without reservation. As long as economic ethics contents itself with moralising from outside *against* economic rationality instead of arguing *for* an ethically well-founded idea of (socio-) economic rationality, it misses its specific philosophical task. Only by pursuing that task we become fully aware why and in which way moral reasoning is "necessary" with regard to all legitimate economic activities, to business policy and political economy.

Such a rational critique of political economy may be done on the methodical base of modern philosophical ethics, if at all. As far as I can see, the approach of integrative economic ethics might be internationally the first one that has fully recognised and more or less worked out the task of bringing economic rationality itself "to reason", proceeding from the oldest until the youngest stages of economic thinking.[13]

---

13 For a critical reconstruction of the most important stages in the history of economic thought cf. ULRICH (1997, pp. 168ff.) and already earlier, with different accents, ULRICH (1986, pp. 173ff.).

IV. The Second Task of Integrative Economic Ethics: The Clarification of an Ethically Integrated Idea of Socio-Economic Rationality

This is the crucial point of integrating ethical reason and economic rationality: How can we define a comprehensive concept of economic reason that includes the normative preconditions of legitimacy and therefore can serve as the *moral point of view in economic ethics*? Such an idea could be the sound base for overcoming the two-worlds (mis-) conception of ethics as the domain of moral arguing on the one side and economics as the "value-free" domain of "pure" economic reasoning on the other side. As we already know, according to the approach of integrative economic ethics the economic logic itself is the paradigmatic "locus" of morality – here we have to reveal and to criticise the fundamental normative content of "pure" economics, as discussed above, and here we have to reconstruct an ethically sound concept of economic rationality in terms of modern philosophical ethics.

The point of integration lies in the simple insight that, in a social economy with division of labour, the question of how to deal with the *scarcity* of economic resources and goods in an *efficient* (i.e. economically rational) way cannot be separated from the question of how to handle the *social conflicts* between all those involved in a *legitimate* (i.e. ethically justified) way. An ethically rational solution of such conflicts is disclosed by modern discourse ethics.[14] It is important to grasp that the problem of rational conflict solutions cannot be reduced to that of rationally dealing with scarcity because these are two basically different *categories* – ignoring this difference precisely means economism. This implies that the idea of an ethically integrated socio-economic rationality has to be conceptualised as irreducibly two-dimensional: it has to comprise an ethically rational discourse on the moral rights (legitimate claims) of all those involved in a social conflict as well as an efficient use of scarce resources or goods *with regard to those legitimate claims*. These two dimensions are no longer separated from or contradictory to each other, rather the efficient use of scarce resources has to be embedded or "kept up" (in a Hegelian sense of the term) in the ethical discourse on legitimate claims (fig. 2).

---

14 Cf. as fundamental approaches APEL (1976, 1988) and HABERMAS (1991).

PETER ULRICH

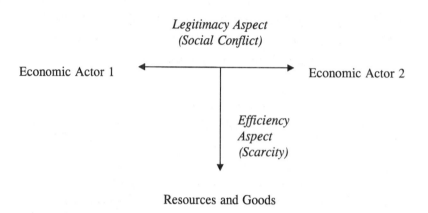

Figure 2: The two dimensions of socio-economic rationality.

This primacy of legitimacy over efficiency is simply the manifestation of the primacy of ethics in the concept of socio-economic rationality, which can now be defined as follows: *Any action or institution is rational in a socio-economic sense which free and mature citizens, in a reasonable process of deliberation, have (or could have) consensually found as a legitimate way of creating value.*

'Legitimate' means that this action or institution impartially respects the moral rights of all those involved, as we have seen above. And the addendum 'or could have' in parentheses reminds us that the methodological status of the concept of socio-economic rationality is that of a regulative idea (that of finding a rational consensus between moral persons who are interested in an impartial and just solution); it does not define a technical procedure of making an agreement between factual or "given" interests (which might be particular interests that turn out not to be legitimate and should therefore be abandoned). This regulative idea defines no more and no less than the moral point of view from which all kinds of socio-economic problems have to be judged *in an ethically reasonable way*.

Two practical dimensions of such socio-economically rational "value creation" can be differentiated, along the two simple questions: *what values* shall be created *for whom* exactly? The first question (what values?), which corresponds the Aristotelian line of ethics, asks for the *vital meaning* of economic activities with regard to the *good life* of the actors themselves. The second question (values for whom?), representing the Kantian line of

48

moral philosophy, asks for the *legitimacy* of the rules of an economy with regard to the *just living-together* of all citizens in a well-ordered society.

Here we cannot enter into a discussion of the manifold contents of those two formal dimensions. They have always to be developed in a concrete historical and situational context, of course. But let me hint at one important point concerning the systematic relation between the two aspects. Again, the primacy of morality means the normative pre-eminence of legitimacy over private projects of the good life, since a well-ordered society aims at the equal freedom of all citizens to choose their personal life-plans. Therefore, legitimate forms of private life depend on respecting (non-violating) the moral rights of other people. This is especially "vital" in the market sphere, because the normative logic of the market is not neutral against different life styles but a priori biased or partial for the benefit of those who have plenty of resources of any kind and prefer an "entrepreneurial" way of life, i.e. who like to invest all their energies and resources in their competitiveness and their economic success. The more intensive and the less restricted market competition is, the more difficult it therefore becomes to fulfil the pre-conditions of a well-ordered society of equally free citizens.

As we have seen, both aspects – the good personal life as well as the just living together – lead to the result that economic ethics, perceived in an uncurtailed way, is inevitably a part of political philosophy and political ethics; and it should join and be aware of the advanced state of affairs in that field. This may sound trivial, but the fact is that until now, economic and business ethics internationally has almost generally neglected its fundamental politico-philosophical nexus. Again, I dare to claim that the "St. Gallen approach" of integrated economic ethics is the first one that consequently understands itself as a part of modern political ethics. And this is essential for really clarifying the normative relations between a well-ordered society of free citizens and a life-conducive market economy.[15]

---

15 It is, for example, essential to clear up the systematic difference between the "free market" and a free society as well as the complex relation between liberalism and republicanism, to redefine the citizens' rights needed to secure their equally real freedom under the dramatically changing socio-economic circumstances of today, and to become aware of the exact meaning of a republican citizens' *ethos* for corporate ethics as well as for the political economy. Cf. the proposed integrative model of a *republican liberalism,* which rethinks political liberalism (RAWLS 1993) from the viewpoint of a republican ethics, in ULRICH (1997, pp. 293ff.).

Now, all well-founded ideas of a well-ordered society and a life-conducive economy remain *u-topian* – that is literally: without a locus – as long as it is not determined who is responsible for taking care of what exactly in that society. For this reason, integrative economic ethics recognises its third systematic task in localising the "loci" of moral reasoning and responsibility with respect to the economy.

V. The Third Task of Integrative Economic Ethics: The Determination of the "Loci" of Socio-Economic Responsibility

According to its politico-philosophical self-understanding outlined above, integrative economic ethics differentiates between three systematic loci of socio-economic responsibility, whereas conventional business ethics knows only two such loci: the individual *economic actor*, be it a person or a business firm, and the *State* as the authority that is responsible for the political framework of the market. The third systematic "locus" of morality, which normally is omitted despite of its fundamental role for a free and democratic society, is the *general public*. In modern political ethics, this term stands for the regulative idea of the unlimited community of all moral persons who are willing to participate as reasonable citizens in the public deliberation on all matters of the *res publica*, i.e. the "public affairs". The more recent political philosophy has developed remarkable approaches to a conception of *deliberative democracy* that keeps the balance between the counterfactual ideal of the general public (as the ethical pole) on the one side and "real politics" (as the factual pole) on the other side, without giving up neither the ethical orientation nor the connection to the political reality.[16]

Here I can give only the general hint that this conception is helpful for clarifying the *ethics of the politico-economic order* as a matter for the citizens' public deliberation on *their* vital priorities; this is *not* a matter of

---

16 Pioneering work in that direction has been done by MANIN (1987), SUNSTEIN (1988), and COHEN (1989); for the German-speaking area cf. HABERMAS (1992). A survey and the specific arguments with regard to the importance of that approach for economic ethics are presented in ULRICH (1997, pp. 305ff.).

"purely" economic expertise.[17] The resulting "vital order" *(Vitalordnung)*[18] of the market defines its life-conducive framework and is therefore essential for the legitimation of the political economy. To reduce the legitimation of the market to nothing but economic criteria like efficiency and international competitiveness would mean to fall into an economistic circle – which is a characteristic feature of presently dominating neoliberalism. Contrary to that, the first task of political economy is to recognise and protect free public deliberation against the interference of economic as well as political power.

Also for *corporate ethics* this enlightened politico-philosophical perspective shows substantial consequences. Integrative corporate ethics does no longer understand ethics either as an antidote to economic rationality (of profit-seeking) or as a means for furthering corporate success but as the constitutive groundwork of any socio-economically rational enterprise (i.e. efficient for legitimate purposes). Integrative corporate ethics aims at clarifying and safeguarding all normative preconditions for a life-conducive corporate "value-creation". This has to be secured on two levels of corporate morality: first, by choosing a *life-conducive corporate mission*, which simply means making money with products or services that have a real value for the "good life" of the customers and do not impose negative externalities upon other people or the community as a whole; secondly, by recognising a *republican co-responsibility* of the business company for the life-conduciveness of the politico-economic framework under which "free enterprise" feels legitimated to do business. Corporate ethics on this second level means that a business firm, as a "corporate citizen", is aware of its responsibilities to initiate and to support "vital" reforms of the politico-economic order, as far as they are necessary to secure the legitimacy and life-conduciveness of market competition, instead of misunderstanding politics only as a continuation of business with different means.

This republican conception of the political process presupposes the idea of the *general public of free and mature citizens as the ultimate locus of morality also for business*. Then the general public is no longer miscon-

---

17 Cf. ULRICH (1997, pp. 359ff.).

18 With reference to RÜSTOW's (1955, p. 74) term *'Vitalpolitik'*, KRÜSSELBERG (1989, p. 59) has introduced the term 'Vitalordnung' for that pre-eminent part of the political economy which does not aim at workable competition (*'Wettbewerbspolitik'*) but at the life-conduciveness of the market economy.

ceived as a special interest group among other stakeholders of the firm; rather it is the figurative place or forum where the "reasoning public" (Kant), in an open ethical and political deliberation, finds out what the general interest really is and how far the claims of special interest groups (including the management of the business firm itself, of course) are legitimate. This results in an *ethical turn of the stakeholder approach:* all stakeholders are part of the general public – from the very moment they raise claims against a firm they, too, have to recognise their moral duty to submit their claims to an open and public deliberation about legitimacy. And this means: in business ethics, it is simply a misconception to define stakeholders in strategic terms of influence and resource power against the company, because only in an open and reasonable deliberation it is possible to find out whose claims against the firm are ethically *justified* instead of being strategically strong only (in the sense that they have the power to *affect* the company so that it is forced to considerate the corresponding special interests).[19]

VI. Conclusions

The purpose of this paper was to outline an approach to economic ethics that does not content itself with the role of an antidote to economic rationality (nor even as a means to further it) but aims at a comprehensive reconsideration and reconstruction of the normative foundations of economic rationality itself. This is not an ivory-towered approach – quite on the contrary, it is the systematic answer to the reality of an exceeding dominance of the "logic of the market" over almost all other aspects of life. Under theses circumstances it is not enough if business ethics deals with the market's symptomatic appearances without critical reflection of the "market logic" itself. The more radical approach (in the literal sense of the term) is to begin at the fundamental roots, and this means: with a critique of the neo-classical two-worlds conception of economic rationality and morality and with the reconstruction of the normative foundations of a conception of

---

19 This ethically critical reconceptualization of the stakeholder approach is developed in ULRICH (1997, pp. 438ff.).

socio-economic rationality which has ethical reason built-in as its prerequisite. This is the approach of *integrative economic ethics:* the approach to a comprehensive ethical re-orientation of "economic reasoning" as such on the basis of today's philosophical ethics and political philosophy. This might be a promising way of renewing the best intentions of the former historical and ethical school of economics without restoring its philosophically obsolete conception of ethics. Economic ethics, conceived in this way, might become the foundation of a practical socio-economics for the future, basically oriented toward the *life-conduciveness* of all economic thinking and acting.

References

APEL, K.-O.: *Transformation der Philosophie*, Frankfurt (Suhrkamp) 1976.

APEL, K.-O.: *Diskurs und Verantwortung. Das Problem des Übergangs zur postkonventionellen Moral*, Frankfurt (Suhrkamp) 1988.

BUCHANAN, J. M.: *The Limits of Liberty. Between Anarchy and Leviathan*, Chicago/London (University of Chicago Press) 1975.

BUCHANAN, J. M.: *Freedom in Constitutional Contract. Perspectives of a Political Economist,* College Station/London (Texas A & M University Press) 1977.

COASE, R.: "The Problem of Social Cost", *The Journal of Law and Economics*, 3 (1960), pp. 1-44.

COHEN, J.: "Deliberation and Democratic Legitimacy", in: A. HAMLIN, P. PETIT (Eds.): *The Good Polity*, Oxford (Blackwell's) 1989, pp. 17-34.

GAUTHIER, D.: *Morals by Agreement*, Oxford (Oxford University Press) 1986.

HABERMAS, J.: *Erläuterungen zur Diskursethik*, Frankfurt (Suhrkamp) 1991.

HABERMAS, J.: *Faktizität und Geltung. Beiträge zur Diskurstheorie des Rechts und des demokratischen Rechtsstaats*, Frankfurt (Suhrkamp) 1992. English translation: *Between Facts and Norms: Contributions to a Discourse Theory of Law and Democracy*, Cambridge, Mass./London (MIT Press) 1996.

HOMANN, K., BLOME-DREES, F.: *Wirtschafts- und Unternehmensethik*, Göttingen (Vandenhoeck & Ruprecht) 1992.

HOMANN, K., PIES, I.: "Wirtschaftsethik in der Moderne: Zur ökonomischen Theorie der Moral", *Ethik und Sozialwissenschaften*, 5 (1994), pp. 3-12.

PETER ULRICH

KOSLOWSKI, P.: *Prinzipien der Ethischen Ökonomie. Grundlegung der Wirtschafts-ethik und der auf die Ökonomie bezogenen Ethik*, Tübingen (Mohr) 1988.

KOSLOWSKI, P.: "Grundlinien der Wirtschaftsethik", *Zeitschrift für Wirtschafts- und Sozialwissenschaften*, 109 (1989), pp. 345-383.

KRÜSSELBERG, H.-G.: "Soziale Marktwirtschaft: Idee und Wirklichkeit", *Orientierungen zur Wirtschafts- und Gesellschaftspolitik*, 41, Bonn (1989), pp. 56-64.

MACPHERSON, C. B.: *The Political Theory of Possessive Individualism. From Hobbes to Locke*, Oxford (Oxford University Press) 1962.

MANIN, B. (1987): "On Legitimacy and Political Deliberation", *Political Theory*, 15 (1987), pp. 338-368.

RAWLS, J.: *A Theory of Justice*, Cambridge, Mass. (Harvard University Press) 1971.

RAWLS, J.: *Political Liberalism*, New York (Columbia University Press) 1993.

RÜSTOW, A.: "Wirtschaftsethische Probleme der sozialen Marktwirtschaft", in: P. M. BOARMAN (Ed.): *Der Christ und die soziale Marktwirtschaft*, Stuttgart/Köln (Kohlhammes) 1955, pp. 53-74.

STEINMANN, H., LÖHR, A.: "Unternehmensethik - eine 'realistische' Idee", *Schmalenbachs Zeitschrift für betriebswirtschaftliche Forschung*, 40 (1988), pp. 299-317.

SUNSTEIN, C. R.: "Beyond the Republican Revival", *The Yale Law Journal*, 97 (1988), pp. 1539-1590.

THIELEMANN, U.: *Das Prinzip Markt. Kritik der ökonomischen Tauschlogik*, Bern/Stuttgart/Wien (Haupt) 1996.

ULRICH, P.: *Transformation der ökonomischen Vernunft. Fortschrittsperspektiven der modernen Industriegesellschaft*, Bern/Stuttgart/Wien (Haupt) 1986 (3rd ed. 1993).

ULRICH, P.: "Towards an Ethically-Based Conception of Socio-Economic Rationality: From the Social Contract Theory to Discourse Ethics as the Normative Foundation of Political Economy", *Praxiology. The International Annual of Practical Philosophy and Methodology*, Vol. 5, ed. by W. W. GASPARSKI & L. V. RYAN, New Brunswick/London (Transaction Publ.) 1996, pp. 21-49.

ULRICH, P.: *Integrative Wirtschaftsethik. Grundlagen einer lebensdienlichen Ökonomie*, Bern/Stuttgart/Wien (Haupt) 1997 (2nd ed. 1998).

WEBER, M.: "Die 'Objektivität' sozialwissenschaftlicher und sozialpolitischer Erkenntnis", in: *Gesammelte Aufsätze zur Wissenschaftslehre*, Tübingen (Mohr) 4th ed. 1973.

WEISSER, G.: "Die Überwindung des Ökonomismus in der Wirtschaftswissenschaft" (1954). Reprinted in: *Beiträge zur Gesellschaftspolitik*, Göttingen (Otto Schwartz) 1978, pp. 573-601.

Chapter 4

Changing Normative Textures
How Discourse-Ethics Meets the Challenge of Historicism

MATTHIAS KETTNER

I. Introduction: The Prose and Pros of a Pragmatist Doctrine of Norms

Normative theories in philosophical ethics rarely invest much effort into scrutinising the very idea of a norm. Norms are usually conceived of as rules with some sort of prescriptive force, or as action guides whose action-orienting content is open to inspection and to some measure of reflective control. Underlying such surface variations in the received view of a norm is a tendency to regard norms as kinds of templates (mental, physical, or otherwise) of performance, resident in agents. Norms are thought to be what determines unilaterally what kinds of thought or action accord with them. They are alleged to guide practice while themselves being independent of the practice they guide and hence without being modified by the practice to which they are taken to be applied. This tendency to view a norm as an isolate locus of unilateral determination is epitomised in the not uncommon view of "principles" as highly abstract norms which determine, but are not determined by, whatever it is that they are held to be principles of. The philosophical elaboration of the common view of norms as templates has led to many perplexities among which is perhaps most conspicuous the question of how there can be evaluation, justification, and rectification of such unilaterally determining entities. Sometimes one can appeal to other, supervening norms; but the need to terminate the regressive procedure typically leads to appeals to dubious "foundations", to conventions, to "intuitions", to supposedly ultimate sources of normativity that allegedly provide governance without in turn being governed by other norms: ungoverned governors. The aporia of this idea is brought home in the notoriously difficult question as to how we can reliably draw the line between arriving at an ultimate source of normativity and arriving at sheer prejudice? (Will 1997, p. 197)

An alternative general view of norms, much more realistic than the standard view of norms as unilateral determiners of right action, has been developed in the tradition of philosophical pragmatism. The pragmatic view of norms concerns the constitutive role played by norms in creating the texture of human life and thought. The view has been shaped by the pragmatic tradition by thoughts developed by Charles Sanders Peirce on the collective fixation of our beliefs, William James (1890) and John Dewey (1922) on the social psychology of habit formation and adaptation, and it has been elaborated more recently by Alasdair MacIntyre's (1988) reflections on tradition and rationality, James Wallace (1996) on normative holism and, with great ingenuity and persuasiveness, in Frederik L. Will's work on reflective and nonreflective governance of norms (Will 1988, 1993, 1997).[1]

This pragmatic view is that norms are intrinsically socio-psychological entities that interlock with each other and are rooted deeply in the practices of individuals and their communities. Embedded in these practices, norms are principally open-textured: i.e. they are open to further definition and revision whenever and wherever serious anomalies in their extant forms are encountered. 'Serious anomalies' are those that are serious for the people

---

1   I discuss Will's views in KETTNER (1998a).

themselves who stand to be affected by the practical consequences of the norms; that is to say, serious enough for them to require scrutiny, modificatory and adaptive efforts.

For a realistic doctrine of norms, it is of the utmost importance to recognise that norms defy an ontology of discrete atomistic entities and to acknowledge the corporate, or compositional, or - if you will - holistic nature of norms. In order to invent a distinctive term for the intrinsically polymorphic nature of norms I propose to speak of "normative textures" of practices. Of course, we can count norms and linguistically or otherwise symbolically represented normative contents one by one, just as we can count linguistically or otherwise symbolically represented propositions or beliefs about what is the case, or just as we can count numbers. The deontic judgement "it is not permitted to park your car here!", whether expressed in words uttered by a policeman or expressed in the form of a pertinent traffic sign, picks out a different norm than the deontic judgement "in Great Britain, drive on the left side of the road!", which translates into action-requirements that evidently differ from those warranted by the aforementioned deontic judgement. However, we should well be aware philosophically that what we single out as some determinate normative content is a symbolically stylised representation that is abstracted from the practice in which the norm is embedded. This representation has determinate identity conditions tailored to the very purpose of sorting things out; whereas to grasp the very point of the norm takes much more in the way of understanding the purposes of the practices in which some particular norm plays a role in conjunction with other norms that are equally part and parcel of the fabric of those practices.[2] Grasping the very point of a norm, however, is necessary in order for there to be something for the operations of practical reason to grasp. After all, the gist of practical reason is not manipulation of symbolic representations, but deliberation about what we have reason to do in practice concretely, i.e. all things considered. Unless practices themselves enter in our practical deliberations, the deontic judgements in which those deliberations may eventually terminate will have no practical import. The following quote from Will neatly sums up the crucial differences in outlook between, on the one hand, the standard view of norms as atomistic templates of action, unilateral determiners whose normative nature comes with clear-cut symbolic identity conditions, and on the other hand a prag-

---

2   Cf. WILL 1997, ch. 4, esp. p. 69.

matic realism that views norms as normative textures constitutive of human practices:

> However valuable it may be for certain scientific purposes, for philosophical purposes it is detrimental to think of norms exclusively as individual patterns connecting specific responses to specific stimulating conditions. Norms are not such patterns, abstracted from each other and from the communal life of which they are features. A norm neither represents nor prescribes a pattern of action or response that can be thought of as existing independently of its relations to other norms though capable also of being brought into relation with them. A norm is not just a form of action. It is a form of appropriate action, of appropriate response; and this appropriateness is something that is determined in its relation with, among other things, other norms: by the role which this or that mode of action or response plays in the constitution of individual and communal life. (Will 1988, p.93)

To sum up this section: For any domain of practices in which some activity is carried out, what makes the activity an appropriate or inappropriate way for one to proceed is to be found in the normative texture of that domain of practices. Normative textures are intrinsically polymorphous, hence many norms will figure in many different domains of practices, hence practices will be more or less porous and overlapping.

II. Normative Textures, Changing Governance, and Governing Change

Historicism, to put it in very popular terms, is the view that "history rules".[3] The same point can be phrased in terms with a respectable philosophic pedigree: historicism is the view that life-world realities are Heracliteian realities. You do not step twice into the same life-worldly situation,

---

3   Ernst Troeltsch, who stands out as perhaps the most important individual figure in the complex epistemological formation of German historicism, put the central point in somewhat more sublime terms when (somewhere in his magnum opus "Der Historismus und seine Probleme") he declared that all meaning and validity reduce to history (*"daß aller Sinn und Geltung historisch sei"*).

since whatever is acknowledged as real in people's life-worlds will turn out on inspection to be governed by history, history being an incessant source-process of multifarious differences that are neither theoretically nor practically ever fully controllable.

What is the drama in this? Why should the admittance a Heracliteian reality of incessant processes of change spell doom for morality and for the corresponding philosophical enterprise of normative moral theorising, as is often supposed? Why should historicism unavoidably lead to "the collapse of morals and religion", as historian Jacob Burkhardt is reported to have said? In my view, the valuable lesson to draw from the historicist enlightenment of the humanities is certainly not that all prescriptive authority ("legitimacy" in the widest sense of this word) pertaining to moral claims and normative claims of other kinds goes up in smoke, but rather, that received views about the sources and bases of prescriptive authority are seriously flawed to the extent that they do not cohere with our best warranted beliefs about the nature of normatively textured social life. What goes up in smoke, and rightly so, is not so much our practices of judgement through which we articulate and determine whatever prescriptive authority we and our cultural peers want to accord to the normative claims we think we have reason to make. What proves untenable, rather, is a set of ill-conceived, metaphysical, platonistic ideas about absolute, unilateral authority from transcendent sources. Instead of abhorring historicism as a force which threatens human values or which can lead to a radical transvaluation of values, we should embrace historicism's descriptive and explanatory powers of discernment concerning the pervasiveness of normative change.

Forces threatening important human values exist, and radical transvaluations of values are under way all the time. Historicism can improve our perception of the extent to which this is true. Historicist knowledge, it is true, can also be enlisted in the service of such forces. But this is platitudinous and there is nothing interestingly intrinsic to historicist knowledge that would seem to condemn such knowledge to be harnessed to such forces.

To think otherwise would be to commit the error of the genetic fallacy. A genetic fallacy, to wit, consists in inferring the validity of a claim from nothing but the genesis of that claim, i.e. of the history of that claim's being raised. Or for short, a genetic fallacy consists in reducing validity to genesis. However, it is no less a fallacy to infer that if the genesis of a claim can be understood, that claim loses whatever validity it was supposed to have beforehand. At times, moralists' warnings against the perils of historicism seem to thrive on this genetic fallacy.

In order not to be misunderstood, let me briefly rehearse three paradigm readings of the term 'historicism':

(1) Historicism, on a first reading, is a methodological maxim linking genetic accounts (descriptions, explanations, narratives) with evaluations, i.e. by giving an historical account of how some valued way of proceeding - for instance, lending money at some reasonable rate of interest (Wallace 1996); classifying according to "natural essences" as opposed to analogies (Foucault 1980) - has come into the position that it actually occupies within some normative texture. Adopting axiological jargon, one might say: historicism (on the reading that we are considering now) operates by giving an historical account of how certain values have been put where we find them amongst all other values that we uphold or repudiate. The Nitzschean and Foucaultean methods of "genealogy" are radicalisations, untenable in some of their less modest claims, of historicism in this first sense.

(2) Historicism, on a second reading, is a search for methodologies that would do justice to the difference between those research interests that are oriented to the quantifiable and nomologically general as opposed to research interests of a kind that are more oriented to the unique and concrete individual case.

Here again, rather than seeing historicism (in the second sense of the term) as a harbinger of social anomie, I think there is more to be said in favour of viewing historicism as promising to make our theories of normativity fit for reality and to make our deontic judgements fit for the kind of fallibilism that we typically cherish as a hallmark of any interestingly rational procedure.

(3) Historicism, on a third reading that has gained currency through the writings of Popper, denotes a group of ontologies of social life, namely those in which certain laws of development (e.g., Marxian "dialectical necessities", or Spenglerian "laws of history") are held to govern social wholes. On the basis of such knowledge (it is held) we can give scientific predictions about the future course of such social wholes.

Historicism in this sense has been so thoroughly and devastating criticised that I will make no more mention of this sense of the term `historicism' in what follows.

Is historicism (in the first or second senses) the deathbed of strong programs of normative ethics? Does historicism imply cultural relativism? Is historicism incompatible with normative universalism? To all these questions the answer is, I submit, clearly no. The pragmatic realistic view of norms (as outlined in section I) can help to reconcile historicism and the pursuit of strong programs of normative ethics. A centre-piece in this reconciliation would be the pragmatist insight that a substantial amount of all the normative change that is always occurring happening is not simply happening, the way radioactive decay is simply happening. A substantial amount of normative change is an effect of the very governance that is the rational point of all norms.

This point deserves a closer look. *Governance* is a broad term covering both the critical and the constructive activities in which we are engaged with the character, establishment, and maintenance of norms, as well as with their disestablishment and elimination. Governance of norms (as I shall employ the term following Will 1993, p.21) encompasses their development, criticism, refinement, reconstruction, reinforcement, weakening, and elimination. Governance in however marginal a way is implicit in the very concept of acting in the light of reasons, when the concept of a norm is taken sufficiently broadly so as to include reasons for appropriate action. Governance comprises the *entire* range of activities, individual *and* collective, deliberate or without much conscious effort, *i.* of fitting norms to each other and to the circumstances in which they are followed; *ii.* of generating new norms and reconstructing already extant norms once they have revealed serious insufficiencies in practice; *iii.* of phasing out the norms that have been rendered anachronistic by substantial change in the very forms of life whose circumstances used to provide contextual fit for the norms; and *iv.*, of revising, extending, or contracting norms in appropriate reaction to the surprises and vicissitudes that we permanently encounter in the practices whose workings are textured by norms.

Piecing together some of Will's acute observations[4] on normative change and the changing of normative textures, the emerging realist view can be rendered somewhat along the following lines:

We experience again and again how norms, or more or less extended components of normative textures for a variety of reasons, and in various degrees, falter and fail in praxis. However, such failures are not always merely "negative". Rather, they often provide stimuli and grounds for change. Bodies of norms inherently and inevitably - sometimes more and

---

4   Cf. WILL (1988, especially pp. 39, 148, 157, 189).

sometimes less - suffer from (1) incompleteness and (2) inconsistency. As to incompleteness, we encounter never our normative repertories as something complete: Occasions for decision, conviction, fixation of opinion and action arise for which there is no ready decision procedure. As to inconsistency, inconsistency appears at various places in the repertory where contrary procedures seem to apply, yielding indecision that can be resolved only if we manage to revise components of the body of norms so that the debilitating opposition is overcome. Further, as a result of the corporate character of these bodies, changes generated or coming to be generated in one set have impacts upon other sets and bodies of norms. Such resonance effects may sometimes include responsive changes and sometimes defensive dispositions to resist change. Always and everywhere, we are faced with having to mutually accommodate determinate sets of norms, once somehow formed and somewhat composed. The stress generated among them, the abrasion and confusion arising in their being jointly followed, as they should, provide motives for this accommodation:

> What may appear in its local environment as merely negative, as the faltering, failure, or confusion in certain readily formalisable procedures, in a larger context may be revealed to play a most important positive role. The faltering, failing, and confusion may provide not only motivation for revision of these procedures, but also indications of the general location where revision is called for and the general direction the revision should take. (Will 1988, p.39)

Let me draw some conclusions for moral theory from the pragmatic, realistic notion of norms that I have been sketching:

(1) The Heracliteian reality of ever changing normative textures as depicted by methodological historicism is largely *a reality of processes of governance*. Processes of governance are multifarious; different forms of governance in different domains of practice may differ drastically in their advantages and disadvantages when compared from an evaluative point of view, and they will differ drastically across different evaluative points of view. Take, for example, bureaucracy as a form of governance and consider what becomes of academic life when universities are predominantly governed by bureaucracies; then compare this rather nasty scenario with the effects of bureaucratic governance in another setting, for instance, think of the indisputable advantages in that historic change which has swept away more arbitrary, whimsical, or feudal modes of governing the affairs that pertain to *state* administration. But then again, think of former "socialist"

state bureaucracies and compare the bureaucratic governance of scarce economic goods or resources by centralised state-planning with the drastically different mode of governance by competitive market exchanges.

(2) Owing to the concrete nature of normative textures as features of the practices they help guide, any effort of reflective and deliberate social reconstruction of normative textures, if it is to be rational, must be sensitive to the holistic and concrete character of normative textures. In its general purport as a social reformist movement that seeks to carry normative moral thinking into diverse domains of practices with a view to morally improving how things get done in those domains, *applied ethics* is completely on the wrong track in conceiving of its operative notions of "application" as implementation or as in the *technical engineering* line of business. Business ethics, e.g., does not inject normativity into a field of practices encountered as a normative void. There are no normative voids in human forms of social life. It would be more adequate to conceive of business ethics as an attempt to intervene with certain moral resources of reflective normative governance into the multifarious normative governance processes, non-moral and moral, which go on all the time in the field of economic practices. Applied ethics has to tap moral resources that are already *in* the practices it seeks morally to ameliorate. It operates from within, internal to the practices, trying to understand and reshape practices for the morally better, otherwise it will invariable appear in the roles of invader, coloniser, or despot, roles which under normal circumstances virtually guarantee that very little will come of such "moralising" efforts.

(3) Business ethics, like all other branches of applied ethics, would be well advised to give up the ill-founded rhetoric of problem solving, as well as the equally ill-conceived dream of problem solving algorithms and of the `one principle fits all' type of theorising.

III. Modes of Transition in Normative Textures

This section sketches how the normative moral theory called Discourse Ethics ties in with the realistic doctrine of normative textures outlined in sections I and II.

In section II I gave some examples of macro transitions in normative textures. Let me add some more examples in order to introduce the concept of a *T1-T2 transition*, i.e. a transition of one state of the normative textures governing a certain practical field to a different state of the normative textures of that practical field: Consider, for instance, of the normative change involved in the transition to the delegitimisation of insider trading. Or think of the normative sea-change that occurred with the transition of business mentality from stakeholder value to shareholder value. To vary the range of practical fields, just consider of the field of medical practices and the transition within this field that occurs when solidaristic practices of blood donation and organ donation are switched to commercialising modes of governance. Graphic examples could be multiplied. We are dealing with reality, after all.

Processes of governance are multifarious, and different forms of governance in different domains of practice may differ drastically in their pros and cons when compared from and across various evaluative points of view. This also holds for moral points of view, since moral points of view are a subset, albeit with some quite peculiar properties, of evaluative points of view. By carefully crafted reflective interventions from within some practical domain, good applied ethics aims at making it the case that in some targeted *T1-T2 transition*, the resulting *T2* is a morally better, or at least not morally less qualified, normatively textured practice than was *T1*.

Discourse ethics grounds a number of constraints on consensus building about normative matters (Apel 1989, 1990a, 1990b, 1993; Rehg 1994). These constraints, if jointly and sufficiently fulfilled, bestow rational moral authority on the corresponding consensus-building process, whereas failure to sufficiently satisfy one or more of these constraints invalidates claims to moral authority for that consensus (Kettner 1993a, 1998b). Discourse Ethics, in my understanding of that approach, articulates and vindicates a moral resource of very minimal morally normative content but with the advantage of being ubiquitously available, namely as an ethics residing in the very idea of argumentative discourse. Discourse Ethics makes this minimal morally normative content explicit - by a heuristics of what is technically called "performative self-contradiction" (Apel 1987; Kettner 1993a), - and from this resource - call it: an ethics in discourse - Discourse Ethics seeks to develop the much richer notion of a fully rational moral discussion - call this the notion of a moral discourse.

Moral discourse is rational argumentation about problems that are perceived specifically as morally perplexing, i.e. problems that are perceived to call for answers in terms of deontic judgements (expressing what we think may or ought or ought not to be done) which are underwritten, not by any sort of reasons, but specifically by reasons that are recognised as moral reasons (thus rendering such deontic judgements morally deontic judgements). The qualification that moral discourse be rational is but a corollary of an aspiration to argue about conflicting moral reasons with a view to (re)making certain morally deontic judgements and their reasons more coherent where they threaten to come apart in the face of disturbing moral perplexities.

If the normative framework of Discourse Ethics can be fashioned into something analogous to what passes as "models of application" in applied ethics, then Discourse Ethics holds the following promise: For any transition of *T1* to *T2*, if this transition is governed by moral discourse, then *T2* will be at least as morally acceptable as *T1*, as judged from all different moral outlooks that are operative in T1. Discourse Ethics then is a morally superb mode of governing transitions in normative textures, whenever the moral qualities that are at stake in such a transition are momentous enough to merit the effort of bringing to bear this very demanding mode of governance on the moral perplexities found in some targeted practical domain.

IV. An Ethics of Responsibility for Discursive Power Among Rational Agents

Discourse Ethics, I maintain, is best conceived of as a set of moral responsibilities accruing to the deployment of a certain form of power, namely discursive power. In order to see the merits of this view it is necessary to get rid of a deep-seated philosophical prejudice, namely the received view that reason and power are totally antithetical. Contrary to this erroneous contemplative idealism, I prefer to take serious the metaphor of reason as being a power of sorts. Argumentation, I maintain, is not only an exercise of some rational "capacities" but also an exercise of power. Call this "discursive power".

To understand the concept of discursive power properly, we must distinguish it from current interpretations of power that are too immediately causal. Admittedly, the *causality interpretation* of power and its various modes is by no means arbitrary: It follows from the quite sound principle that "if someone has power then it must imply something for others. [...] Yet it is clearly possible to conceive of power as a capacity of a power holder to make a difference without causing any power subject to do anything; in the decisional" - and likewise in the discursive - "interpretation of power what matters [...] is less the impact that a power holder has upon the behaviour of some power subject, but [...] the capacity to make a difference in decision making, the outcomes of which may or may not cause another actor to behave in certain ways" (Lane and Stenlund 1984, p. 395). Discursive power, then, is the power to modify via argumentation, to change or to keep from changing the beliefs people have about what is right and wrong in their employment of the authority of good reasons in their actions. Discursive power operates on our interpretations of reasons as better or worse, and in the measure in which our ways of life give importance to how we match our actions to our interpretations of reasons as better or worse, discursive power operates albeit indirectly on our actual conduct. Discourse Ethics, then, is the intrinsic morality of the use of discursive power in the governance of (moral or non-moral) norms.

In order to get clear about the sense in which some intrinsic elements of the normative texture of argumentative discursive practices amount to a minimal *morality* it is helpful first to consider the general notion of a morality.

V. Morality, Moralities

Morality in the most general sense of the term can be characterised as a social practice of governing our doings by a concern for (certain aspects of) the well-being of (certain sorts of) beings. In all commonly recognised moralities, the set of beings with moral standing includes but need not be exhausted by people. Usually these "bearers" or "subjects" of moral beliefs will be the members of the same community of moral concern, i.e., one's moral peers. Different moralities draw the boundaries of their respective communities of moral concern in different ways.[5]

The definition, common among sociologists, of (any particular) morality as a (particular) "normative system" that regulates action by classifying actions for "praise and blame" is too general, for there are many different action guiding normative systems (e.g. law, religion, prudence, mores, etiquette) none of which is identical with, though each is somehow related to, morality as we know it (Castaneda 1974).

Moralities are complex socio-evolutionary constructions: A morality is a more or less integrated yet open-textured (Brennan 1977) web of knowledge, emotional dispositions ("moral feelings"), action skills ("virtues"), motivational propensities ("altruism"), and interpretative resources ("moral thinking") (Gibbard 1990). This web provides us with moral reasons (Dancy 1993; Copp 1995; Gert 1998), moral judgements, and moral norms.

Moral reasons are reasons why certain things may or ought or ought not to be done, where failing to do what one ought to do is *morally wrong*. Moral reasons in turn support our practice of moral judgements. Moral judgements are judgements about the moral rightness or wrongness of claims concerning what morally may (or ought or ought not to) be done. That something may (morally) or may not (morally) be done is usually expressed in the format of a (moral) norm. A (moral) norm presents some way of acting in some circumstances as (morally) required of certain agents. There is, of course, a wide variety of norms only some of which are moral norms. Legal rules, rules of games, traffic regulations, etc., are all norms. Moral norms, as opposed to other sorts of norms, are norms which are intersubjectively recognised as "categorical" (Gewirth 1978) i.e., to the extent that people are unwilling or unable to respect them (minimally as negative constraints, maximally as positive ideals) in their deliberations about what they shall do, such people will either be taken to act immorally

---

5   Where "particularist" moralities draw the boundary narrowly it is also possible to extend the community of one's moral peers "universalistically" so as to encompass all human beings indifferent of cultural differences and spatial or temporal distances between them. Such universalism, far from being a lofty idealism, is a built-in possibility of people's moral-cognitive development. This development is patterned into a number of stages in an invariant sequential order. There is ample cross-cultural evidence for this in cognitive developmental psychology (COLBY, KOHLBERG 1987; WREN 1990).

("morally wrong") or will not be counted as moral agents by other moral agents.

To bring out more clearly the sense in which moral reasons, judgements and norms differ from non-moral reasons, judgements, and norms, consider the notion of *moral responsibility*. Moral agents are persons who bear, and take their moral peers to bear, moral responsibility (Ladd 1982; Frankfurt 1983; French 1985). An agent's moral responsibility is a responsibility that is neither exhausted by that agent's *causal* role in the outcome of actions nor in that agent's liability that is relevant to *juridical* assessment of actions. Rather, the bearing of moral responsibility consists specifically in collectively taking seriously how the outcome of one's conduct, i.e. of possible actions or omissions, affects oneself or relevant others for their good or ill.

Different moralities, of course, assign different contents to the structure of such responsibility: different ways of acting ("conduct"), different reference groups ("others"), different significant values ("good or ill"). This diversity of interpretations implies moral pluralism. From pluralism we must distinguish moral relativism. Diversity and pluralism do not as such imply relativism. Consider: Like natural languages, moralities are a pervasive feature of human culture. Yet whereas cross-translatability between any two natural languages seems to be feasible in principle without any limitation, the fact of moral diversity (and value pluralism) has been taken to support the view that it makes sense to speak of justified moral claims or commitments only with reference to particular cultures: cultural moral relativism. However, strong moral relativism (and incommensurability of values across deeply different cultures or across subcultures) is a self-refuting theoretical view, as is the view that understanding across different value-horizons is impossible. I cannot discuss these points here. Suffice it to say that the world-wide recognition of those deontic reasons and morally significant values that we abbreviate as human rights in fact contradicts any strong relativism and incommmensurabilism. At a sufficiently abstract level where moral deontic reasons take the form of "moral principles", there is considerable overlapping consensus across diverse cultures despite disagreement over their more fine-grained interpretation and ranking and to what extent which real social practices ought to be governed by which principles.[6] A certain range of values (e.g. freedom, the provision of basic needs, integrity of primary affective bonds, sanity) bear moral significance

---

6   OUTKA, REEDERS (1993). For a less sanguine view, see SNARE (1989).

virtually everywhere (Gert 1990, 1998). Yet their determinate interpretations in terms of moral action requirements, moral norms, may vary dramatically across drastically different cultures.

The fact of moral diversity (even at the level of principles) should not obscure the fact that the common object of any morality is the facilitation and enhancement of human flourishing (Mackie 1977) - even in borderline cases where such flourishing is interpreted, e.g., in some "cosmocentric" ethical outlooks, as amounting to a concern for the integrity of inanimate components of nature.

The fact of moral diversity needs to be accommodated sensibly in any "rational" morality and normative moral theory with universalistic aspirations. To see why, consider that universalistic moral claims make a claim on everyone who properly takes them into account intellectually. They purport to command the assent of whoever is a morally responsible rational agent. Yet the people making such claims are always members of some particular community in space, time, and culture. Hence they run the risk of imposing claims of what they take to be their universalistic morality on others whose moral views, if only they were allowed to express themselves, could be seen to differ from or even to defy the imposed claims. Owing to the universalism inherent in our notion of rational validity, any markedly "rational" morality will also aspire to universalism. Yet a sensible universalism in morality, it seems, must not impose rigid moral principles on an unruly moral world of heterogeneous moral views. If it would, it would be buying uniformity at the cost of dogmatism or paternalism. Both dogmatism and paternalism concerning the imposition of alien moral views spell unnecessary "moral costs". They are therefore wrong according to the very standards of a truly rational morality. To the extent that an allegedly rational morality or moral theory is insensitive to its own impact, or lacks the conceptual resources for the moral assessment of such impact in its application, it is seriously inadequate to the modern pluralist condition.

VI. Moral Horizons, Discourse Ethics, and Other Moral Paradigms

A moral point of view or horizon (as I would prefer to say) is the evaluative stance of someone who identifies with some morality M (e.g., by "having been brought up" in the spirit of M, by finding M convincing, etc.) for assessing practical activities and the reasons for which people take themselves to be justified in doing what they do. A moral horizon discloses the "moral costs" (according to the particular value standards that are acknowledged in M) which accrue to people's transactions. By considering things in a moral horizon, one assesses impacts of, and reasons for, actions with an eye to minimising whatever moral costs they are seen to have. A moral horizon, being a *moral* point of view, discloses what is right or wrong (as judged by its avoidable moral costs) and what thus ought to be done or ought not to be done (on moral grounds). Being a point of view, no moral horizon is all-encompassing. Being a *point* of view, any moral horizon, to the extent that it can be called rational, must admit of controversy and consensus, of questions and answers, of argument and counter-argument.

Naturally, there are many different evaluative perspectives, only some of which are moral horizons. We can assess actions and the reasons for which they are performed from the prudential, the legal, the moral, the economic, the technical, the religious and, no doubt, from many other points of view. For instance, some new medical technique may be ingenious and highly recommendable on prudential grounds when seen from a techno-economic point of view (e.g., because it saves resources) and yet be disreputable and wrong on grounds of its moral costs when seen from a moral point of view (e.g., because it subverts patient autonomy). A new law might be legitimate from a juridical point of view (e.g., because it has passed parliament) and yet be illegitimate morally considered (e.g., because it violates human rights). A new financial instrument (e.g., derivatives) for all the sense it may make economically, may be found wanting in fairness (i.e. morally) when the patterned distribution of risks and benefits engendered by that instrument is assessed.

For the reasons I give in the next section I believe that Discourse Ethics and its moral horizon - the horizon of taking seriously how the consequences of argumentative uses of discursive power affect peoples' capacities for governing all normative textures on which they perceive their well-being to depend - is centre-stage among moral horizons. This is not to say that Discourse Ethics replaces extant moral horizons. It is to say, rather, that Discourse Ethics is central in its capacity to synthesise and gauge *more or less different other* moral horizons.

Roughly, four paradigms of normative moral theory and their respective central principles are presently in the foreground of philosophical ethics.[7] These paradigms are: (1) Kantian deontologism with it principle that persons ought to be respected as ends-in-themselves (O'Neill 1989), (2) utilitarianism with its principle that utility ought to be impartially maximised (Sen & Williams 1982; Hare 1981), (3) contractualism with its principle that explicit or tacit agreements for mutual benefits ought to be honoured (Gauthier 1990), and (4), consensualism with its principle that all normative arrangements ought to be procedurally governed through free and open argumentative dialogue ("discourse"), ideally of everyone concerned (Apel 1980 and 1990; Habermas 1993). Of these, consensualism as developed into a "communicative" or "Discourse Ethics" (Apel, Habermas) is the most integrative and most flexible position. The initial stimulus behind the philosophical development of Discourse Ethics is the intuition that the reasons for which people claim that something is morally right must be such as to be conceivably acceptable from the first-person plural perspective ("we") of everyone concerned by the practice, activity or regulation whose moral rightness is at stake. Call this the *discourse principle*. Moral rightness then is a property of action-norms, a property ultimately dependent on the cooperative discursive practice of free and open dialogue between rational evaluators about discordant *appreciations* of allegedly good reasons.

This is not to say that all moral content is held to be generated in dialogue[8] or that we would have to devote all our moral life to argumentation. Instead, the discourse principle is a problem-driven principle; i.e. its critical force is invoked only when particular issues cannot be satisfactorily handled by the conventional resources that the people concerned usually take for granted. Hence it operates on subject matters that are always already pre-interpreted by whatever moral intuitions the participants happen to bring to the fore.

Discourse is the medium to modify and reshape them. In moral discourse, people work through their various moral perplexities in a cooperative effort at reaching a maximally value-respecting practical deliberation which everyone can support, even though it need not coincide completely with what each claimant would judge as the right way to go, given only each claimant's own moral horizon and supposing that other moral

---

7   For the first three, see HARMAN (1977).

8   For this misunderstanding see esp. pp. 7-15 in WALZER (1994).

horizons were not part of the problem at hand. In fact, it may deviate considerably from "the" right exclusively within one's own moral horizon. However, there is the possibility of integrity preserving genuinely moral compromise (Benjamin 1990).

A second point deserves mentioning. Consensus building constrained by Discourse Ethics can emulate central principles of other moralities. For instance, if all people whose needs and interests are affected by some practice *p* were to agree in a practical discourse to regulating *p* by, say, utilitarian standards, then the discursively prompted consensus about the morally right way of regulating *p* will result in *p*'s being regulated so. Yet whatever substantial moral principle people would want to adopt (e.g., a utilitarian principle of maximising the average satisfaction of individuals' preferences) will become constrained in Discourse Ethics by respect for the capacity of people to reach a common understanding about how they want to treat and be treated by others, regardless of egocentric positional differences.

VII. Disputing Norms, Values, and Facts

There are no moral problems *per se*, i.e. independent of people who are morally perplexed by what taking a moral point of view discloses to them about some of their practices. As substantive interpretations of moral responsibility differ, what is a moral problem to one person is not always a moral problem to another, though both parties view things in moral horizons.[9] We find moral problems when we find people in doubt about whether a course of action is right or wrong. Hence if we want to under-

---

9 E.g., an atheist will have no moral qualms about sacrilege, because for her the concept of the holy (on which the characterisation of a certain transaction as sacrilege depends) will be an altogether empty concept. A roman catholic woman's belief, that one ought not engage in sexual activity unless the two values of possible procreation and marital affective solidarity are jointly served, will bear heavily on her moral evaluation of the impact of contraception practices as such practices ply apart ("de-naturalise") procreation and the pursuit of sexual happiness, two endeavours whose natural nexus is a morally significant fact when considered from the perspective of catholic faith.

stand moral problems, we must find out the rationale why people are perplexed about what is right or wrong.

Disputing what people take as proper responses to their moral perplexity, to the extent that it is rational, is governed by a logic of discourse. This logic of discourse revolves around our powers of raising and answering

i. questions of fact (senses in which something to believe can be the case),

ii. questions of value (senses in which something to appreciate can be good),

iii. questions of norms (senses in which something to do can be required of someone).

Questions of fact and their associated truth-claims can be disputed by reference to the availability and persuasiveness of the evidence for establishing what is the case. Questions of value and their associated claims of evaluative commitment can be disputed by reference to the appropriateness and importance of the properties in virtue of which something is held to be valuable in the disputed sense of good. Whether the purported good-making or value-giving properties are really present is in turn again governed by questions of fact. Questions of norms can be disputed by reference to the values a norm is held to subserve or express. Whether the values in virtue of which it is claimed that certain agents ought to do certain things really authorise the norm in the disputed sense of requiredness is in turn governed by value questions and by factual questions.

Two people in disagreement about what one ought to do must consider whatever other norms they subscribe to that link up with the norm in question. Norms face the tribunal of discourse and experience corporately: commitment to some component normative texture N may turn out to involve, on pain of incoherence, subscription to (or refusal to accept) some other component normative texture N'. Furthermore, people turn to what each of them takes as the relevant values that bear on the norms in question, i.e. on what one ought to do. And two people in disagreement about the sense in which they have reason to take something to be good must be prepared to be led into scrutinising as many other of their evaluations as are found to be somehow related to the one in question. Values, like norms, face the tribunal of discourse and experience corporately; hence someone cherishing some value V may find himself committed, on pain of incoherence, to some other value V'. Furthermore, people discuss what they take to be the relevant facts and their relations on the basis of which they suppose something in question to be in some sense good. The unfolding dialogical dynamics of relating factual, evaluative and normative questions, reiterated if need be, make for rational inquiry in the processes of perplexity-driven discourse.

Using technical terminology, we can sum up this section by saying that normative differences supervene on evaluational differences which in turn supervene on factual differences. 'Supervenience' here is a conceptual relation such that if properties of kind x supervene on properties of kind y then there can be no difference in x without some relevant difference in y.

VIII. Conclusion: Five Parameters of Moral Discourse

In some target domain where a reflective mode of governance, like argumentation, can be brought to bear on normative change (as applied ethics presumes it can), the corresponding processes of argumentation represent moral discourse if they embody and express a set of parameters that jointly guarantee the moral integrity of the discursive power that is exercised by the respective community of argumentation.

I can only list five normative parameters that are necessary elements in the idea of a moral discourse. Space does not permit to elaborate on their formulation and vindication. Each parameter can be introduced as a well-grounded partial answer to a general question. The general question can be framed thus: Are there recognisable proprieties, such that if they were not mutually required among co-subjects of argumentation, then argumentation in the face of conflicting reasons specifically representing moral responsibility for them would not make sense?[10]

Parameter 1: Autonomous Articulation of Need-Claims:
All participants in a discourse should be capable of articulating rationally any need-claim they take to be morally significant.

---

10 I discuss the notion of a moral discourse more fully in KETTNER (1998a).

Parameter 2: Bracketing Power Differentials:
Differences in (all sorts of) power which exist between participants (both within and outside of argumentation) should not give any participants a good reason in discourse for endorsing any moral judgement.

Parameter 3: Nonstrategic Transparency:
All participants should be able to convey their articulations of morally significant need-claims truthfully, without strategic reservations.

Parameter 4: Fusion of Moral Horizons:
All participants should be able sufficiently to understand articulated need-claims in the corresponding moral horizons of those who articulate them.

Parameter 5: Comprehensive Inclusion:
Participants should make it a constraint on what their community of discourse can accept as good reasons, that participants must anticipate whether their reasons can be rehearsed by all nonparticipant others who figure specifiably in the content of any moral judgement that the participants determine everyone should take seriously.

Note that discourse ethical consensus-building does not require unanimity, or majority vote, or any preference-aggregative decision procedure (e.g. bargaining). The dynamics of consensus-building in practical discourse does not guarantee a unique "solution" to all moral issues. Staking out a range of permission is often the best we can come up with. No morality is an algorithm for solving problem cases. To some extent, morality must countenance tragic choices and persistent tensions. Such choices and tensions at best admit of alleviation, not of total resolution, and considerable "moral costs" are bound to remain. However, a consensus sufficiently reflective of the parameters of moral discourse guarantees to all parties who mutually recognise one another as having a credible stake in the outcome of the discourse that they are mutually aware of all their different "moral costs", and that they are also mutually aware of the right-making reasons from every participant's moral horizon. Realistically, no rational morality can guarantee anything stronger than that. The possibility of reasonable disagreement (dissent) exists alongside the possibility of reasonable agreement (consensus), notwithstanding the conceptual truth that the latter envelopes the former.

On this basis, a morally-discursively prompted consensus may well integrate some amount of justified dissensus. Depending on whether such dis-

75

sensus expresses mutual, omnilaterally justified concessions, a morally-discursively prompted consensus may as such express a moral compromise. In such a compromise, however, no-one's morally significant need-claims will have been compromised intolerably.

To sum up: Discourse ethics is a two-tiered normative moral theory. On the first tier, completely general yet morally significant norms of argumentation are identified. This yields a minimal morality ("ethics in discourse") whose claims range over, and whose grounds can be ascertained by, all subjects of argumentation. On the second tier, moralities are meta-ethically characterised as variations of a common basic structure of moral responsibility. Moral reasons represent how moral communities fill out this basic structure with determinate content. By tracing normative requirements that are arguably necessary for argumentation about moral reasons to have a rational point in the face of moral perplexity and moral pluralism, a set of five parameters is proposed which together define as a normative ideal type the notion of a moral discourse. Moral discourses are reflective modes of governance. If governed by moral discourse, normative textures in transition would not deteriorate and might even progress in their moral qualifications. Moral discourse as specified by Discourse Ethics is a medium in which our moral convictions can face the tribunal of historical experience and divergent moral horizons without ceding to cultural relativism and historicism. Historicism awakens us to the vast Heracliteian reality of normative change. Historicism, however, does not spell the futility of strong programs of normative moral philosophy. Rather, if historicism is reconstrued in terms of a pragmatic and realist conception of norms and normativity, historicism may mark the beginning of their wisdom.

References

APEL, K.-O.: *Towards a Transformation of Philosophy*, London (Routledge) 1980.
APEL, K.-O.: "The Problem of Philosophical Foundations in Light of a Transcendental Pragmatics of Language", in: K. BAYNES, J. BOHMAN, T. MCCARTHY (Eds.): *After Philosophy. End or Transformation?*, Cambridge (MIT Press) 1987, pp. 250-290.

CHANGING NORMATIVE TEXTURES

APEL, K.-O.: *Diskurs und Verantwortung*, Frankfurt (Suhrkamp) 1989.

APEL, K.-O. (1990a): "Is the Ethics of the Ideal Communication Community a Utopia?", in: S. BENHABIB, F. DALLYMAR (Eds.): *The Communicative Ethics Controversy*, Cambridge (MIT Press) 1990, pp. 23-60.

APEL, K.-O. (1990b): "Universal Principles and Particular (Incommensurable?) Decisions and Forms of Life - a Problem of Ethics that is both post-Kantian and post-Wittgensteinian", in: R. GAITA (Ed.): *Value & Understanding. Essays for Peter Winch*, London (Routledge) 1990, pp. 72-101.

APEL, K.-O.: "Do we need universalistic ethics today or is this just eurocentric power ideology?", *Universitas*, 2 (1993), pp. 79-86.

BENJAMIN, M.: *Splitting the Difference*, Kansas (Kansas University Press) 1990.

BRENNAN, J. M.: *The Open-Texture of Moral Concepts*, London (MacMillan) 1977.

CASTANEDA, H.-N.: *The Structure of Morality*, Springfield, Ill. (Charles Thomas) 1974.

COLBY, A., KOHLBERG, L.: *The Measurement of Moral Judgement*, Vol. 1, 2, Cambridge (Cambridge University Press) 1987.

COPP, D.: *Morality, Normativity, and Society*, Oxford (Oxford University Press) 1995.

DANCY, J.: *Moral Reasons*, Oxford (Blackwell) 1993.

DEWEY, J.: *Human Nature and Conduct. An Introduction to Social Psychology*, New York (Random House) 1922.

FOUCAULT, M.: *Die Ordnung der Dinge. Eine Archäologie der Humanwissenschaften*, Frankfurt (Suhrkamp) 1980.

FRANKFURT, H. G.: "What we are morally responsible for", in: L. S. CAUMAN (Ed.): *How many questions?*, Indianapolis (Hackett) 1983.

FRENCH, P.: "Fishing the red herrings out of the sea of moral responsibility", in: E. LePORE (Ed.): *Actions and Events*, Oxford (Basil Blackwell) 1985.

GAUTHIER, D.: *Moral Dealing. Contract, Ethics, and Reason*, Ithaca (Cornell University Press) 1990.

GERT, B.: "Rationality, Human Nature and Lists", *Ethics*, 100 (1990), pp. 279-300.

GERT, B.: *Morality. Its Nature and Justification*, Oxford (Oxford University Press) 1998.

GEWIRTH, A.: *Reason and Morality*, Chicago (Chicago University Press) 1978.

GIBBARD, A.: *Wise Choices, Apt Feelings: A Theory of Normative Judgement*, Cambridge (Harvard University Press) 1990.

HABERMAS, J.: *Justification and Application: Remarks on Discourse Ethics*, Cambridge (MIT Press) 1993.

HARE, R.: *Moral Thinking. Its Levels, Methods and Point*, Oxford (Clarendon Press) 1981.

HARMAN, G.: *The Nature of Morality. An Introduction to Ethics*, Oxford (Oxford University Press) 1977.

77

JAMES, W.: *The Principles of Psychology*, Vol. 1, New York (Henry Holt) 1890.

KETTNER, M. (1993a): "Ansatz zu einer Taxonomie performativer Selbstwider-spräche", in: A. DORSCHEL, M. KETTNER, W. KUHLMANN, M. NIQUET (Eds.): *Transzendentalpragmatik*, Frankfurt (Suhrkamp) 1993, pp. 187-211.

KETTNER, M. (1993b): "Nuclear Power, Discourse Ethics, and Consensus Forma-tion in the Public Domain", in: E. R. WINKLER, J. R. COOMBS (Eds.): *Applied Ethics. A Reader*, London (Blackwell) 1993, pp. 28-45.

KETTNER, M. (1998a): "Neue Perspektiven der Diskursethik", in: A. GRUNWALD, C. F. GETHMANN (Eds.): *Ethik technischen Handelns. Praktische Relevanz und Legitimation*, Heidelberg (Springer) 1998 (in print).

KETTNER, M. (1998b): "Reasons in a World of Practices. A Reconstruction of Frederick L. Will's Theory of Normative Governance", in: K. WESTPHAL (Ed.): *Pragmatism, Reason, and Norms*, New York (Fordham University Press) 1998, pp. 255-296.

LADD, J.: "Philosophical remarks on professional responsibility in organizations", *International Journal of Applied Philosophy*, vol. 1, No. 2 (1982).

LANE, J.-E., STENLUND, H.: "Power", in: G. SARTORI (Ed.): *Social Science Con-cepts. A Systematic Analysis*, Beverly Hills (SAGE) 1984, pp. 315-402.

MACINTYRE, A.: *Whose Justice? Which Rationality?*, Indiana (University of Notre Dame Press) 1988.

MACKIE, J. L.: *Ethics. Inventing Right and Wrong*, London (Penguin) 1977.

O'NEILL, O.: *Constructions of Reason. Explorations of Kant's Practical Philosophy*, Cambridge (Cambridge University Press) 1989.

OUTKA, G., REEDERS, J. P. (Eds.): *Prospects for a Common Morality*, Princeton (Princeton University Press) 1993.

REHG, W.: *Insight and Solidarity. The Discourse Ethics of Jürgen Habermas*, Ber-keley (University of California Press) 1994.

SEN, A., WILLIAMS, B. (Eds.): *Utilitarianism and Beyond*, Cambridge (Cambridge University Press) 1982.

SNARE, F. E.: "The Diversity of Morals", *Mind*, 89 (1980), pp. 353-369.

WALLACE, J. D.: *Ethical norms and particular cases*, Ithaca (Cornell University Press) 1996.

WALZER, M.: *Thick and Thin. Moral Argument at Home and Abroad*, Notre Dame (Notre Dame University Press) 1994.

WESTPHAL, K. (Ed.): *Frederick L. Will's Pragmatic Realism*, Chicago (University of Illinois Press) 1998.

WILL, F. L: *Beyond Deductivism. Ampliative Aspects of Philosophical Reflection*, London (Routledge) 1988.

WILL, F. L.: "The Philosophic Governance of Norms", *Jahrbuch für Recht und Ethik*, 1 (1993), pp. 329-361.

WILL, F. L.: *Pragmatism and Realism*, ed. by K. R. Westphal, Lanham (Rowman & Littlefield) 1997.

WREN, T. E. (Ed.): *The Moral Domain. Essays in the Ongoing Discussion Between Philosophy and the Social Sciences*, Cambridge (MIT Press) 1990.

80-114

Chapter 5

Ethics, Corporate Culture and Economic Modelling

LORENZO SACCONI

I. Introduction

A well known result in the economic theory (Coase 1960) states that, when exclusive property rights are settled, and transaction costs (i.e. the costs related to the negotiation and enforcement of contracts and property rights) are equal to zero, then the market - market of rights, not only of goods - is always able to internalise all the costs, obtaining socially efficient outcomes. As it often happens, the most interesting implication of this finding is represented by its negative complement. In other words, it suggests considering what happens when transaction costs are not equal to zero. In this case, in fact, property rights have to be optimally designed and - if necessary - enforced by means of an authority or a public choice mechanism, as they cannot be optimally transferred through costly market exchanges. Optimal designing of economic institutions and, in particular, of property rights are therefore a crucial task in the context of real economies, where transaction costs are effective.

It is the purpose of this paper to suggest that the design of economic institutions, and property rights in particular, may be not a sufficient condition to overcome the problem of transaction costs. There are distributive inequalities and efficiency losses (*less* than second best solutions) still asking to be accounted for, as they are generated by opportunistic behaviours that the property rights design exercise leaves unsolved. Moreover, these opportunistic behaviours can even destabilise the compliance with the same economic institutions of market societies. For these reasons, it seems necessary to integrate the efforts towards the optimal design of contracts and property rights with the study of self-regulatory codes of ethics, acting as a flexible mechanism to prevent opportunism, by means of self-imposed patterns of behaviour. Between the failures of the market's 'invisible hand' and those of the encumbering foot of Government, the importance of the visible - but discreet - hand of morality in the economy should be also acknowledged.

Codes of ethics can be seen as *rules of conduct* that are a necessary prerequisite for rational calculations underlying the functioning of the market. However, contrary to what Hayek says - which is currently recognised as the major theorisation of rules of conduct sustaining the market order - these rules do not simply exist because of a spontaneous and evolutionary process (in biological sense). They can also be the focus of *implicit social contracts* among firms and their stakeholders, who agree to delegate part of their sovereignty to those intermediate social institutions (firms), in exchange for expectations of well being. This is the interpretation of self-regulatory codes of ethics that I want to put forward here: they define the duties of *responsibility* the corporate governance has towards all its stakeholders (clients, suppliers, workers, employees, shareholders, creditors and the public in general). It is because who governs the corporation bears these responsibilities that he is entitled to exercise authority based on the property right over the physical assets of the firm.

In order to be complied with, these rules of conduct have to be 'incentive compatible' - or, in the jargon of game theory, must correspond to a Nash equilibrium. However, the typical rules and moral conventions underlying the economic institutions of capitalism cannot be insensitive to considerations of "fairness" (as far as fairness is understood in the terms of a social contract for mutual advantage). In fact, if corporate ethical codes did not embody some fundamental criteria of justice, the resulting level of trust towards the economic institutions of capitalism would inevitably be low, thereby endangering and representing a threat to their stability and efficiency. One could therefore affirm - *pace* the liberal-conservative Hayek - that "social justice" is not a utopian dream for market economies. Distributive justice - at least in the sense of contractarianism - must be already embodied within corporate ethical codes if economic institutions have to work.

The paper is organised as follows: Section 2 presents the New Institutional Economics approach and discusses the explanation of the authority relationship set up by this theory of the firm. Section 3 analyses two answers to the problem of abuse of authority that can be traced back in the economic literature (*ex-ante* co-operative bargaining and repeated games of reputation), pointing out their limitations. Section 4 outlines the hypothesis that the codes of ethics are the correct solution to this problem. This hypothesis is further discussed in section 5, where I suggest that the moral code, by making explicit the social contract underlying the firm, contributes to clarify a notion of fairness, therefore making possible the common pre-understanding and identification of the abuses of authority within incomplete contracts and bounded rationality situations. Section 6 considers again the role of reputation effects in explaining the incentives to comply with the social contract on the part of the player in a position of authority and, as a matter of consequence, the incentives of adhering to the organisational authority on the part of any other stakeholders of the firm. Adherence to organisational authority, in fact, is seen as stable only once the code has established the criteria for measuring reputation in the presence of unforeseen contingencies and information incompleteness. In the following section 7 there is an attempt to explain how codes of ethics (and the 'constitutional' ethical norms of the firm as well) may serve as a way to establish *commitments* that are conditional on *ex-ante* unforeseen contingencies. This sounds somewhat paradoxical: how could one take a commitment conditional upon some states of the world that he cannot even figure out? I attempt to give an answer through an explorative definition of unforeseen contingencies as states of the world that can be handled by means of the fuzzy sets corresponding to the domain of general moral norms, i.e. sets of states of the world (some of them being the unforeseen ones) which belonging to the domain of a general moral norm, can be defined by means of gradated membership functions. By this route I get to a provisory definition of *fuzzy reputation*. Finally, section 8 provides an application of the foregoing theorising to a case of great significance: the privatisation of state-owned firms.

II. The Firm as Hierarchy: What Is There and What Is Missing in the New Institutional Economics?

The role of corporate ethical codes can be comprehensively understood by referring to the theory of the firm. According to the new institutional approach, efficiency of the firm as a social institution is based on the virtues of the unified governance system for a wide range of exchanges and transactions, i.e. on the virtue of authority relationships that, in their turn, are based on the firm's ownership and control structure. I want to argue that this is only half an answer: the other half is that the firm is an efficient social institution because the authority relationship is legitimised by the agreement of all those who are subjected to that authority. Legitimisation, in turn, is not any longer generated by the ownership structure (which needs to be legitimised itself), but rather by corporate cultures and corporate ethical codes. In other words, an optimal control structure is not the sole key element to evaluate the efficiency of the firm's governance: we have to look as well at the corporate culture and ethical code, as they play the crucial role in promoting trust in those agents who are in a position of authority.

The point will be made by going through a sequence of analytical steps. To begin with, consider a hypothetical exchange situation, in which different "patrons" (Hansmann 1988) rely on simple contracts to carry out separate transactions of goods or services, before any elaborate governance structure of transactions has been worked out.

Then add the typical assumptions of transaction-costs economics (Williamson 1986, Kreps 1990, and Ch. 20):

i) *Specific Assets*. Different patrons make specific investments, that is

-*Labour*: the productivity of labour depends on the acquisition of specific technical skills for the given productive process, learning organisational codes and particular organisational routines, maintaining good working relations, environment and climates; much of these are highly specific assets.

- *Consumer's trust*: if the quality of goods is not observable, the consumer invests to acquire information not about the physical commodity, but about the producer. After having acquired enough information about her, if positive, he will trust her. Trust is a specific asset that loses its value outside the specific relation with the given producer.

- *Investors' trust*: supply of credit or financial investments are complex activity; being not able (or, simply, not willing) to exercise direct control, investors need to get information about the reliability of the producer to be financed. The value of such investment is, again, specific, as it can be only rewarded by the success of the producer about whom the relevant information has been gathered, but it is, however, useless with respect to trust in other producers.

Other typical assumptions are (Williamson 1986, Kreps 1990):

ii) *Opportunism of the agents*, that is the usual utility maximising hypothesis plus the disposition to cheat any unenforced agreement.

iii) *Contract incompleteness* (or *bounded rationality* of the agents), which means that contracts cannot include conditional provisos for any possible event, as unforeseen or inconceivable events may occur.

To comment on the last assumption we may say that the problem lies in the fact that we cannot completely describe all the possible states of the world, i.e. we cannot give an internally coherent, mutually exclusive and jointly exhaustive description for every state of the world. Moreover, we cannot *ex-ante* establish the set of possible consequences for each action belonging the set of each agent's choices. In decision theory terms, each event is a set of states of the world. Each action is a mapping from the state-set to the set of consequences - each of these being generated for a given state by an alternative action (Savage 1972). If some events have not been foreseen, because the states of the world belonging to them are non-conceivable or badly specified, then we are simply unable to figure out the consequences of our actions. This is to say that the real meaning of those actions escapes us. Then we cannot even say we have a specified set of action when we are lacking the representation of some states of the world. Note, incidentally, that this is the most radical characterisation of contract incompleteness. Some economic models – typically the *Grossman-Hart-Moore model,* which I assume as the main reference in the rest of this section - often tends to 'tame' contract incompleteness with notions that make it more manageable according to the standard maximisation techniques: for example, statistic uncertainty, linguistic complexity in writing complete contracts, and non-verifiability by a third part (Grillo 1994).

From these assumption it follows that there is the risk that investments made in bilateral contracts are expropriated. In fact, agents have some *discretion*, due to the occurrence of unforeseen events. Moreover, once specific investments are settled, each agent will be forced to acquiesce in a certain amount of opportunism in order to avoid the risk of losing the entire value of his investments. Once specific investments have created a dependency relationship (the *'lock-in'* effect) and unforeseen events have occurred, the agents may try to re-negotiate the contract in order to change the distribution of the transaction's surplus. One part will gain a rent to the detriment of the counterpart. To minimise the costs of re-negotiation, the latter will endorse a sub-optimal incentive to invest.

Transaction costs economics defines the firm as a governance structure meant to solve this problem. This endeavour is accomplished by setting up authority relationships designed so that the party endowed with the authority will have control upon the *ex-ante* non-contractible decision variables. By 'authority' I mean the fact that one party receives from the others the right to control the actions' set physically belonging to those other parties. Hence, the agent in the authority position will command the action to be picked out from a given set of alternatives that other parties will perform at the proper time in the future. Consider, for example, the employees. By signing the labour contract they delegate to the firm's management or to the employer authority of establishing which actions they will perform, within the limits of their organisational role and working time specified in the contract (Simon 1951). However it is not required that a formal delegation of authority has taken place for the phenomenon of substantive authority to hold. Even though it is usually overlooked, the relevant aspects of an authority relationship also hold between firm on one hand and consumers, creditors and stockholders on the other hand, where they undergo specific investments but do not exercise control:

- *Authority towards consumers*: in the case of complex services, whose quality is not observable, the consumer accepts that his generic willingness to consume will be led by the services' supplier toward some particular object of consumption.

- *Authority towards creditors and sponsors*: financial resources invested or lent are possibilities of acting delegated to the controlling group (the management), who is entitled to establish how to use them, within the limits of its appointment.

According to the economic model of a firm's control structure, these authority relationships are established by allocating to a specific part - among all the parts participating in the exchange – the property right upon the physical assets of the firm. (This is a characteristic assumption in Grossman and Hart 1986, Hart and Moore 1988, see also Hansmann 1988.) Consequently:

a) The agent who *ex-post* will be in the state of best information for deciding, is given formal discretion about *ex-ante* non-contractible variables, i.e. authority is assigned to the part that, after unforeseen events have occurred, will hold the relevant knowledge for choosing optimal allocation of inputs provided by the various stakeholders' specific investments;

b) Investments made by the party entitled with authority are safeguarded, as he can obtain the most advantageous solution in the case of re-negotiation threatening to exclude the counterparts.

c) If the choice of the party to be entitled with authority is optimal, a big amount of transaction costs is saved; in fact discretion is assigned to the agent who would have incurred the maximum loss by expropriation of its investments and at the same time would incur the lower costs for monitoring, controlling and - if necessary - sanctioning the opportunistic behaviours of the others.

This solution does not allow achieving a Pareto-efficient allocation of investments. A position of authority itself can be exploited by those who hold it in order to obtain a rent through re-negotiation. Assume that specific investments related to an economic transaction are made by several parties - such as investors, workers, managers, consumers etc. Then those parties who are *not* safeguarded by the settlement of property rights against the risk of opportunistic behaviour - and, consequently, remaining subject to expropriation of benefits (that they consider unfair) - will not have *ex-ante* adequate incentives to contribute to the joint production of the surplus. This will induce them to under-invest. Nevertheless, if authority is given to the party which is *more important* for producing the surplus, the constitution of the firm will, in any case, allow a positive shift towards Pareto-efficiency. Residuals will be large enough to allow the owner to offer the counterparts a margin not inferior to that which they would obtain under alternative contractual arrangements, in exchange for their acceptation of the control structure over the firm. The outcome will be what Transaction Costs Economics calls a *second-best* governance structure for the transactions at issue.

To be sure, there are several reasons to doubt whether this foundation of the concept of authority is really sound:

(i) There is a conceptual asymmetry between the content of claim implicit in the property right on the firm's physical assets and the content of claim implicit in the notion of authority. Property right implies a negative claim on forbearance from interfering in the use of the firm's assets held by the owner; i.e. the owner has the power to exclude the others from every use of firm's physical assets he does not consent to. Authority, by contrast, implies a positive claim on compliance with commands put forward by the agent in the position of authority (typically, the management), i.e. the claim that those who are subject to authority should accept those commands as the premises of their own deliberation. Authority, therefore, includes a claim on positive action, not only a claim on forbearance and exclusion. So we talk about *managerial* authority even if the management is not the owner of the firm; *political* authority even if the politician is not the owner of the public assets; *professional* authority even if the professional is not the owner of the physical resources he uses.

(ii) A threat of exclusion is not a satisfactory explanation for the establishment of an authority. To be sure, any explanation of organisational authority uniquely focused on the power of inflicting sanctions, would result too superficial (Arrow 1974). Each time the possibility of enforcing sanctions is limited to a relatively small number of infractions. It would be impossible to sanction all the members of an organisation if everybody chose to disobey. At least compliance from those who are designed to enforce sanctions cannot be based on the sanctions themselves.

(iii) Any explanation of authority based on property rights is unsatisfactory, because it ultimately rests on compliance with the authority of law, i.e. on the decision to obey the law. But this, in turn, would require an explanation of the reason why members of the organisation decide to comply with the law, instead of resorting to forms of explicit disobedience or tacit defection.

These remarks concur to rise the main point I want to make here about the economic model of the firm grounded on the analysis of costs and benefits of ownership. Being one agent in the role of an authority, in effect, does not prevent this same agent from resorting to the re-negotiation of the initial pre-investments contract. The assumption that whenever unforeseen events occur it is possible to share a surplus through re-negotiation remains unchanged. What makes the difference is the fact that authority based on property right settles the *status quo* for re-negotiating - through bargaining - the terms of exchange, in front of unforeseen events that were not provided for by the contract. That is what in fact allows discretionary decisions essentially by the owner. Given the power to settle the *status quo*, the owner will bargain according to his best interests. As a matter of fact, the owner has the authority to impose base-line conditions that may be quite unpleasant for the counterpart. So re-negotiation will favour him. This means that the owner will be able to safeguard his earning expectations, making it possible not only to allocate an optimal level of investment, but also to exceed this level and gain a rent through the opportunistic exercise of authority. Grossman and Hart (1986) conclude that there will be a tendency to over-invest by the party entitled with the authority - the owner - and a tendency to under-invest by the parties whose relationships with the firm are regulated by incomplete contracts. These two simultaneous incentives identify what I call *abuse of authority*.

III. Abuse of Authority: Is There Any Solution Within the Existing Economic Theory?

I call what has been identified at the end of the foregoing section the *abuse of authority problem*. It has not been tackled by the economic literature because of the appearance that it would only imply distributive effects, without affecting the property of second-best efficiency of economic solutions. Soon we will see that this is not the case. Two lines of argument can be found in the economic literature that could be expected to answer this problem. The first employs the model of co-operative bargaining games. The second resorts to the model of iterated non-co-operative games.

1. Co-operative Bargaining Games

In Grossman and Hart's theory of ownership of the firm (Grossman and Hart 1986) an answer to the abuse of authority problem could be construed as follows. Effects of the opportunistic exercise of authority in the re-negotiation of contracts are anticipated and neutralised, before unforeseen events may occur, through a utility side transfer. *Ex-post* a bargaining game will take place whose pay-off will measure the cost of re-negotiation to the players. But they can anticipate these costs by an *ex-ante* contract upon the allocation of property rights. This will prescribe the utility side-payment to the players forgoing control. Due to this utility transfer, one part agrees to delegate ownership to the other i.e. the control upon all the *ex-ante* non-contractible decision variables. In such a way the problem of fairness would be reabsorbed by a preventive *ex-ante* compensation. What can be obtained is a second best efficiency solution, because incentives under any control structure cannot accomplish the first best allocation of idiosyncratic investments. However this answer underestimates the difficulties arising from contract incompleteness. *Ex-ante* the parties will fail to negotiate the value of the side transfer that *ex-post* they would recognise as the proper compensation for any opportunistic exercises of authority that will eventually occur. In fact, as it is impossible to establish *ex-ante* all the decisions that will prove to be available and relevant when unforeseen events have occurred, neither the limits to discretion nor their price can be explicitly defined. Being impossible to specify exactly the sphere of exercise of authority, it is also impossible to exclude opportunistic behaviour when the time for re-negotiation comes. That is what, in effect, Grossman and Hart's model explicitly predicts, as it proves that each governance structure implies some incentive distortions. What is at fault with this theory, however, is that the amount of these distortions cannot be predicted. The amount of costs that abuse of authority would impose upon the damaged parties will result to be contingent on *ex-ante* not even conceivable events.

To give an example, the labour contract could define the set of orders X that A, the owner of a firm's physical assets, can legitimately give the employee B. However, some of the orders $x_i \in X$ may, under some circumstances, represent a heavy cost or damage for B, who has not already been compensated for that. In fact this cost or damage only occurs under a particular state of the world s_i that was not included within the description of all the possible states of the world when B signed the labour contract. Therefore, the abuse of authority in the re-negotiation setting is possible. Why, then, should I not suppose that the property right itself could be denied and re-negotiated when unforeseen events transpire? Why, moreover, should I not consider that the parts that can be subject to abuse of authority could even choose not to enter the authority relationship?

2. Repeated Non-Co-operative Games

An attempt to answer the abuse of authority problem within the theory of iterated non-co-operative games rests upon the concept of *reputation effects*. The reference situation is given by a game in which one long-run player A - for example the management of the firm - meets an infinite sequence of short-run players $B_1,...,B_n \cdot$ ($n \to \infty$) - for example consumers - each staying in the game only one play (Fudenberg and Levine 1989, 1992). (See figure 1 for the constituent game).

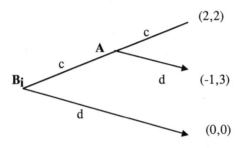

Figure 1: The strategy combination (d, d) is the sole Nash equilibrium and it is in dominant strategies.

Each time, firstly a consumer chooses whether to buy or not; afterwards, the management chooses whether to supply high or low quality services. Each time decisions are taken in sequence, but only communicated after both of them have been taken.

In the one-shot constituent game the dominant strategy for the management is always to supply low quality services. This induces the consumer's best reply, i.e. not to buy, leading to the sub-optimal equilibrium solution (*d, d*) of the constituent game. Nevertheless, the infinite iteration of the game allows us - except for an initial finite sequence of periods - to obtain an infinite sequence of co-operative exchanges (solution (*c, c*) in figure 1). This requires the assumption that each short-run consumer B_i is not sure about the 'type' of player A, i.e. he puts a positive probability p on the possibility that A is not the standard fully rational, strategic utility maximiser, but a non-strategic follower of a code of honesty that is a code as King, requiring him to always supply high quality services. The probability p measures the reputation of A as an 'honest' player in the eyes of the B_i

players. Assume that the initial p is positive but very small. The idea is that each B_i chooses on the basis of his expected utility, given the current probability that A is an honest player. This probability inductively increases every time a short-run player B_i observes that player A at the immediate foregoing repetition supplied high quality services. At any time player A were seen to be choosing d, his/her reputation would become zero, because this move would be incompatible with his/her being the 'honest' type. On the contrary, if A were seen to be supplying high quality services from the beginning on, then, however small the initial p might be, after a certain number N of repetitions, in which the various B_i have not bought, the expected utility of buying would increase enough - together with the p - that the following B_i would find more advantageous to buy. Assuming for simplicity only two possible types of player A, this means that $2p + (-1)\ 1\text{-}p$ >0.

Therefore, if player A is patient enough (i.e. he/she does not excessively discount future utilities), even if he/she is a strategic rational 'type', then he has an equilibrium strategy consisting of 'sustaining his reputation' of being an honest player, always offering high quality services. Assume he has been employing this strategy for a number of times, beginning from the first play of the game, then the consumers shall eventually begin to buy and later on the payoffs (2,2) will become accessible each time. To sum up, there exists an entire set of equilibria of the game supporting some co-operation among a number of players B_i and player A. The upper boundary of this set consists of the equilibrium point where both players co-operate all the time but the first N times, where players B_i still do not co-operate but player A nevertheless invests in the reputation (Fudenberg and Levine 1989, 1992).

It is quite problematic, however, to apply this result to hierarchical transactions taking place within the firm, that is when the player A is in the role of an authority. *Ex-ante* the optimal decision cannot be identified because of unforeseen events. Otherwise *ex-post* - after some unforeseen event has occurred - player A has real discretion. Nothing prevents him from undertaking some action, given that the decision taken is drawn from the set of actions that are under his control after the delegation of authority. To be sure, whether one of these decisions constitutes an abuse cannot *ex-post* be identified unambiguously on the basis of the content of the contract. This only determines a set of action the authority can order to be performed, no provisos or constraints being settled conditionally upon the occurrence of unforeseen events. Nevertheless the party suffering hardness of discretion may guess it has been abused. Lots of fuzziness and dissent can be expected after a single player in the position of a B_i reports having been abused by the counterpart A. Let us consider the following game situation: an infinite number of workers (short-run players) $B_1,.....,B_n$ have to decide, through an infinite sequence of identical iterations of the same basic game, whether to enter a dependency relationship with the long-run management A. The management, dealing with unforeseen events, will take a discretionary decision concerning the tasks it wants the workers to perform. Some of these decisions constitute - *under some circumstances* - an abuse of authority, as they take away from the workers a part of the fair share of the surplus generated - among other things - by their own investments in human capital (Grossman and Hart 1986; Hart and Moore 1988). I assume that the strategy "to abuse" is dominant for the management in the constituent game (see Fig. 1). However, it is not possible to recognise as abusive these decisions on the basis of the labour contract. Due to labour contract incompleteness, player A is free to take *ex-ante* non-contractible decisions at his/her discretion.

In other words, in the game described in figure 1 the action d has a unique description (to *'defect'*) and a well specified meaning (i.e. to offer low quality services). In the context of hierarchical transactions, however, the action d may represent an act that in normal circumstances belongs to the set of admissible behaviours but, under unforeseen circumstances, constitutes an abuse. In standard terms of economics, the player A's action not only will be *ex-post* not verifiable by a third party, it will also be not 'observable' by the players themselves. This is so not because they cannot observe *ex-post* the acts performed *per se*. But because *ex-post*, in the face of unforeseen events, these acts do not have clear meaning, that is the players are not able to specify without ambiguity which consequences are associated with those acts. This amounts to saying that under unforeseen events actions become *vague*. Therefore, being impossible to unambiguously identify the abusive actions, the basis itself for assessing player's A reputation is lacking. But this would imply that A has no way to establish a positive reputation that could induce the various $B_1,...,B_n$ to enter into the authority relationship. Consequently, relationships of trust, that should back the constitution of the firm, will breakdown, endangering both the emergence and the stability of the firm as an institution.

IV. Codes of Ethics

Corporate ethical codes are the main tool for implementing ethics within firms. In the United States there has been a rapid diffusion of written documents clearly recognisable (in spite of their differences in form and structure) as ethical codes of conduct, promulgated and periodically revised by the firm's top management and aimed to incorporate ethical values and concerns about the way firms do business. According to some empirical surveys while in 1980 only 8% of American largest companies (the *Fortune 1000* list of industrial and service corporations) had an ethical code, in 1990 they already reached 85%. Although it is less extensive, nevertheless the phenomenon is clearly recognisable also in Europe. This apparent success of the codification option suggests an interpretation in terms of "evolutionary stability": corporate ethical codes are an advantageous "mutation" that tends to spread over the population of companies. Usually, a well structured code of ethics clearly reflects the idea of corporate responsibility towards all the firm's stakeholders, and is divided into different chapters defining the corporate duties towards customers, employees, suppliers, government agencies, competitors, local communities, political representatives etc. My suggestion is that this is so because of the abuse of authority problem.

In fact, what is the function of a corporate ethical code? My answer is that it allows us to solve the above-described problem of breakdown of trust that makes the authority relationships within the firm unstable. To ensure stability of the firm's authority relationships, a common pre-understanding of the legitimate exercise of authority is needed. This is so in order to make a focus of mutual expectations possible revolving around the belief that those limits will not be exceeded by any party in the organisation. It has been suggested that the underlying corporate culture, rather then the firm's legal structure, is the key element favouring this common pre-understanding of mutual commitments, establishing each party's rational expectation that others will comply with those commitments. (Kreps 1990; Tirole 1987; Simon 1991). I want to argue that the corporate ethical code, even more than the generic corporate culture, is what gives shape to such a pre-understanding.

Analytically, the purposes of corporate ethical codes are:

a) To settle very general but not void moral principles that could rationally be agreed upon by all the organisation participants and that would be used to identify the abusive exercise of authority. These principles give a common understanding of the constraints limiting each stakeholder's prerogatives and legitimate claims with respect to many ill defined situations, as these constraints cannot be *ex-ante* specified by concrete statutes, contracts and regulations. How the code can achieve this purpose can be explained by resorting to the model of the Social Contract as a hypothetical agreement on the fair constitution' of the firm.

b) To provide incentives for compliance with the code itself, which thus becomes a self-enforcing system of norms. I call self-enforcing a code under which players calculate that their best response to the expected behaviours of the counterparts is compliance with the commitments embodied in the code itself. The achievement of this purpose can be explained only if we add to the model of reputation effects a specific account of how a moral code may constitute a parameter for reputation within incomplete information contexts.

I shall explain how an ethical code can favour the achievement of these goals in the following two sections. Before going through these subjects a remark is in order to specify the kind of cognitive function that is provided by the social contract model of an ethical code (point a), it being instrumental also to the incentive nature of the code (point b). The social contract model works as a *default reasoning system*: It provides agents with a hypothetical agreement model from which they can infer a set of normative statements. These have already proved to be sound within the domain of states of the world the agents are able to describe and account for. However, reasoning by default logic the agents assume it is legitimate to extend the validity of this normative system also to states of the world that they cannot accurately describe. They draw some additional statements from the system and assume that these statements are valid by default, i.e. until a contrary proof has been given (Reiter 1980). Validity of these inferences is not warranted against mistakes. In fact, the validity of extensions of the model to situations not accounted for before, is not proved by an effective procedure answering yes or not to the question of whether these sentences hold in each of the logically conceivable worlds.

So these extensions are fallible. However they are not at all irrational. Can we really be sure of reasonably believing only sentences that we have effectively ascertained to be true by means of a recursive procedure of decision? On the contrary, these extensions express that we are doing our best in outlining our beliefs in the light of consistency with what we positively know about the situations we are able to figure out. They transform the absence of any negative answer into the provisory statement that a given sentence does positively hold.

The cost for these extensions of our beliefs system is the 'non-monoticity' of the system itself: it may change without retaining the entire old beliefs set under the after-change system. The logic of default reasoning implies that we have to be ready to correct our systems of normative beliefs as an unforeseen contingency transpires in which a given normative sentence clearly does not hold. A good normative system (a good 'Constitution') can be defined as a set of norms requiring, as time goes by, minimal contractions in terms of renunciation of a body of sentences and postulates in order to keep coherence and soundness of the remaining part. The better the normative system, the larger the set of default extensions which do not have to be 'contracted' in the light of new information (Gärdenfors 1988). The social contract model employs default reasoning to provide instructions for behaving in the presence of incomplete contracts. So it can also be defined as a *filling gap* rule, i.e. an abstract model of hypothetical rational agreement from which instructions can be drawn for filling the holes of contracts (Coleman 1992).

V. Hypothetical Social Contract and the "Constitutional Chart" of the Firm

The first function of ethical codes can be explained by referring to the typical social contract model in political philosophy: the firm is understood as an institution endowed with a formal organisation. Under it transactions are governed *via* authority relationships. This institution, in turn, is based on a social contract among all the agents participating in the transactions. Through the social contract they establish the 'constitution' of the firm. The social contract provides, therefore, a hypothetical model of ideal agreement that can constitute the criterion for assessing real economic institutions. The definition of 'abuse of authority' therefore does not rely on the real contracts, but on an implicit contractarian ideal of fairness. This ideal is based on the hypothetical model of impartial agreement, negotiated by the parties in absence of power and fraud and without the dependency effects generated by specific investments. Thus, social contract defines the ideal benchmark for identifying the non-abusive exercise of authority. It provides for partici-pation of each member of the organisation in a joint co-operative strategy in exchange for an efficient, fair share of the surplus. The code can then be seen as the "constitutional chart" that makes the implicit social contract explicit. This way a general notion of fairness is set up, affirming the crite-rion of sharing costs and benefits in the case of re-negotiation due to un-foreseen events.

There is, in fact, a strict analogy between the firm, understood as an in-stitution, and the idea of the State underlying the theory of social contract. According to contractarianism, the starting point to explain and justify any institution (the State as well as the firm) is an hypothetical situation of choice ("state of nature") where rational, self-interested agents have to face the risk of undergoing reciprocal opportunism if they enter the potentially mutual advantageous co-operative relationships. Were a constitutional order not established, in the above described situation no particular agreement or commitment would be complied with, because each agent would find it individually rational to cheat. If he thinks the other will co-operate, he will try to take advantage of the others' co-operation, without doing his part in the agreement. On the other hand, the fear of suffering the other's oppor-tunism will also drive each agent to find it rational to protect himself and choose a non-co-operative strategy as well. Game Theory formalises this situation as the well-known "Prisoner's Dilemma", a game where distrust, cheating or mutual non co-operation represent the sole equilibrium - and robustness of this solution is underlined by the fact that it is an equilibrium in dominant strategies. (See Figure 2.)

	C	D
C	(2,2)	(0,3)
D	(3,0)	(1,1)

Figure 2: The strategy combination (D, D) is the sole Nash equilibrium, but sub-optimal.

ETHICS, CORPORATE CULTURE AND ECONOMIC MODELLING

Market relationships, characterised by contracts under incompleteness and information asymmetry, are instances of a "quasi-state-of-nature" situation, where no appropriate constitutional order has yet been agreed upon and, consequently, a non co-operative equilibrium tends to prevail. Protagonists of the "state of nature" are, in this case, the patrons of the firm who really hold specific investments (workers, stockholders, consumers, and suppliers). We equate here the term "patrons" - used in the 'Law & Economics' literature (Hansmann 1988) - with the term "stakeholders" - used in the Business Ethics literature, the idea being that they hold stakes on the firm's outcome *because* of the specific investments they make. At the same time, due to contract incompleteness, they undergo the risk of expropriation.

According to contractarianism, escaping the mutually destructive outcome of the "state of nature" requires the agents to set up, by unanimous agreement, a central authority entitled to disincentivate opportunistic behaviours and protect each agent's ownership. A similar interpretation can be given to the decision of calling an agent, external to the group of workers, to carry out the role of 'guard' of Pareto efficiency (Alchian, Demsetz 1972, Holmstrom 1982). Similarly, we can give a "social contract" interpretation of the delegation of authority upon the *ex-ante* non contractible decisions to the part able to minimise transaction costs (Williamson 1975, Grossman, Hart 1986). However, unlike the typical transaction-costs model, contractarianism does not explain the emergence of authority simply by comparing the aggregate costs and benefits of each institutional governance structure. Aggregate efficiency - or transaction costs minimisation - has no influence *per se,* but as one of the components of the fair/efficient agreement. Authority arises only if all the holders of specific investments rationally accept a governance structure by a constitutive agreement, in the perspective of a mutual advantage. Legitimacy follows from the unanimous acceptance of the establishment of an authority by 'social contract'. This does not exclude the fact that authority might be allocated to the owner of the physical means of production. But in the contractarian view authority does not rest simply on the prerogative implicit in the property right. As already said, a property right on goods and assets is a *negative claim* that simply forbids transfer without consent of the owner. On the contrary the holder of hierarchical authority in the firm lays a *positive claim* on employees' compliance with his directives concerning the use of the firm's assets.

Why should the holders of specific investments sign the social contract? Given the utility level of the *status quo* - what each part gets if the attempt to reach an agreement fails - the additional product of the joint activity can be defined as *co-operative surplus*. Participants will rationally bargain about how to split the co-operative surplus, taking the agreed outcome of bargaining as the necessary pre-condition for their participation in the joint activity. This approach naturally leads to the theory of Bargaining Games. This theory proves that the social contract will be signed on a joint action plan allowing the production of a *socially efficient* co-operative surplus. The optimal additional amount (with respect to the *status quo*) will be shared in such a way that each agent will have the highest possible share given the share obtained by the counterpart. Several bargaining solutions can be calculated as outcomes of different bargaining processes. Under any of these each part makes rational claims and concessions in response to the rational claims and concessions carried out by the counterpart - i.e. each bargaining model ends up with the reaching of a bargaining equilibrium. However, most celebrated bargaining solutions - namely Nash (1950), Kalai-Smorodinsky (1975) and Gauthier (1986) - have in common that, if the payoff space of the game is a symmetric bargaining set - i.e. the set of possible bargaining outcomes is invariant under the permutation of the players' names - they share the surplus in equal parts.

Identifying the *status quo* suitable to the end of a social contract theory is quite controversial. I follow here Gauthier in assuming that suitability of the bargaining model for ethical theory requires the identification of the *status-quo* with the baseline of a hypothetical bargaining situation between rational agents who negotiate *before* any social interaction could have advantaged or disadvantaged one party over the other. A fair *status quo* must therefore forbid outcomes depending upon force and fraud, free riding and parasitism that could take place only in unfair transactions (Gauthier 1986). It can be identified only by imagining a joint productive venture that begins at a starting point from which all these distortions have been erased. Turning back to the firm context, this hypothesis means that the situation resulting in specific investments and characterised by contract incompleteness cannot be taken as the appropriate baseline for measuring the co-operative surplus. Nor can the re-negotiation situations, where one or both parties in the contract are locked-in, due to the costs of their specific investments be a fair *status quo*. The appropriate baseline is the situation coming *before* the cost of any specific investment having been paid. We can find a rationale for this assumption: the parties anticipate that they will undergo the burden of specific investments if they enter the joint co-operative venture. Consequently they want to be assured that their payoff will be at least neutralised with respect to these costs. Each of them legitimately claims as *status-quo* payoff at least the amount of utility he had before entering the effort of the joint co-operative production. Therefore each player's co-operative surplus must be calculated at the *net of all* the costs of specific investments made by each player.

I shall now consider how the social contract model applies to the decision of establishing the firm. The world of economic institutions (firms and markets) is an imperfect world. In fact, property rights on a firm's assets held by agents who carry out the most important investments, gives them an advantage. They are not only permitted to protect themselves, but allowed to seek a rent through re-negotiation - i.e. abuse of authority. From the point of view of contractarian ethics, this solution is arbitrary. In order for the constitution of an authority and the allocation of property rights on the firm's assets to be justified, each patron - who waives the firm's control on behalf of the one who will be entitled with the authority role - has to be compensated with a fair share of the surplus net of any specific investment cost. 'Fair' means that shares must correspond to what they can expect on the basis of the rational bargaining game solution, calculated from the appropriate *status quo*. For example, take the case of the surplus generated by a co-operative joint action between a single capitalist and a single worker, where the feasible set of outcomes is symmetric. Then, each of them will make a rational claim on half of the expected surplus, calculated on the basis of the value (in terms of expected utility of risky prospects and their certain equivalents) of the return net of all specific investment costs, that at minimum has to be repaid if each of them is to be ready to enter the joint venture. The patron waiving control - let it be the worker or the capitalist depending on case specific governance costs - holds a legitimate claim on a fair share of the benefits generated by the firm. In this sense he is a 'stakeholder': he holds a legitimate claim independently of the fact that this claim is not protected by the property right - i.e. in spite of the fact that he is not a 'stockholder'.

A social contract is an impartial agreement. Firstly, as far as the *status quo* is concerned, nobody may complain that a failure of the agreement would represent a more serious threat to him than his own refusal to agree with the others. What each is entitled to before co-operation takes place, is not subject to the moral requirements of fair co-operation. However, each party is guaranteed that it will not be put under duress by an agreement failure due to the lock-in effects of *ex-ante* investments. Secondly, surplus is shared in such a way that any one, putting himself in everybody else's shoes, would recognise the rationality of her claim to the share she effectively gains. The solution (the agreed upon outcome that distributes shares of surplus) is rational according to everybody's view. In fact rational acceptance of the shares of surplus each agent gets under the bargaining solution is invariant with the replacement of each agent in the position of everybody else. Therefore, it satisfies a requirement of anonymity and universalisability.

From this construction a scheme for the "constitutional chart" of the morally justified firm follows, i.e. the set of rights and duties governing transactions within and outside the firm. This "constitutional chart" would provide for

1. the owner's legitimate residual claim and exercise of authority, this including authority on *ex-ante* non-contractible decisions and on the choice to exclude anyone form the use of the firm's physical assets. At the same time, it allows the owner to delegate monitoring and control to the managers, with the aim of disincentivating opportunistic behaviours, thereby maximising the value of co-operation among the patrons/stakeholders.

2. the owner's responsibility towards other stakeholders: to respect their legitimate claims to fair shares of the surplus - as fixed by the hypothetical social contract.

If the management of the firm is so constrained by the constitutional contract (and if the constraint is made explicit by a corporate ethical code) then all the stakeholders would willingly enter the co-operative relationships with the firm.

VI. Self-enforceable Ethical Codes:
A Parameter for Reputation Effects

The foregoing explanation is not sufficient in the *ex-post* perspective. Once the firm's stakeholders have entered the constitutional contract that allocates discretionary power to a specific part, why then should the holder of such discretion respect its duties of responsibility? If this expectation cannot be supported, why should the stakeholders trust the institutions that assign discretionary power to that party? This problem refers to the second purpose of a corporate ethical code: How can it create the incentives to comply with the code itself?

In the economic literature "corporate culture" (Kreps 1990) is explained in the light of the theory of "reputation effects" (Kreps and Wilson 1982; Kreps, Milgrom, Roberts and Wilson 1982, Fudenberg and Levine 1988. Fudenberg and Tirole 1991). I extend this explanation to corporate ethical codes arguing that this application of the game theoretical analysis to explain corporate ethical norms is even more appropriated than the one resting on the somewhat obscure notion of "culture" (Sacconi 1991, Sacconi 1994, Sacconi 1997). This theory can be traced back to Hume's moral conventionalist view, a typical example of rational choice ethics. I will not consider here other approaches that explain ethical codes as rational-moral constraints "interiorised" on the basis of a rational choice, as they do without any reference to reputation effects (Gauthier 1986; McClennen 1990), which is my focus in this section.

I showed in section 3 that some difficulties arise in applying the theory of reputation effects within hierarchical contexts. Essentially, what generates these difficulties is the discretionary nature of decisions taken by the agent endowed with authority. Given the set X of allowable decisions, some of them may turn out to be abusive *ex-post*, without the possibility providing for them *ex-ante*. Nevertheless, whether abuse were identifiable at least *ex-post*, it could be argued that reputation effects as such would be able to discourage abusing because of the threat to the prospective abuser of losing his face forever (i.e. in the following repetitions of the game). This is not the case however. Neither the contract, nor the law provides a unique criterion to identify these abuses. *Ex-post* there will be a large amount of dissent among the players entering the game after the abused one. Apparently this problem also prevents us from resorting to the hypothetical social contract as a parameter to identify abusive actions. If, in fact, an agreement is signed in the *ex-ante* hypothetical constitutional phase, *ex-post* the contract may not account for unforeseen costs or benefits, which have not been agreed upon *ex-ante*. Nevertheless, we can resort here to the difference between *ideal* and *real* contracts and more generally between moral/constitutional general norms on the one hand and detailed regulations on the other. This possibility relates to the general nature of the moral language used in "writing" the social contract and embodied within the corporate moral code.

By definition, the social contract model (a general ethical model of fair/efficient agreement) is not intended to regulate each specific and concrete case. It addresses strategic interactions as a whole, characterised by only a few structural features. Taking the social contract point of view, players put themselves under the *Archimedean point*: any rational agreement will be assessed independently of any personal, historical, empirical features about the participants and the contexts - the only salient features being the few characterising the abstract bargaining interaction. One could say that the social contract is a cognitive device to focus only on a few ethically relevant variables among the many that could be considered in a more concrete account of the same situations. This enables us to abstract from many details of the concrete bargaining situations in which the structural features, focused by the social contract, are embedded. Thus, the validity of the social contract is not limited to the occurrence of *ex-ante* known cases in point. Situations presenting cases that we were not even able to figure out, can then be subjected to the social contract machinery, because they display at a significant level the pattern of its structural variables. Indeed, it works as a device for 'pattern recognition'.

Moreover the social contract, and the code incorporating it, specify which procedures the firm must adopt every time an event occurs that calls over a principle - that is when the event displays the same pattern of the concerned structural variables. It is not necessary to have already provided exactly for that event. It is enough that it satisfies the criterion of belonging to the class of cases to which the given procedure applies, even if the elements of this class are not entirely *ex-ante* known. In other words, the code of ethics provides a standard procedure of behaviour which is not conditional upon the occurrence of specific events. Instead it depends on the occurrence of situations whose borders are not univocally determined in set theoretical terms. These are situations that, at a certain level of approximation, display the pattern of a given ethical principle. An incomplete description of the world is enough to recognise that an unexpected event belongs to the class of cases morally relevant in the light of a given principle (this is exactly what we termed before as the 'pattern recognition' function of social contract). Thus, moral language applies to *ex-ante* unforeseen events.

For instance, the corporate ethical code may request "safeguarding the job of a worker every time he is in conditions of real need and is not responsible for wrongs to the firm", where the conditional is wide enough to include a range of situations *ex-ante* impossible to specify. Or it can request "sharing gains in equals parts, every time an unforeseen advantage can be achieved thanks to the investments both of the client and the supplier, or both of the worker and the employer". "Being co-responsible for the production of the surplus" is a characteristic that can be found in several situations whose *ex-ante* description is not complete. Once norms settle patterns of the morally relevant events, again it becomes possible to exploit reputation effects. Compliance with commitments announced, i.e. implementation of a settled procedure, can be verified and judged by all the subordinate agents and stakeholders. On that basis they will update probability assigned to the owner types ('honest' vs. 'opportunistic'). Then it will become rational again for the agent endowed with authority to support his reputation by acting according to the norms of the code. This, in turn, will lead the subordinate to accept her authority and invest within the firm.

VII. Code of Ethics, Bounded Rationality and "Fuzzy Reputation"

The crucial but very problematic point of Kreps' theory of corporate culture (Kreps 1990) is the suggestion that we treat "general principles" of a given corporate culture (i.e. what I mean by the principles of a corporate code of ethics) as a way of *ex-ante* defining the behaviours to be implemented *ex- post*, when unforeseen events have occurred. This requires a model of rationality under unforeseen contingencies. This section gives a sketch of this model (see Sacconi 1997 for more details).

If rationality were unbounded, the players would have all the complete alternative descriptions of the possible states of the world at their disposal. Consequently, there would be no unforeseen events any longer. Unfortunately it is not so. Human rationality is bounded, and we do not have all the complete alternative descriptions of the states of the world at disposal.

To explain, imagine that we want to describe a set of alternative state of affairs given a language endowed with n individual variables and m monadic predicates. We could describe for example a state of the world where the individual i is white, not black nor yellow, the individual j is black, not white nor yellow, the individual k is white... another state where the individual i is black, not white, nor yellow, the individual j is yellow, not white, not black, the individual k is black... etc. We would like these alternative and mutually exclusive descriptions of the state of the world to prove to be exhaustive as a whole. But, as a matter of fact, the language in use would not be rich enough to express every possible property that could transpire through time and experience.

Now, assume that we discover a state of the world in which a surprising property occurs. It can be seen as an unforeseen event occurring only in that state of the world. This property is not accounted for by the repertory of predicates included in our current language. Accordingly, the individual showing the "new" property is not properly white, not properly black, not properly yellow....but nevertheless it is in some sense both white, black yellow etc... In other words we are unable to establish for this state of the world whether each predicate has to be affirmed or denied with reference to the relevant individual. Consequently this state will not be clearly specified, in the sense that we may not be able (in this state of the world) to understand whether some event occurs or not, simply because under that description the relevant characteristic is not clearly specified with reference to the relevant individual. My suggestion (in a very exploratory way) is that a code of ethics works as the appropriate tool to prescribe behaviours in situations like these.

A moral code can be seen as the settlement of a set of general principles and statements announcing that the firm will perform some pre-defined procedure when (generic) events satisfying morally relevant characteristics occur. Consider for instance the general sentence "The firm A follows the principle of compensating any loss or damage suffered by the client/employee when it realises that a client/employees is in conditions of real need". Assume that, if it is the case, the firm will apply the aid procedure Y without request for compensation. The problem, of course, is that the event "the client/employee is in conditions of real need" is a *vague* event. Therefore we are unable to say exactly in which states of the world this event occurs. This situation can be expressed in terms of *fuzzy set theory*. Considering a reference set W, composed by n elements, a fuzzy sub-set E of W is given by a set of membership functions that are defined for each element belonging to W. Each function defines the degree of membership of a single element of W to E and takes its values in the ordered set $[0,1]$. In other terms, the set E is a set of elements of W which are members of E at a certain degree x ($0 \le x \le 1$). The set E is therefore a set with fuzzy or vague borders that can be used to deal with vague concepts like "to be near", "to have a reddish colour", etc. - i.e. defining the set of things having these vague characteristic.

This definition can be used to give an account of unforeseen contingencies in terms of their impact on the events we are *ex ante* able of conceiving within the existing system of knowledge. Some events are *vague* because their occurrence is not clearly defined in some state of the world and this typically happens for the unforeseen ones. Consider Ω as the all encompassing set of states of the world that appears to be possible in the *ex-post* perspective. Given the resources of our current language (the language we already had at hand in the *ex ante* perspective), W will include the set of all the alternative accurate description of the state of world *relative to that language*. Nevertheless, Ω will also include the *ex-ante* unforeseen states that *ex-post* we cannot accurately describe by means of the existing language. These are states that we were not even able to imagine in the *ex-ante* perspective. Thus as a whole we have only a superficial and incomplete description of the states elements of Ω. We may assume to know their number (this is not a painless assumption) but have only a partial description for them. A *fuzzy event* then is defined as the set of membership functions which associate each of the *n* states of the world to the degree to which the given state belongs to the event in point - the degree to which the characterising property of the event in question does occur in the given state. For example, the event "a client is in conditions of real need" is the set of states in which for at least one individual (a client) the propriety "to be in need" is predicated. Then the state ω_1 may be a state in which we are able to describe exactly an individual with the relevant characteristic (degree of membership 1, i.e. the state of the world w_1 unambiguously belongs to the event in question). On the contrary the state of the world ω_2 may be a state in which we are unable to describe an individual that clearly displays the characteristic in point. The way the man under observation relates to the firm is too unusual to say that he is clearly a "client", his desires are too unusual to say that these desires are clearly "needs". In this case it may be impossible a sharply assign of ω_2 to the extent of the event "a client is in conditions of real need". Nevertheless we may assign a *grade* of membership of ω_2 into the event. The resulting event is a *fuzzy event*, to which the state ω_2 belongs only to a certain *degree*. A fuzzy event expresses the idea that we may be unable to clearly define the states of the world in which a given event occurs and, consequently, it corresponds to an incomplete description of the states.

Let me consider again the code of ethics. A conditional strategy – according to standard decision theory - is a rule that provides an action conditional upon the occurrence of each non fuzzy event, i.e. upon the occurrence of events with respect to which the relation of being a member for different states of the world is clearly defined (0 or 1). Events like these are, however, quite artificial and their semantic content is very poor. They presuppose a world that could satisfy the clear-cut sentences expressed by means of a language conventionally reduced to a limited number of individual constants, variables and predicative letters to be affirmed or denied with reference to the individual variables and constants. Moral language, on the contrary, refers to "open" worlds, in the sense that *ex-ante* we do not have for each of these states a complete description enabling us to say whether any event occurs in it. That is, we do not know every mode in which a given event can take place. Saying that we are unable to specify in which states of the world the event "a client is in conditions of need" does occur simply means that we are unable to clearly conceive the situations, contexts and modalities in which it may occur that a client is in conditions of need. However a fuzzy event, that is the set of situations belonging to the domain of a moral norm at a certain degree, asks for less than so. By means of this sort of events we express that some *ex-ante* unexpected situations ('worlds') belong to the relevant badly specified moral category to a vague but nevertheless quantifiable degree. An ethical code provides for the firm's behaviour in relation to fuzzy events like this.

We call these events *moral events* and understand them as sets of situations ("worlds") belonging to the domain of a given moral norm. We notice that the prescriptive meaning of the command embodied in a moral principle may be perfectly clear-cut. (For example the following: "in any interactive situation satisfying the definition of a co-operative game, share payoffs according to the *Nash Bargaining Solution*"). Where vagueness comes about however is in the descriptive characteristics required by the moral principle requires in order to make the inference that the situation falls into the domain of the principle itself, i.e. in the domain of objects such as "co-operative games". So to say, the game having mixed interests, non-zero-sum (endowed with a super-additive characteristic function) with enforceable agreements or not etc., all this may be a matter of vague description, which needs to be answered before deciding whether the *Nash Bargaining Solution* has to be employed.

Assume that the degree of fuzziness associated with any given state of the world, when it occurs for the first time, is common between every two adjacent players entering at immediately consecutive times the game described in fig.1 in the role of the short-run player. This means that, for any value of *n,* the membership functions do not dramatically undergo dynamic changes during the time lags between the time when the *n-ary* short-run player learns the outcome of the repetition *n* and the time when the *n+1-ary* is called to participate according to his *ex-ante* perspective in the repetition *n+1* of the game. Assume moreover that the firm (i.e. the long-run player) is capable of capturing the fuzziness degree assigned by any two adjacent short-run players. Thus an ethical code will provide that, for all the states of the world in which the event E, presenting the morally relevant characteristic *C*, occurs with a degree no less than a (i.e. all the states that belong to E with a membership degree $\mu(w_i) \geq \alpha$, where a identifies a constant inside the values $x \in [1,0]$) then the firm *will adopt the procedure Y.* Define this as a *fuzzy (default) commitment.* Given the same degree of fuzziness between the two adjacent short-run players assumed above, the stakeholders will be able to recognise, as well as the firm, the degree z to which this state belongs to the event. If the degree is $z > \alpha$ but the firm still does not apply the procedure Y, then the stakeholders will be able to update the firm's reputation down-rating the firm. This will imply that each player in the role of a B_i (i = 2,...,*n,* where *n* goes to infinitum) matching the firm during the continuation of the game, will punish it (the player A) not entering the relation. I call *fuzzy reputations* those reputations whose variance is a direct function of the compliance with the fuzzy (default) commitments defined above.

VIII. Privatisation and Moral Responsibility

Some recent works by Tirole and Laffont (see Laffont and Tirole 1993) suggest analysing the comparative costs and benefits of state-owned companies and private firms according to a regulatory approach based on the theory of property rights. According to these authors, the relationship between the Government and the managers of the state-owned company on one side, or among the Government, stockholders and the managers of the privatised firm on the other side, can be captured by the incomplete contract model. The manager settles specific investments in human capital, creating surplus. But decisions concerning the appropriation of the fruits of such investments are *ex-ante* non-contractible. The Government, in particular, cannot undergo binding pre-commitments on the appropriation of the firm specific investments. Relative costs of the two forms of ownership are therefore to be assessed in terms of the incentives that the two different governance structures give the firm's managers to choose the optimal level of investments. The difference being that under State ownership the rights to claim the residual and to expropriate it are assigned to the Government, while under the private governance structure these rights are held by stockholders *and* the Government - through *ad hoc* regulations.

The costs of the public property arrangement are pointed out very clearly in this approach. In the case of a benevolent State, the problem lies in the fact that the Government will appropriate the fruits of specific investments made by managers for the sake of social wellfare. This may lead to an optimal *ex-post* allocation of resources, but will induce the managers not to invest, as the returns on their specific investments are expropriated. Even more intuitive is the case – which is not addressed by Laffont and Tirole - of a non benevolent Government. The right to take discretionary decisions will be exploited to expropriate the state-owned company of the fruits of specific investments made by the management, because of the self-interest of politicians and the pressure put on the Government by particular interests groups. This is also so in the cases analysed by the theory of *rent seeking* (Buchanan 1980) and "influence costs" (Milgrom and Roberts 1990), as well as by the theory of collusion (Tirole 1987). What Tirole and Laffont suggest is an approach in terms of incomplete contracts.

The costs of regulation under stockholders ownership are, on the contrary, created by the existence of two principals (the Government and the shareholders). These have conflicting interests, interaction of which may be unable to provide for adequate incentives to the management. However, we should also consider a further type of costs arising in privatised companies, financed through the stock market. These costs are linked to the problem of disciplining managerial behaviours in presence of the risk of opportunism. There are three qualifications for such a risk:

1. The need to rely on the stock market to finance the firm implies a total or partial (in the case of the existence of a control group) separation

between ownership and control of the firm: shareholders - or, at least, the minority group - are excluded from the effective control over the management.

2. The relationship between firm and top managers is not characterised by a complete - even if imperfectly monitored - agency contract, but, more in general, by an incomplete contract: part of the *ex-ante* non-contractible decisions are delegated to the top managers. It is a case of authority without ownership. This generates additional problems with respect to those cases analysed by the theory of optimal agency contract. Top managers can, in fact, exploit their discretionary power to seek a rent – on behalf of their own interests or a dominant coalition of shareholders. This rent will normally expropriate benefits due to investments made by other shareholders or other members of the firm (internal or external stakeholders). The problem seems particularly relevant when the investment decisions of the firm are essential for several economic agents, such as clients, suppliers, etc. (e.g. choices concerning policy options on alternative sources of energy and in their production technology). These decisions are said to be "essential" (Hart and Moore 1988) in the sense that the value of many specific investments made by several other agents depends upon them – they are 'sunk cost' with a lock-in effect. Control over *ex-ante* non-contractible decisions of this type gives, therefore, a relevant re-negotiation power to the managers that they can use for their abusive purposes.

3. As institutional investors become shareholders of large public companies, these shareholders tend to be less willing than the traditional dispersed investors to rapidly liquidate their shares on the stock market, even if they suspect that the behaviour of management is opportunistic. Such investors have a more idiosyncratic relationship with their investments and can consequently undergo a lock-in effect. In the presence of incomplete contract and discretionary power delegated to the management such investments can be subject to expropriation. Thus, those investors, not willing to be involved in direct management decisions, may devise various forms of indirect control, for example by the impersonal authority of internal regulations constraining the management and the control group.

These remarks lead us to consider two types of opportunistic behaviour by the top managers of the privatised public company:

a) Opportunism towards shareholders who do not exercise effective control over the management. (Also in the form of abuse of the majority power by the group of control in the stock company.)

b) Opportunism towards the holders of specific investments (stakeholders) both internal (workers) and external (suppliers, customers) or the Government in the case of the privatised but regulated company.

Ethical self-regulation of firms seems, at this point, a necessary complement to any decision of privatising the control structure of the firm. Let me consider, firstly, the possibility that the contractarian model gives a clear meaning of the notion of abuse of the majority power in stock companies (what the civil law cannot do). Therefore, the social contract ethical model would allow us to understand the notion of "bona fide" (good faith) in the conduct of top managers (Preite 1992). Secondly, corporate social responsibility would result better defined, because the ethical code specifies a criterion for recognising the different stakeholders' legitimate claims. What they can claim exactly are the fair shares of the surplus that are calculated by the moralised bargaining solution. Finally, the responsibilities towards middle managers and workers are also made clear. The model of an ideal contract answers all this points, by establishing the general criteria that make legitimate claims and abuses of authority inherently related to contract incompleteness recognisable. While the management of the privatised firm appeared at a first glance not really trustworthy, after it has undergone the commitment to an ethical code, subjecting its power to disciplining force of the reputation effects mechanism, the picture changes. Deciding for privatising makes the management the trustee of stakeholders - an agent to whom they would accept to delegate the guidance of their common affairs.

To sum up, it is fairly clear that this view requires for the emergence of a new type of management for privatised large stock companies. The manager should become a professional agent who responds not only to the discipline of the contract and to the threat of take-over, but also to the professional deontology construed out of its fiduciary duties which are based on the corporate social contract. Moreover, the model of reputation effects applied to corporate ethical codes shows that seeing the manager not as an egoistic agent, constrained only by contractual incentives and the fear of a take-over, but as a professional trustee constrained by a code of ethics is not wishful thinking. The corporate ethical code gives the management the opportunity of accumulating reputation that otherwise it would never get. Thus complying with the corporate ethical code can be also in the best interest of the management.

Finally the theory of a self-enforceable ethical code throws a clear distinction between two distinct view of the firm. The contractarian ethical view of the firm on one hand, and the view of the firm as an organic community on the other. This view is sometimes presented as the 'Japanese view' on corporate governance or as the coming back of the Aristotelian view of society, as interpreted for example in Virtue Ethics (McIntyre 1981) and its applications to business ethics (Solomon 1992). On the contrary, the firm, in my view, remains an institution based on the agreement of rational individuals carrying on separate lives. They see the firm simply as an instrument to reach their aims, an institution they entrust with their aims, but, still, a structure which *per se* has no aims (Keeley 1986, Sacconi 1991, Vanberg 1992).

References

ALCHIAN, A., DEMSETZ, H.: "Production, Information Costs and Economic Organisation", *American Economic Review*, 62 (1972), pp. 777-795.

AOKI, M.: *The Co-operative Game Theory of the Firm*, Oxford (Oxford University Press) 1984.

ARROW, K.: *The Limits of Organisation*, New York (W. W. Norton and Company) 1974.

ARROW, K.: "Business Codes and Economic Efficiency", in: BEUCHAMP, T. and BOWIE, N. (Eds.): *Ethical Theory and Business*, Englewood Cliffs, N.J. (Prentice Hall) 3rd ed. 1988.

BLAIR, M.: *Ownership and Control*, Washington, D. C. (The Brooking Institutions Publisher) 1995.

BUCHANAN, J.: *The Limits of Liberty*, Chicago (Chicago University Press) 1975.

BUCHANAN, J.: "Rent Seeking and Profit Seeking", in: BUCHANAN, TOLLISON and TULLOCK (Eds.): *Toward a Theory of Rent-Seeking Society*, College Station, Texas (A&M Press) 1980.

CASSON, M.: *The Economics of Business Culture*, Oxford (Oxford University Press) 1991.

CENTRE FOR BUSINESS ETHICS: "Are Corporations Institutionalising Business Ethics?", *Journal of Business Ethics*, 8 (1988).

COASE, R.: "The Problem of Social Cost", *Journal of Law and Economics*, III (1960), pp. 1-44.

COLEMAN, J.: *Market Morals and the Law*, Cambridge (Cambridge University Press) 1988.

COLEMAN, J.: *Risks and Wrongs*, Cambridge (Cambridge University Press) 1992.

FREEMAN, R. E., EVANS, W.: "Stakeholder Management and the Modern Corporation: Kantian Capitalism", in: T. BEUCHAMP and N. BOWIE (Eds.): *Ethical Theory and Business*, Englewood Cliffs, N.J. (Prentice Hall) 3rd ed. 1989.

FREEMAN, R. E., GILBERT, D. R.: *Corporate Strategy and the Search of Ethics*, Englewood Cliffs, N.J. (Prentice Hall) 1988.

FUDENBERG, D., LEVINE, D.: "Reputation and Equilibrium Selection in Games with a Patient Player", *Econometrica*, 57 (1989), pp. 759-778.

FUDENBERG, D., LEVINE, D.: "Maintaining Reputation When Strategies Are Imperfectly Observed", *Review of Economic Studies*, 59 (1992), pp. 561-579.

GÄRDENFORS, F.: *Knowledge in Flux*, Cambridge, Mass. (The MIT Press) 1988.

GAUTHIER, D.: *Morals by Agreement*, Oxford (Clarendon Press) 1986.

GRILLO, M.: "Teoria economica dell'organizzazione", *Economia politica*, 3 (1994).

GROSSMAN, S., HART, O.: "The Costs and Benefit of Ownership: A Theory of Vertical and Lateral Integration", *Journal of Political Economy*, 94 (1986), pp. 691-719.

HANSMANN, H.: "Ownership of the Firm", *Journal of Law Economics and Organisation*, 4, 2 (1988), pp. 263-304.

HARDIN, R.: *Morality Within the Limits of Reason*, Chicago (Chicago University Press) 1988.

HARSANYI, J. C.: *Rational Behavior and Bargaining Equilibrium in Games and Social Situations*, Cambridge (Cambridge University Press) 1977.

HART, O. MOORE J.: "Property Rights and the Nature of the Firm", *Journal of Political Economy*, vol. 98, n. 6 (1988), pp. 1119-1158.

HAYEK, VON F.: *Law, Legislation and Liberty*, vol. 1: *Rules and Order*, London (Routledge) 1973.

HOLMSTROM, B.: "Moral Hazard in Teams", *Bell Journal of Economics*, 13 (1982), pp. 324-340.

KALAI, E., SMORODINSKY, M.: "Other Solution to Nash's Bargaining Problem", *Econometrica*, vol. 43, 3 (1975), pp. 880-895.

KAUFMANN, A.: *Introduction to the Theory of Fuzzy Subsets*, New York (Academic Press) 1975.

KEELEY, M.: *A Social-Contract Theory of Organisation*, Notre Dame (University of Notre Dame) 1988.

KREPS, D., WILSON, R.: "Reputation and Imperfect Information", *Journal of Economic Theory*, 27 (1982), pp. 257-279.

ETHICS, CORPORATE CULTURE AND ECONOMIC MODELLING

KREPS, D., MILGROM, P., ROBERTS, J., WILSON, R.: "Rational Co-operation in the Finitely Repeated Prisoner's Dilemma", *Journal of Economic Theory*, 27 (1982), pp. 245-252.

KREPS, D. (1990a): "Corporate Culture and Economic Theory", in: J. ALT, K. SHEPLSE (Eds.): *Perspectives in Positive Political Economy*, Cambridge (Cambridge University Press) 1990.

KREPS, D. (1990b): *A Course in Microeconomic Theory*, New York (Harvester Wheatsheaf) 1990.

LAFFONT, J. J., TIROLE, J.: *A Theory of Incentives in Procurement and Regulation*, Cambridge, Mass. (MIT Press) 1993.

MAITLAND, J.: "The Limits of Business Self-Regulation", in: T. BEUCHAMP and N. BOWIE (Eds.): *Ethical Theory and Business*, Englewood Cliffs, N.J. (Prentice Hall) 3rd ed. 1988.

MARCH, J. G., SIMON, H.: *Organizations*, New York (Wiley & Sons) 1958.

MCINTYRE, A.: *After Virtue*, Notre Dame (University of Notre Dame) 1981.

MCMAHON, C.: "Managerial Authority", *Ethics*, 100 (1989).

MILGROM, P., ROBERTS, J.: "Bargaining Costs, Influence Costs and the Organisation of Economic Activity", in: J. ALT and K. SHEPSLE (Eds.): *Perspectives on Positive Political Economy*, Cambridge (Cambridge University Press) 1990.

MOLANDER, E.: "A Paradigm for Design, Promulgation and Enforcement of Ethical Codes", *Journal of Business Ethics*, 1987, pp. 619-631.

NASH, J.: "The Bargaining Problem", *Econometrica*, 18 (1950), pp. 155-162.

PREITE, D.: *L' "abuso" della regola di maggioranza nelle deliberazioni assembleari*, Milano (Giuffr Ed.) 1992.

RAWLS, J.: *A Theory of Justice*, Oxford (Oxford University Press) 1971.

RAZ, J.: "Authority and Justification", in: *Philosophy and Public Affairs*, 1985, pp. 3-29.

REITER, R.: "A Logic for Default Reasoning", *Artificial Intelligence*, 13 (1980), pp. 81-132.

SACCONI, L.: *Etica degli affari. Inividui, imprese e mercati nella prospettva di un'etica razionale*, Milano (Il Saggiatore) 1991.

SACCONI, L.: "Codici etici e cultura di impresa", in: S. ZAMAGNI (Ed.): *Enciclopedia dell'impresa, vol. Politica economica*, Torino (UTET) 1994.

SACCONI, L.: *Economia, etica, organizzazione. Il contratto sociale dell'impresa*, Roma-Bari (Laterza) 1997.

SIMON, H.: "A Formal Theory of Ownership Relationship", *Econometrica*, 19 (1951), pp .293-305.

SIMON, H.: "Organisations and Markets", *The Journal of Economics Perspectives*, 5 (1991), pp. 25-44.

SIMS, R. R.: "The Institutionalisation of Organisational Ethics", *Journal of Business Ethics*, Vol. 10, n. 7 (1991), pp. 493-506.

LORENZO SACCONI

SOLOMON, R. C.: *Ethics and Excellence*, Oxford (Oxford University Press) 1992.
TIROLE, J.: "Hierarchies and Bureaucracies", *Journal of Law, Economics and Organisation*, 2 (1987), pp. 235-259.
TIROLE, J.: *The Theory of Industrial Organisation*, Cambridge, Mass. (MIT Press) 1988.
VAMBERG, V. J.: "Organisations as Constitutional Order", *Constitutional Political Economy*, vol. 3, n. 2 (1992), pp. 223-255.
WILLIAMSON, O.: *Market and Hierarchies*, New York (The Free Press) 1975.
ZIMMERMAN, H. J.: *Fuzzy Sets Theory*, Dordrecht (Kluwer Academic. Press) 1990.

Part B

Business Ethics

117 – 47

MI4
AI3

Chapter 6

Historicism, Communitarianism, and Commerce: An Aristotelean Approach to Business Ethics*

ROBERT C. SOLOMON

I.   An Aristotelean Approach to Business
II.   Aristotle, Happiness and Virtue
III.   The Corporation as Community
IV.   An Aristotelean Metaphor: Corporate Culture
V.   Trust and the Dynamics of Community
VI.   Conclusion: A Different Kind of Conception of Business?

> Corporations are places where both individual human beings and human communities engage in caring activities which are aimed at mutual support and unparalleled human achievement. (R. Edward Freeman and Jeanne Liedtka[1].)

Historicism, in one of its more modest meanings, is the meta-view that ideas and knowledge are "relative" to human practices, which, quite naturally, change with the times, with new technology, with alterations in the environment and in demography, in short, with history.

Communitarianism, in its more modest meaning, involves a rejection of what is sometimes called "liberalism" and in particular the assumption of

---

*   This essay was written especially for the Fifth Annual SEEP Conference on Economic Ethics and Philosophy, Marienrode, 2-4 November, 1997. Portions of this essay have been adapted from my book: *Ethics and Excellence*, Oxford (Oxford University Press) 1991.

1   R. EDWARD FREEMAN and JEANNE LIEDTKA: "Corporate Social Responsibility: A Critical Approach", *International Association for Business and Society Proceedings*, New York (IABS) 1991.

ROBERT C. SOLOMON

self-interested individualism that has come to dominate a good deal of the social sciences, economics and business language and literature especially. It takes human relationships and the sense of community to be at least as important as any isolated sense of self or self-interest. It is, one might say, Confucianism come to roost in the bowels of contemporary Western thought. Or, closer to home, we might say that it is Aristotle, the great Greek philosopher, reconditioned for modern, democratic society.

I think both historicism and communitarianism, in these modest senses, are true, or, at any rate, important meta-theses to hold as this millennium come to an increasingly irrational end.

There are other senses, in which historicism and communitarianism invoke the utter incommensurability of ideas, views, and cultures and can be used to defend authoritarian, divisive and intolerant practices, which I reject. But I do not want to talk about those meta-views here. What I do want to talk about is a particular aspect of economics and philosophy, namely, business ethics, and the way in which communitarian thinking-- or, thinking in terms of community - is influencing the current historical moment in business ethics thinking and theorising.

Historicism has played very little role in the business ethics literature, except, perhaps, for the common observation that business thinking is socially acceptable in much of the world today whereas it was condemned by many of the world's religions (more in the West than the east, one might argue[2]) for most of history. Communitarianism has played even less of a role, in part because liberalism and individual self-interest have so often been taken as central to business and economics. But the fact is, as Adam Smith so forcefully pointed out (even if it was subsequently ignored), a flourishing market presupposes a civil and civilised society, one in which there is some sense of community, fellow-feeling, compassion and justice. And, in modern times (that is, in the last half of this century), business depends on community in yet another sense, one which Smith did not talk about. Much of the world's business goes on in especially organised communities called "corporations" (literally, "embodiments"), both large and small, multi-national or very local. However much press the entrepreneur and entrepreneurship may command, the fact is that most of business con-

---

2   Confucian Chinese society has had a healthy respect for commerce for over two thousand years. Hinduism has never expressed shame about the desire for wealth. Even the Jains have long been pretty good businessmen.

sists of people *working together*. It is this phenomenon that I want to understand.

I. An Aristotelean Approach to Business

I have called the theoretical framework I have developed "an Aristotelean approach to business." As Aristotle is famous largely as the enemy of business, some justification of this approach would seem to be in order. True, he was the first economist. He had much to say about the ethics of exchange and so might well be called the first (known) business ethicist as well. But Aristotle distinguished two different senses of what we call economics, one of them " *oecinomicus*" or household trading, which he approved of and thought essential to the working of any even modestly complex society, and "*chrematisike*," which is trade for profit. Aristotle declared the latter activity wholly devoid of virtue. Aristotle despised the financial community and, more generally, all of what we would call profit-seeking. He argued that goods should be exchanged for their "real value," their costs, including a "fair wage" for those who produced them, but he then concluded, mistakenly, that any profit (that is, over and above costs) required some sort of theft (for where else would that "surplus value" come from.) Consequently, he called those who engaged in commerce "parasites" and had special disdain for money-lenders and the illicit, unproductive practice of usury, which until only a few centuries ago was still a crime. ("Usury" did not originally mean excessive interest; it referred to any charge over and above cost.) Only outsiders at the fringe of society, not respectable citizens, engaged in such practices. (Shakespeare's Shylock, in *The Merchant of Venice*, was such an outsider and a usurer, though his idea of a forfeit was a bit unusual.) All trade, Aristotle believed, was a kind of exploitation. Such was his view of what we call "business." Aristotle's greatest medieval disciple, St. Thomas Aquinas, shared "the Philosopher's" disdain for commerce, even while he struggled to permit limited usury (never by that term, of course) among his business patrons. (A charge for "lost use" of loaned funds was not the same as charging interest, he argued.) Even Martin Luther, at the door to modern times, insisted that usury was a sin and a profitable business was (at best) suspicious. Aristotle's influence on business, it could be argued, has been long-lasting - and nothing less than disastrous.

In particular, it can be argued that Aristotle had too little sense of the importance of production and based his views wholly on the aristocratically proper urge for acquisition, thus introducing an unwarranted zero-sum thinking into his economics.[3] And, of course, it can be charged that Aristotle, like his teacher Plato, was too much the spokesman for the aristocratic class and quite unfair to the commerce and livelihoods of foreigners and commoners.[4] It is Aristotle who initiates so much of the history of business ethics as the wholesale attack on business and its practices. Aristotelean prejudices underlie much of business criticism and the contempt for finance that preoccupies so much of Christian ethics even to this day, avaricious evangelicals not withstanding. Even defenders of business often end up presupposing Aristotelean prejudices in such Pyrrhonian arguments as "business is akin to poker and apart from the ethics of everyday life" [3] (Alfred Carr) and "the [only] social responsibility of business is to increase it profits" (Milton Friedman).[4] But if it is just this schism between business and the rest of life that so infuriated Aristotle, for whom life was supposed to fit together in a coherent whole, it is the same holistic idea-- that business people and corporations are first of all part of a larger community, that drives business ethics today.

We can no longer accept the amoral idea that "business is business" (not really a tautology but an excuse for being socially irresponsible and personally insensitive). According to Aristotle, one has to think of oneself as a member of the larger community - the *Polis* for him, the corporation, the neighbourhood, the city or the country (and the world) for us - and strive to excel, to bring out what was best in ourselves and our shared enterprise. What is best in us - our virtues - are in turn defined by that larger community, and there is therefore no ultimate split or antagonism between individual self-interest and the greater public good. Of course, there were no corporations in those days, but Aristotle would certainly know what I mean when I say that most people in business now identify themselves - if tenuously - in terms of their companies, and corporate policies, much less cor-

---

3   ALFRED CARR: "Is Business Bluffing Ethical?", *Harvard Business Review*, 1968.

4   MILTON FRIEDMAN: "The Social Responsibility of Business Is to Increase its Profits", *New York Times*, September 13 (1970).

porate codes of ethics, are not by themselves enough to constitute an ethics. But corporations are not isolated city-states, not even the biggest and most powerful of the multi-nationals (contrast the image of "the sovereign state of ITT"). They are part and parcel of a larger global community. The people that work for them are thus citizens of (at least) two communities at once, and one might think of business ethics as getting straight about that dual citizenship. What we need to cultivate is a certain way of thinking about ourselves in and out of the corporate context, and this is the aim of ethical theory in business, as I understand it. It is not, let me insist, anti-individualistic in any sense of "individualism" that is worth defending. The Aristotelean approach to business ethics rather begins with the two-pronged idea that it is individual virtue and integrity that counts, but good corporate and social policy encourage and nourish individual virtue and integrity. It is this picture of community, with reference to business and the corporation, that I want to explore here. One might speak of "communitarianism" here, but it is not at all evident that one must give up, at the same time, a robust sense of individuality (as opposed to self-interested individualism). Community and virtue will form the core of the thesis I want to defend here.

To call the approach "Aristotelean" is to emphasise the importance of community, the business community as such (I want to consider corporations as, first of all, communities) but also the larger community, even all of humanity and, perhaps, much of nature too. This emphasis on community, however, should not be taken to eclipse the importance of the individual and individual responsibility. In fact, the contrary is true, it is only within the context of community that individuality is developed and defined, and our all-important sense of individual integrity is dependent upon and not opposed to the community in which integrity gets both its meaning and its chance to prove itself.

One of the most important aspects of the "Aristotelean" approach is the emphasis on the purposiveness (or "teleology") that defines every human enterprise, including business. But that purposiveness transcends the realm of business and defines its place in the larger society, though the popular term "social responsibility" makes this sound too much like an extraneous concern rather than the purpose of business as such. On both an individual and the corporate level, the importance of the concept of **excellence** is intricately tied to this overall teleology, for what counts as excellence is defined both by its superiority in the practice and its role in serving larger social purposes. "Aristotelean" too is a strong emphasis on individual character

121

and the virtues (where a "virtue" is all-round personal excellence"), embedded in and in service to the larger community. It is the role of the individual in the corporation (and of the corporation in society) that concerns me, not the individual alone, not the structure of the corporation abstracted from the individuals that are its members (and not the nature of "capitalism," abstracted from the character of particular corporations and the communities they serve.) That is why the idea of business as a practice is absolutely central to this approach: it views business as a human institution in service to humans and not as a marvellous machine or in terms of the mysterious "magic" of the market.

Finally, it may be theoretically least interesting but it is polemically, perhaps, most important, I prefer the name "Aristotelean" just because it makes no pretensions of presenting something very new, the latest "cutting-edge" theory or technique of management but rather reminds us of something very, very old, a perspective and a debate that go all the way back to ancient times. What Aristotle gives us, I want to suggest, is a set of doctrines that both conforms to and goes beyond historicism, namely, the incessant appeal of ethics (including business ethics) to the standards of a particular community but at the same time the standards of community as such, that is, the very possibility of human beings living and working together. What the Aristotelean approach promises is not something novel and scientific but an approach that is very staid and above all very human. The idea is not to infuse corporate life with one more excuse for brutal changes, a new wave of experts and seminars and yet another down-sizing bloodbath. It is to emphasise the enduring importance of continuity and stability, clearness of vision and constancy of purpose, corporate loyalty and individual integrity for both financial success and (more important) a decent life.

II. Aristotle, Happiness and Virtue

Aristotle's central ethical concept, accordingly, is a unified, all-embracing notion of "happiness" (or more accurately, *eudaimonia*, perhaps better translated as "flourishing" or "doing well"). The point is to view one's life as a whole and not separate the personal and the public or professional, or duty and pleasure. The point is that doing what one ought to do, doing one's duty, fulfilling one's responsibilities and obligations is not counter but conducive to the good life, to becoming the sort of person one wants to become. Conversely, becoming the sort of person one wants to become - which presumably includes to a very large extent what one does "for a living" - is what happiness is all about. Happiness is "flourishing," and this means fitting into a world of other people and sharing the good life, including "a good job," with them. A good job, accordingly, is not just one that pays well or is relatively easy but one that means something, one that has (more or less) tangible and clearly beneficial results, one that (despite inevitable periods of frustration) one enjoys doing. Happiness (for us as well as for Aristotle) is an all-inclusive, holistic concept. It is ultimately one's character, one's integrity, that determines happiness, not the bottom line. And this is just as true, I want to insist, of giant corporations as it is of the individuals who work for them.

There is no room in this picture for the false antagonism between "self-ishness" on the one hand and what is called "altruism" on the other. For the properly constituted social self, the distinction between self-interest and social-mindedness is all but unintelligible and what we call selfishness is guaranteed to be self-destructive as well. And "altruism" is too easily turned into self-sacrifice, for instance by that self-appointed champion of selfish-ness Ayn Rand. But altruism isn't self-sacrifice; it's just a more reasonable conception of self, as tied up intimately with community, with friends and family who may, indeed, count (even to us) more than we do. What the Aristotelean approach to business ethics demands isn't self-sacrifice or submerging oneself to the interests of the corporation, much less voluntary unhappiness. What it does say is that the distinctions and oppositions be-tween self and society that give rise to these wrong-headed conceptions are themselves the problem, and the cause of so much unhappiness and dissatis-faction. So, too, the most serious single problem in business ethics is the false antagonism between profits and social responsibility. There is an aca-demic prejudice, for example, against clever profit-making solutions - the obviously optimal solution to "social responsibility"-type problems. It is as if moralists have a vested interest in the nobility of self-sacrifice (that is, self-sacrifice by others). (This is the same problem, philosophy students will recognise, once raised by the theory of egoism in ethics, e.g. in the famous exchange between Thomas Hobbes and Bishop Butler.) According to all such views, either an action is selfish or it is selfless, and the Aristo-telean synthesis of self-interested, noble behaviour is eliminated from view.

Once one introduces such artificial oppositions between self-interest and shared interest, between profits and social responsibility, the debate becomes a "lose-lose" proposition, either wealth and irresponsibility or integrity and failure. Yet I do not want to say that the Aristotelean approach offers us a "win-win" proposition, since that popular formulation already assumes a self-interested (albeit mutual self-interest) game theoretical situation. The truth is closer to this: by working together *we* are better off (and woe to the corporation or society that too long keeps all of the rewards at the top of the pyramid and allows only a "trickle-down" of benefits to most of those in the "we".

What is worth defending in business is that sense of virtue which stresses co-operative joint effort and concern for consumers and colleagues alike. Aristotelean ethics is an ethics of virtue, an ethics in which personal and (corporate) integrity occupy the place of central concern and focus. But virtue and integrity are not to be found in a vacuum. They do not appear miraculously in the atomistic individual, they cannot be contracted or commissioned, nor are they the special province of saints. They are not (except cynically) the result of a cost/benefit calculation of utility, and they cannot be dictated according to abstract rules or principles (thus the nagging vacuity of such principles as "be courageous!" or "be generous!"). A virtue has a place in a social context, in a human practice, and accordingly it is essentially part of a fabric that goes beyond the individual and binds him or her to a larger human network. Integrity - literally "wholeness" - also has to be understood (in part) in the context of a community, and in business life the corporation. It consists not just of individual autonomy and "togetherness" but of such company virtues as loyalty and congeniality, co-operation and trustworthiness. Of course, this also means that the corporation itself must be viewed as a morally and socially responsible agent, a view which does not, however, compromise the ultimate importance of the responsibility and integrity of the individuals who work within it.[5] Nothing is more damaging

---

5 This two-level view of the individual and the corporation, integrity and virtue **in** and **of** the corporation, has its classic analogue in the imagery of Plato's *Republic*, and many of my themes will echo where they do not repeat Plato's insistence on the importance of harmony and proper perspective in both the good society and the healthy individual soul. It is this presumption of essential participation and co-operation that is the heart of the Aristotelean perspective as well. Despite the cheerleading emphasis on "team work" in the modern corporation,

to business ethics (or to ethics in business) than the glib dismissal of corporations as agents because they are "legal fictions" or the equally fatuous if familiar insistence that the sole purpose of corporations (and, therefore, the sole responsibility of their managers) is to turn a profit and fulfil their "fiduciary obligation to the stockholders."[6] The pursuit of integrity is undermined from the start, I have argued, by such dangerous myths and metaphors about business, corporations, and the people who work for them. Corporations are neither legal fictions nor financial juggernauts but communities, people working together for common goals. That seemingly simple realisation, which so much of corporate life has seemingly rejected in recent years, is the first principle of Aristotelean business ethics. And with that emphasis on integrity and community comes not only the fulfilment of obligations to stockholders (not all of them "fiduciary") but the production of quality and the earning of pride in one's products, providing good jobs and well-deserved rewards for employees and the enrichment of a whole community and not just a select group of (possibly short-term) contracted "owners."[7]

So, too, Aristotelean ethics presupposes an ideal, an ultimate purpose, but the ideal of business in general is not, as my undergraduates so smartly insist, "to make money." It is to serve society's demands and the public good and be rewarded for doing so. This ideal in turn defines the mission of the corporation, and provides the criteria according to which corporations and everyone in business can be praised or criticised. "Better living through chemistry," "Quality at a good price," "Productivity through people," "Progress is our most important product." - these are not mere advertising slo-

---

however, it is just this sense of harmony and co-operation that gets systematically undermined.

6   MILTON FRIEDMAN: "The Social Responsibility of Business", *op. cit.*

7   ALISTAIR M. NACLEOD: "Moral Philosophy and Business Ethics: The Priority of the Political", in: E. WIAKLEN, J. COOMBS (Eds.): *Applied Ethics*, Oxford (Blackwell) 1993, pp. 222-228. On the importance of institutional arrangements: "once institutions are seen, not as relatively unmalleable, quasi-organic structures which it would be perilous to try to modify, but as elaborate human artefacts serving a wide range of human purposes, the question whether they ought to be preserved in something like their present form or changed in some way--radically transformed, even, if they no longer secure the interests, private or public, which provided their raison d'etre is bound to win an important place on the moral theorist's agenda."

gans but reasons for working and for living. Without a mission, a company is just a bunch of people organised to make money while making up something to do, (e.g. "beating the competition"). Such activities may, unintentionally, contribute to the public good, but Adam Smith's "invisible hand" never was a very reliable social strategy,[8] and the difference between intending to do good and doing good unintentionally is not just the special sense of satisfaction that comes from the former. Contrary to the utterly irresponsible and obviously implausible argument that those ("do-gooders") who try to do good in fact do more harm than good, the simple, self-evident truth is that most of the good in this world comes about through good intentions. Meaningful human activity is that which intends the good rather than stumbling over it on the way to merely competitive or selfish goals.

III. The Corporation as Community

The Aristotelean approach begins with the idea that we are, first of all, members of organised groups, with shared histories and established practices governing everything from eating and working to worshipping. We are not, as our favourite folklore would have it, first of all **individuals**, that is, autonomous, self-sustaining, self-defining creatures who, ideally, think entirely for ourselves and determine what we are. The "self-made man" [or woman] is a social creature, and he (or she) "makes it" by being an essential part of society, however innovative or eccentric he or she may be. To say that we are communal creatures is to say that we have shared interests, that even in the most competitive community our self-interests are parasitic on and largely defined in terms of our mutual interests. To think of the corporation as a community is to insist that it cannot be, no matter how vicious its internal politics, a mere collection of self-interested individuals. To see business as a social activity is to see it as a practice that both thrives on competition and presupposes a coherent community of mutually concerned as well as self-interested citizens.

---

8   a metaphor he used exactly once in the whole of *Wealth of Nations* (and once prior in his *Theory of the Moral Sentiments*).

HISTORICISM, COMMUNITARIANISM AND COMMERCE

To be sure, communities in the contemporary "western" world are anything but homogeneous or harmonious, but the claim I am making here is more metaphysical than nostalgic, and the claim is that what we call "the individual" is socially constituted and socially situated. "The individual" today is the product of particularly mobile and entrepreneurial society in which natural groups (notably the "extended" family or tribe) have been replaced by artificial organisations such as schools and corporations. Movement between them is not only possible (as it is usually not between tribes and families) but encouraged, even required. Human beings are not, as such, individuals. They are separated by the boundaries of their epidermises, to be sure, and there is some rather (philosophically confusing) sense in which each one "has" his or her own thoughts and emotions, even if these are prompted by, learned from and the same as the thoughts and emotions of other people. "The individual" was an invention of the eleventh and twelfth centuries in Europe, when families were separated by war and the tightly arranged structures of feudalism were breaking apart. "The individual" became increasingly important with the advent of capitalist and consumer society, but (as so often in the overly materialist history of economics) he or she became important first because of changing religious conceptions, with increased emphasis on personal faith and individual salvation. But "the individual" was always a relative, context-dependent designation. An individual in one society would be a sociopath in another. ("The nail that sticks out is the one that gets hammered", goes a traditional Japanese proverb.)

What we call "the individual" is, from even the slightest outside perspective, very much a social, even a conformist conception. To show one's individuality in the financial world, for example, it may be imperative to wear the same tie as everyone else, usually of a colour (red, yellow, pink) or a pattern (paisley) that only a true eccentric would have chosen on his own. To further emphasise individuality (which connotes creativity, even genius), one might sport a moustache or a beard (though the range of styles is very strictly circumscribed). But getting beyond trivial appearances, even our thoughts and feelings are, it is obvious, for the most part defined and delineated by our society, in our conversations and confrontations with other people. Princeton anthropologist Clifford Geertz once wrote that a human being all alone in nature would not be a noble, autonomous being but a pathetic, quivering creature with no identity and few defences or means of support. Our heroic conception of "the individual" - often exemplified by

127

the lone (usually male) hero - is a bit of bad but self-serving anthropology. There are exceptional individuals, to be sure, but they are social creations and become exceptional just because they serve the needs of their society, more often than not by exemplifying precisely those forms of excellence most essential to that society.[9]

We find our identities and our meanings only within communities, and for most of us that means - at work in a company or an institution. However we might prefer to think of ourselves, however important we (rightly) insist on the importance of family and friends, however much we might complain about our particular jobs or professional paths, we define ourselves largely in terms of them, even if, in desperation, in opposition to them. Whether a person likes or hates his or her job will almost always turn on relationships with the people one works for and works with, whether there is mutual respect or animosity and callousness or indifference. Even the lone entrepreneur - the sidewalk jeweller or the financial wizard - will succeed only if he or she has social skills, enjoys (or seems to) his or her customers or clients.

The philosophical myth that has grown almost cancerous in many business circles, the neo-Hobbesian view that business is "every man[sic] for himself" and the Darwinian view that "it's a jungle out there" are direct denials of the Aristotelean view that we are first of all members of a community and our self-interest is for the most part identical to the larger interests of the group. Competition presumes, it does not replace, an underlying assumption of mutual interest and co-operation. Whether we do well, whether we like ourselves, whether we lead happy productive lives, depends to a large extent on the companies we choose. As the Greeks used to say, "to live the good life one must live in a great city." To my business students today, who are all too prone to choose a job on the basis of salary and start-up bonus alone, I always say, "to live a decent life choose the right company." In business ethics the corporation becomes one's immedi-

---

9   There is always the *Star Trek* myth, of course, the benign "outsider" who brings to a civilisation some virtue that is sorely missing but wholly lacking (e.g. Kirk's courage, Spock's rationality), and the more generic Joseph Campbell myth of the hero who leaves his society and wanders off on his own, later returning with new virtues to save the society. But the fact that these are **myths** should already tell us something about their sociological status. The virtues supposedly imported are already celebrated as such.

ate community and, for better or worse, the institution that defines the values and the conflicts of values within which one lives much of one's life. A corporation that encourages mutual co-operation and encourages individual excellence as an essential part of teamwork is a very different place to work and live than a corporation that incites "either/or" competition, antagonism, and continuous jostling for status and recognition. There is nothing more "natural" about the latter, which is at least as much the structuring of an organisation (whether intended or not) as the co-operative ambience of the former.

The first principle of business ethics, in my book, is that the corporation is itself a citizen, a member of the larger community and inconceivable without it. This is the idea that has been argued over the past few decades as the principle of "social responsibility," but the often attenuated and distorted arguments surrounding that concept has been more than enough to convince me that the same idea needed a different foundation.[10] The notion of "responsibility" (a version of which will, nevertheless be central to my argument here too) is very much a part of the atomistic individualism that I am attacking as inadequate, and the classic arguments for "the social responsibilities of business" all-too-readily fall into the trap of **beginning** with the assumption of the corporation as an autonomous, independent entity, which **then** needs to consider its obligations to the surrounding community. But corporations like "individuals" are part and parcel of the communities that created them, and the responsibilities that they bear are not the products of argument or implicit contracts but intrinsic to their very existence as social entities. There are important and sometimes delicate questions, of course, about what the social responsibilities of business or of a particular corporation might be, but the question whether they have such responsibilities is a non-starter, a bit of covert nonsense. Friedman's now-infamous idea that "the social responsibility of business is to increase its profits" betrays a wilful misunderstanding of the very nature of both social responsibility and business. (Not surprisingly, the author of that doctrine has elsewhere protested, alienating his friends along with his critics, that he is "not pro-business but pro-free enterprise.")

---

10 E. FREEMAN has made much the same argument with a more radical conclusion, that we should abandon the overworn concept of "social responsibility" altogether.

ROBERT C. SOLOMON

These claims are closely akin to the ideas captured in the pun-like notion of a "**stakeholder**," that broadening conception of the corporate constituency which includes a variety of affected (and effective) groups and all sorts of different obligations and responsibilities.[11] The term has become something of a cover-all, and so what considerable advantages it has provided in terms of breadth are to some extent now compromised by the uncritical over-use of the word. For example, the notion of "stakeholder" suggests discrete groups or entities whereas the primary source of dilemmas in business ethics is the fact that virtually all of us wear (at least) "two hats," e.g. as employees and as members of the larger community, as consumers and as stockholders, as a manager and as a friend, and these roles can come into conflict with one another. As a programme for ethical analysis in business, the standard list of stakeholders is notoriously incomplete where it concerns one's competitors rather than one's constituents. In an obvious sense, no one is more affected by one's actions (and, sometimes, no one is more effective in determining one's actions) than one's competitors. "Good sportsmanship" and fair play are essential obligations in business ethics. And yet it seems odd to say that the competition "has a stake" in the company. The idea of community thus goes beyond the idea of particular responsibilities and obligations although it embraces the same impetus toward larger thinking and citizenship endorsed by stakeholder analysis.

If we consider corporations as first of all communities - not legal fictions, not monolithic entities, not faceless bureaucracies, and not matrices of Price/Earnings ratios, net assets, and liabilities - then the activities and the ethics of business become much more comprehensible and much more human. Shareholders are, of course, part of the community, but most of them only marginally rather than, as in some now-classic arguments, the sole recipients of managerial fiduciary obligations. The concept of community also shifts our conception of what makes a corporation "work" or not. What makes a corporation efficient or inefficient is not a series of "well-oiled" mechanical operations but the working interrelationships, the co-ordination and rivalries, team spirit and morale of the many people who work there and are in turn shaped and defined by the corporation. So, too, what drives a corporation is not some mysterious abstraction called "the

---

11 The term "stakeholder" began floating around the Business Roundtable about a decade ago, but it gained currency in E. FREEMAN: *Corporate Strategy and the Search for Ethics*, Englewood Cliffs, NJ (Prentice-Hall) 1988.

130

profit motive" (which is highly implausible even as a personal motive, but utter nonsense when applied to a fictitious legal entity or a bureaucracy). It is the collective will and ambitions of its employees, few of whom (even in profit-sharing plans or in employee-owned companies) work "for a profit" in any obvious sense. What the employees of a corporation do, they do to "fit in," to do their jobs and earn the respect of others, and self-respect as well. They want to prove their value in their jobs, they try to show their independence or their resentment, they try to please (or intentionally aggravate) their superiors, they want to impress (or intimidate) their subordinates, they want to feel good about themselves or they try to make the best of a bad situation. And, of course, they want to bring home a paycheque. To understand how corporations work (and don't work) is to understand the social psychology and sociology of communities, not the logic of a "flow-chart" or the "organisational" workings of a cumbersome machine.

What is a corporate community? To begin with, it is a heterogeneous conglomerate that is bound to be riddled with personality clashes, competing aims and methodologies, cliques and rivalries and criss-crossed loyalties. The very fact that a corporation requires specialisation and the division of labour makes inevitable such heterogeneity. Two young men working in a garage, pooling their resources and their knowledge to produce a successful commodity may, in the throes and thrills of development and struggle, experience an uninterrupted sense of one-ness that would impress even a Buddhist. But once the product is launched and marketing people and managers are brought in to do the job, that primeval corporate unity is shattered and, as in the most famous recent case of this kind, one or both of the founders of the company may find themselves displaced or even fired by the assistants they brought in to help them. There is an intrinsic antagonism - to be explained in terms of social class rather than economics and in terms of our mythologies of work rather than the nature of the work itself - between the shoproom floor and the managerial office, just as there is an obvious opposition (not entirely financial) between those divisions of the corporation that always need to spend more money (advertising and research and development teams, for example) and those whose job it is to save it. Add to this the many different characters and personalities who populate even the most seemingly homogeneous company (although these differences too are already pre-established in the social types and classes who tend to one or the other position or profession) and one can appreciate the foolishness in our popular treatment of corporations as monolithic entities with a single mind and a single motive.

And yet, there is an emergent phenomenon, that does often speak with a single voice and deserves to be treated (and not just by the law) as a singular entity, "the corporation." Groups have personalities just as individuals do, and heterogeneous, even fragmented groups can nevertheless have a singular character just as conflicted people do. What this means, in terms of collective responsibility, for example, is that it is a mistake to speak of corporations as only collections of individuals, both because the "individuals" in question are themselves the creatures of the corporation and because the corporation is one of those sums that is nevertheless greater than its many constituent parts. Aristotelean ethics takes both the corporation and the individual seriously without pretending that either is an autonomous entity unto itself. Corporations are made up of people, and the people in corporations are defined by the corporation. Business ethics thus becomes a matter of corporate ethics, emphatically **not** in the sense that what counts is the ethics of the corporation, considered as an autonomous, autocratic agent, ruling over its employees (perhaps exemplified by its "corporate code"), nor in the more innocent but naive sense that the ethics of the corporation is nothing but the product of the collective morality of its employees. The morals of the executives, particularly the exemplary morals of those who are most visible in the corporation, are an important influence on corporate morality, but it is the nature and power of institutions - particularly those in which a person spends half of his or her adult waking life - to shape and sanction the morals of the individual. There may well be (and often is) a gap or dichotomy between a person's sense of ethics on the job and his or her sense of right and wrong with friends and family. There may well be real ethical differences within a company, particularly between its various departments and divisions. But even in diversity and conflict the ethics of a corporation becomes clearly and often soon visible to those most closely attached to, affiliated with or affected by it. Corporations can (and often do) get "a bad rap," an institutional black eye caused by a tiny percentage of its employees. (Hertz Rent-a-Car was caught up in a monumental scandal a year or so ago, which turned out to involve some 20 dealers out of 20,000. Nevertheless, it was the name "Hertz" that took the brunt of the abuse, and numbers were simply not the issue.) Such apparent injustices throw a revealing light on a company and its ethical standards, however, and give the best corporations a chance to show their moral mettle. Communities are essential units of morality, and corporations are ultimately judged not by the numbers but by the coherence and co-operation both within their walls and with the larger communities in which they play such an essential social as well as economic role.

IV. An Aristotelean Metaphor: Corporate Culture

It is a sign of considerable progress that one of the dominant models of today's corporate thinking is the idea of a "corporate culture". As with any analogy or metaphor, there are, of course, disanalogies, and the concept of corporations as cultures too quickly attained the status of a "fad" - thus marking it for easy ridicule and imminent obsolescence.[12] But some fads nevertheless contain important insights, and while those who insist on keeping up with the latest fashion may soon have moved on the virtues of this recent change in thinking may not yet have been fully appreciated.

---

12 E.g. see MARK PASKIN: *The Hard Problems of Management*, San Francisco (Jossey-Bass) 1986: "why corporations should have weak cultures and strong ethics." But one is tempted to speculate whether Paskin, who learned ethics under the tutelage of Roderick ("ideal observer theory") Firth at Harvard, might not have too little respect for the shared mores that come of participation of cultural life and too little concern for the dispassionate negotiations of the social contract (p. 129). "The lesson is clear. Forget culture and think about fair agreements" (p. 144), arguing that cultures are intrinsically "conservative" and strong cultures "put basic beliefs, attitudes and ways of doing things beyond question." Cultures are hard to change, but this, I want to argue, is precisely their strength. Sometimes, ignoring the culture works best. But only within the confines of the culture (cf. families) tends to blend ethics into culture (or vice versa) so opposition not as pronounced as initial pronouncement would suggest trivial sense of culture: on cadbury schweppes 'few corporate symbols, none of the bells and whistles characteristic of strong-culture companies, and no need to do things 'the cadbury way'. The corporate environment is free from ceremony, (p. 140) open to ethics, respect for individual, participatory and consensus-aimed decision-making procedures. (Sir Adrian Cadbury himself, quoted on the same page, "the one thing I'm sure about ... is that the way it's done must be related to the culture' (against the 'mandarin culture)".

ROBERT C. SOLOMON

The concept of a corporate culture, first and foremost, is distinctively and irreducibly **social**. It presupposes the existence of an established community and it explicitly rejects atomistic individualism. Individuals are part of a culture only insofar as they play a part in that culture, participate in its development and fit into its structure. Cultures are by their very nature (more or less) harmonious, that is, they are not possible unless people co-operate and share some minimal outlook on life. (There could not be a completely competitive culture, only a Hobbesian jungle of mutually disagreeable animals.[13]) Cultures have rules and rituals, particular modes of dress and address; and most important of all (for our purposes) every culture has an ethics, including those basic rules which hold the society together and protect it from itself. (Which of these are essential and which are "mere custom," of course, is sometimes more easily determined by an outsider than by a member of the culture itself. The various "taboos" of every culture, including our own (and most corporate cultures), may indeed (for reasons now forgotten) protect the integrity of the community, blocking out some dreadful secret or preventing some now-unpredictable disaster. But they may be only "the way we do things around here" and of significance only because they are part of the values that are accepted by and thus help define the membership of the culture. The difference here may become extremely important in the midst of corporate upheaval and cultural change, but for day to day purposes it is a difference that makes very little practical difference. The important point is that cultures presuppose shared knowledge, experience and values and they are thus co-operative enterprises. A corporate culture is an essentially co-operative enterprise with public as well as private purposes. It cannot be reduced to a legal "fiction" or an economic

---

13   The most famous modern counter-example, the infamous Ik tribe of the mountain ranges of Africa, has been often abused for this purpose. Colin Turnbull's careful description of the comparative callousness and competitiveness of the Ik shows quite clearly that beneath their selfishness there is a cultural method, a sense of coherence even in the face of a hostile and alienating environment. Within the context of a culture, the Ik do indeed strike us as shockingly indifferent to one another's well-being (even to the welfare of their own children), but nevertheless the culture itself displays the requisite structure of mutual attention, shared goals and minimally harmonious cohesion if not exactly co-operation. See COLIN TURNBULL: *The Mountain People*, New York (Simon and Schustel) 1972.

mechanism or the numbers in the annual report or anything else that is not first and foremost an established group of people working together.

Needless to say, there are make-shift corporations that are neither cultures nor communities at all, just as there are nations by fiat (usually of other nations, e.g. the amalgamation of Czechoslovakia and Yugoslavia in Europe and the carving up of Africa across and in violation of tribal lines by European colonialists) and "organisations" put together just for the sake of some external benefit, e.g. the "travel clubs" that were organised in the 1970s in order to charter airline passage to Europe.) The problem arises when theorists take these deviant examples and elevate them to the status of paradigms, as if the existence of such merely formal organisations proves that what constitutes an organisation, after all, is not its people or its shared values but the legal charter that defines and limits its purpose and activities. To the contrary, what I want to insist on here is just that such purely formal arrangements are both deviant and exceptional, and that corporations (and most other human organisations) are defined first of all by their communal and cultural status and only secondarily (and not essentially) by any formal or legal process.

It is important to appreciate the significance of the "culture" metaphor against the backdrop of the more vulgar, sometimes brutal and either atomistic and mechanical metaphors we have been discussing. Just as business (in general) has been saddled (and saddled itself) with unflattering and destructive images, thus misunderstanding itself, corporations - both in general and as individual entities - have too often tended to present themselves (despite all of their public relations work and advertising to the contrary) as giant juggernauts, mechanical monsters as faceless as the glass and steel buildings that typically form their headquarters. Consumers are so many numbers and employees are only so many replaceable parts. Even top management is only part of the mechanism. It is no wonder that most Americans who do not work for corporations think of them as inhuman and as inhumane places to work, and those millions who do work in and for corporations find themselves at a serious conceptual disadvantage. What kind of a life is this, being a replaceable part in a giant machine, for which the only virtue is mere efficiency?

The conception of a corporate culture, though relatively recent, has its origins in the more familiar model of the **bureaucracy**, developed during the French revolution and the Napoleonic era as a correction to inherited privilege and incompetence (but with its roots back in Rome, in the labyrinthine organisation of the medieval catholic church and, long before that, in the ancient civilisation of the Middle East). The concept of the bureaucracy was extensively promoted and popularised (though with considerable misgivings) by the great German sociologist Max Weber at the turn of this century. The imagery of the bureaucracy provided something of a compromise between the juggernaut and machine imagery of the eighteenth century enlightenment on the one hand and the Renaissance and romantic demands for "humanisation" on the other. (Indeed, the whole of the Western enlightenment was something of an odd mix of machine metaphors and humanism, but that is another story, e.g. see Toulmin's *Cosmopolis: The Hidden Agenda of Modernity*.)[14] But "bureaucracy" has become something of a "dirty word" for us, suggesting inefficiency instead of the model of efficiency it was once intended to be. It calls up images of Soviet ineffectiveness and Kafkaesque catacombs. And yet, modern corporations are in large part bureaucracies, and this is not necessarily to say something against them. But what is important and progressive about bureaucracies is not just their traditional and now largely discredited emphasis on efficiency or even their still essential emphasis on meritocracy. It is rather the humanisation of the bureaucracy as "culture" and the all-important shift of emphasis from machine-like efficiency to inter-personal co-operation and human productivity.[15]

Bureaucracies, like cultures and unlike machines, are made up of people, not parts. Bureaucracies have purposes. Bureaucracies involve people in making judgements, employing their skills, working together in an organised way to produce results. Those results may be the maintenance of the status quo, no easy trick in modern societies. For all of the obsessive talk about "innovation" and "competition," the essential function of most corporate bureaucracies-- that is, the larger part of the corporation by far--

---

14 S. TOULMIN: *Cosmopolis: The Hidden Agenda of Modernity*, New York (Fice Press) 1990.

15 The familiar misunderstanding of the nature of bureaucracy extends even to those who are most sympathetic with the idea of corporate culture, notably, T. DEAL and A. KENNEDY: *Corporate Cultures*, Reading, Mass. (Addison-Werley) 1982, p. 108: "The process culture. A world of little or no feedback where employees find it hard to measure what they do; instead they concentrate on how it's done. We have another name for this culture when the processes get out of control - bureaucracy." (This book began the recent "culture" fad.)

is just this maintenance of the status quo. One can understand and sympathise with the fear and uncertainty about the future that is part of most markets without joining the myth-making chorus of "future shocks" and "megatrends." To be sure, change these days is both very real and very fast. Maintaining the status quo in a fast changing society requires being adaptive and organically tuned to the times, but it also requires a durable structure and a stable organisation. Over-emphasis on change and the sacrifice of stability - as evidenced in so many corporate "shake-ups" and "restructurings" today - weakens the corporation and makes it a far less efficient competitor. However "leaner" (and often "meaner") it may be, this "new" corporation - is likely to be far more embroiled in internal politics and the personnel problems of coping with insecurity and anxiety than facing the competition or improving its products. What maintains the stability within a corporation, however, is precisely that much-despised locus of inefficiency - the bureaucracy. Or, now in more enlightened terms, this essential continuity is provided by what we recognise as the corporate culture, an enduring security founded on inter-personal co-operation and mutual respect.

The idea of a corporate culture is an improvement over the more staid image and impersonal of the bureaucracy in several respects, but in one respect in particular. A "culture" is first of all a structured community of individuals and their interrelationships. Bureaucracies, on the other hand, remain subtly individualistic as well as mechanistic. People may work together in their various capacities but this "togetherness" is a function of the organisation and not a relationship between them. They may not be cogs in a machine but they are functionaries who are readily replaced by anyone else with the same skills and knowledge. Our image of the bureaucracy, accordingly, is lots of people isolated in little offices (or "bureaus") doing their jobs and, if they are conscientious and efficient, not stopping to talk to one another or chit-chat over the coffee machine. Our image of a culture, by way of contrast, essentially involves people talking with one another (probably dancing, cooking and worshipping together as well). Thus the image of the bureaucracy carries over the machine image of facelessness and an attitude of indifference toward individuals. In a culture, by contrast, individuals are essential, not just as impersonal parts but as members with personalities as well as functional roles.

In a corporate culture, people, not functions or mere functionaries, work together for their shared and not merely mutual benefit. People, unlike functions and mere functionaries, have personalities, personal ambitions,

137

and "outside" interests. They make friends (and enemies). They need a moment to unwind, catch their breath, relieve themselves, express themselves, and daily renew their personal contacts around the office. (How quickly an office can be disrupted when a manager just fails to say "hello" to everyone that morning.) Anal compulsive types may see this (wrongly) as inefficient, and such interpersonal behaviour as gossip and "chit-chat" as a distraction, but this betrays a fatal misunderstanding of both people and organisations. That is why I have insisted, with such seeming innocence and insistence, that corporations are first of all communities. They are social groups with a shared purpose (or rather purposes). A person's position is not just a function defined by duties but a role in the community, a role which comes to have as its attributes (whether by design or evolution) such strictly interpersonal virtues as charm, attractiveness and a good sense of humour as well as this or that job to be done.

But "community" is a very general term for interconnected and mutually interested individuals and it contains no commitment or even a suggestion of development or internal structure. A community may be just a particular bunch of people gathered together for some period of time to enjoy themselves and each other. Indeed, it is not altogether clear whether the same community exists over time, as individual members enter and leave the group. Thus the importance of the additional concept of a culture, a corporate culture. Corporate cultures are not only distinctively and irreducibly social and opposed to atomistic individualism. Cultures have a history and a structure, and thus a culture can remain "the same" over a substantial period of time despite the coming and going of any or even all individuals in the culture. And among those essential structures are the various demands of ethics. It is, above all, shared values that hold a culture together. And these values concern not only the "internal" cohesion and coherence of the culture. They also concern the sense of mission that the corporation embodies, its various stakeholder obligations and its sense of social responsibility and social (not just corporate) values.

We should always remember that the free market economy and the prominence of business and business-thinking is an on-going experiment not an indelible aspect of society or a writ of God. We might not have the best way of doing it. We could even be wrong. A colleague of mine at an international conference in Bucharest recently heard a West German businessman, after listening to a number of suggestions concerning the exportation of American management skills to Eastern Europe, argue that American management was too rigid, mechanical and hierarchical to work well even in America, much less in the more humanistic cultures of Europe. The Americans, of course, were shocked. Not only was their paradigm of a corporate culture being thrown back in their faces as inhuman; it was also declared to be dysfunctional. If no philosophical or humanitarian concerns are sufficient to prompt a new way of thinking about business, the new American situation in the world market should be ample motivation. One more management fad or marketing miracle is not going to do it, and the continuing denial of our own humanity and sociability is only going to leave us more isolated and more desperate, when what we really need is a renewed sense of solidarity and shared cultural significance.

V. Trust and the Dynamics of Community

Trust, it is now widely acknowledged, is the "glue", the basic "medium" of a successful business enterprise, - or a successful business society. But, until very recently, the business ethics literature was almost silent on the topic of trust. There were the necessary nods to trust, for example, in discussions of management-employee relations and agency relationships[16] but the nature of trust went unanalysed, as if no analysis were needed. So, too, Francis Fukuyama's *Trust: The Social Virtues and the Creation of Prosperity* and John Whitney's *The Trust Factor* have both attracted considerable attention in the business world. Each has its virtues, and their central theme - that trust is essential for prosperity and business - is undebatable. But what they fail to do is to say anything much about trust itself, and they assiduously avoid the red-flag term "ethics". It is as if the point of trust is mere efficiency, the elimination of wasteful "transaction costs", with no moral or ethical implications. Whitney, for example, starts and essentially ends his analysis with the Random House Dictionary definition of trust-- as if that "official" definition of the word were sufficient to grasp the complexities

---

16 For example, FRANCIS SEJERSTED: "Managers and Consultants as Manipulators", *Business Ethics Quarterly*, vol. VI, n. 1, January 1996, esp. pp 77-78; NANCY B. KURLAND: "Trust, Accountability, and Sales Agents' Dueling Loyalties", *Business Ethics Quarterly*, vol. VI, n. 3, July 1996, esp. pp 293-295.

and nuances of the phenomenon.[17] Fukuyama dubiously redescribes trust as "spontaneous sociability" which is found in some cultures but not in others. Perhaps the single most important feature of his book is the subordination of economics to culture (which is why, I hypothesise, most economists have abandoned Fukuyama). But then Fukuyama turns (against his own insight) to an overly economic analysis of the consequences of trust and distrust, narrowly confined to large corporations instead of (as in China) broad networks of communal ties and business arrangements.

In this essay, I only want to introduce the notion of trust as a *dynamic process*, a function of communal practices and relationships rather than a static cultural "medium" or "ingredient", even "glue".[18] These metaphors reflect, I think, the fact that business people usually feel uncomfortable talking about trust, except, perhaps, in the most abstract terms of approbation. When the topic of trust comes up, they heartily nod their approval, but then they nervously turn to other topics. Executives are talking a great deal about trust these days, perhaps because they rightly suspect that trust in many corporations seems to be at an all-time low. One of our associates, who also consults for major corporations, recently gave a lecture on the importance of trusting your employees to several hundred executives of one of America's largest corporations. There was an appreciative but stunned silence, and then one of them - asking for all of them - queried, "but how do we control them?" It is a telling question that indicates that they did not understand the main point of the lecture, that trust is the very opposite of control. Or, perhaps, they understood well enough, but suffered a lack of nerve when it came time to think through its implications. Like the first-time sky-diver who had eagerly read all of the promotional literature about the thrills of the sport and had listened carefully to instructions, they asked, incredulously, "but now you want us to *jump out of the plane!?*" We all know the importance of trust, the advantages of trust, and we all know how terrible life can be without it. But when it comes time to put that knowledge into practice, we are all like the novice skydiver. Creating trust is taking a

---

17 JOHN WHITNEY: *The Trust Factor*, New York (McGraw-Hill) 1994.
18 These metaphors come from Benjamin Barber, Sisela Bok, Fukuyama and Kenneth Arrow, respectively. BENJAMIN BARBER: *The Logic and Limits of Trust*, New Brunswick (Rutgers) 1974; SISELA BOK: *Lying: Moral Choice in Public and Private Life*, New York (Random House) 1978; KENNETH ARROW: *The Limits of Organization*, New York (Norton) 1974.

risk. Trust entails lack of control, in that some power is transferred or given up to the person who is trusted. It is leaping from the dark, claustrophobic fuselage of our ordinary cynicism into what seems like the unsupported free-fall of dependency. And yet, unlike sky-diving, nothing is more necessary.

Today, there is a danger that trust is being over-sold. There is such a thing as too much trust, and then there is "blind trust", trust without warrant, foolish trust. Trust alone will not, as some of our pundits promise, solve the problems that our society now faces. Thus we think there is good reason to listen to doubters like Daryl Koehn, who rightly asks, "should we trust trust?"[19] But the urgency remains, we believe, on the side of encouraging and understanding trust. There is a lot of encouraging going on today. What is lacking, we want to suggest, is understanding. The problem is not just lack of an adequate analysis - like Augustine's puzzlement about time (he understood it perfectly well when he didn't think about it, but understood nothing at all when he did). The problem is an aggressive *mis*understanding of trust that pervades most of our discussions. The problem, if we can summarise it in a metaphor or two, is that trust is treated as if it were a "medium" in which human transactions take place, alternatively, as "ground", as "atmosphere" or, even more vaguely, as "climate". Benjamin Barber, for instance, who is one of the early writers on trust and often appealed to by the current crop of commentators, says that trust is "the basic stuff or ingredient of social interaction". But as "stuff" or "ingredient", as a "resource" (Fukuyama[20]), as "medium", "ground", "atmosphere" or "climate", trust all too easily tends to seem inert, simply "there" or "not there", rather than a dynamic aspect of human interaction and human relationships.

This misunderstanding of trust provides a dangerous rationalisation. Trust(ing) presupposes trustworthiness. Either the other person is trustworthy or he or she is not. So trusting takes the form of a kind of knowledge, the recognition (which may, of course, be fallible) that this person is trustworthy. So, if one trusts, so the rationalisation goes, then nothing need be said, and it is much better that nothing be said. That is the core of our problem. Trust is rendered inarticulate, unpresentable. According to this

---

19 DARYL KOEHN: "Should We Trust Trust?" - unpublished paper read at SBE Quebec, August, 1996.

20 Francis Fukuyama: *Trust: The Social Virtues and the Creation of Prosperity*, New York (Free Press) 1996.

view, to even raise the question, "Do you trust me?" or "Can I trust you?" is to already instigate, not only indicate, distrust. (Blaze Starr's mother warns her, "never trust a man who says, 'Trust me.'"[21]) If one does not trust, then nothing much is accomplished by saying so, except, perhaps, as an insult, a way of escalating an already existing conflict or, perhaps, as a confirming test ("If you tell me that I should trust you, then you are doubly a liar.") When a politician or a business leader says, "trust me", he takes a considerable risk. Those who support him may well wonder why he needs to say that, and become suspicious. For those who are already suspicious of him, such an intrusive imperative confirms their suspicions.[22] On the other hand, when someone says "I trust you", there is always the possibility of some sense of manipulation, even the unwanted imposition of a psychological burden, one of whose consequences may be guilt. In his speech to the Czech people in 1990, Vaclav Havel says "we must trust one another". He does not say "trust me" or "I trust you". The circumstances in which a politician (or anyone else) would or should say such a thing are worth analysing, but here we will only say that the primary reason for talking about trust is not just to "understand" the concept philosophically but to put the issue of trust "on the table" in order to be able to talk it through in concrete, practical situations. By talking through trust, trust can be created, distrust mitigated. Not talking about trust, on the other hand, can result in continuing distrust.

Economic approaches to trust, while well-intended and pointing us in the right direction, are dangerously incomplete and misleading. Trust in business is not merely a tool for efficiency, although it does, as Nicholas Luhmann argues at length, have important implications for dealing with complexity and therefore efficiency.[23] Moreover, it would hardly be honest to guarantee (as many authors do these days), that more trust will make business more efficient and improve the bottom line. Usually, of course, trust

---

21 Blaze Starr was the long-time mistress of Louisana governor Earl Long. The line occurs in the movie, starring Paul Newman and Lolita Davidovich, *Blaze* (1989).

22 E.g. DICK MORRIS on Bill Clinton's campaign strategy: *Behind the Oval Office*, New York (Random House) 1997.

23 NICHOLAS LUHMANN: "Trust: A Mechanism for the Reduction of Social Complexity", in: NICHOLAS LUHMANN: *Trust and Power*, New York (Wiley) 1980, pp. 4-103.

has this effect, but there is no necessary connection between trust and efficiency, and this is neither the aim nor the intention of trust. Indeed, trust as a mere efficiency-booster may be a paradigm of **inauthentic** or phony trust, trust that is merely a manipulative tool, a facade of trust that, over the long run, increases *dis*trust, and for good reason. Employees can usually tell when the "empowerment" they receive like a gift is actually a noose with which to hang themselves, a set-up for blame for situations which they cannot really control. Managers know what it is like when they are awarded more responsibility ("I trust you to take care of that") without the requisite authority. Like many virtues, trust is most virtuous when it is pursued for its own sake, even if there is benefit or advantage in view. (Generosity and courage both have their pay-offs, but to act generously or courageously *merely* in order obtain the pay-offs is of dubious virtue.) To think of trust as a business tool, as a mere means, as a lubricant to make an operation more efficient, is to not understand trust at all. Trust is, first of all, a central concept of ethics. And because of that, it turns out to be a valuable tool in business as well.

Philosophers, too, have only recently begun to talk about trust.[24] Trust is not just another abstraction but a rich, "thick" social and ethical phenomenon. Not surprisingly, philosophers all-too-often tend to interpret trust as a phenomenon of belief, and thus in terms of one more question about justification, but trust is not primarily about belief (although clearly it may involve any number of beliefs), nor does it readily invite anything like the

---

24 The most notable exception is Annette Baier, who wrote a series of provocative articles in the mid-Eighties, and credited her own interest to David Hume. Baier's recent work on Hume and on trust can be found in ANNETTE BAIER: *A Progress of Sentiments: Reflections on Hume's Treatise*, Cambridge (Cambridge University Press) 1991; and ANNETTE BAIER: *Moral Prejudices*, Harvard (Harvard University Press) 1994, esp. "Trust and Antitrust", pp. 95-129. Hume's views on ethics are too often restricted to his (in)famous discussion of reason versus the passions (perhaps the weakest of his views) and the problems he raises about moral motivation. Hume's work on sentiments has only recently come back into view, for example, at the conclusion of Stephen Darwall's *The British Moralists and the Internal 'Ought' 1640-1740*, Cambridge (Cambridge University Press) 1995; but Hume's theory of the sentiments is also brought up only to take something of a pounding, for instance, in ALASDAIR MACINTYRE: *Whose Justice? Which Rationality?* Notre Dame (Notre Dame University Press) 1988.

usual evidential grounds for justification (which is not to say that trustworthiness, which is usually the basis for trust, does not require evidence). Trust, I would argue, is first of all an attitude, a feeling, an emotion, an affect, topics which make many philosophers uncomfortable. In one of the most prestigious philosophy journals, *Ethics*, three distinguished ethicists - Karen Jones, Russell Hardin, Lawrence C. Becker[25] have taken on the phenomenon of trust full-tilt and attempted to remedy some of these shortcomings, but, perhaps, nothing they say is as important as the very existence of the symposium itself, which signifies the emergence of trust as a full-blooded philosophical topic.

It is particularly important to clarify the distinction and the relationship between trust and trustworthiness, both of which are usually subsumed under the heading of "trust." These form an obvious complementary pair. In the ideal case, one trusts someone because they are trustworthy, and one's trustworthiness inspires trust. But "trust as a virtue" is usually understood in terms of trustworthiness as a virtue.[26] To be sure, trustworthiness is a virtue, - the compound virtue of being dependable, capable, responsive and responsible, but trust(ing) is a virtue of a different sort, and one not limited to cases of trustworthiness. One can and sometimes must or should trust someone who is untrustworthy or untried. (There are numerous points in parenting, at which the parent must trust a child to do something he or she has never done before.) Trust(ing) is a virtue both because it is often useful and necessary (and thus utilitarian), and because it opens up possibilities in a relationship (and for each of its members) which would be impossible without it. Inability to trust, in a situation in which trust is appropriate or necessary, is a moral defect.[27] Inability or refusal to trust does not violate any ethical principle, although one can argue that the consequence of

---

25 KAREN JONES, RUSSELL HARDIN, LAWRENCE C. BECKER: "A Symposium on Trust," *Ethics*, vol. 107, n. 1, October 1996, pp. 4-61.
26 HARDIN: *ibid*.
27 Hardin, in particular, occasionally goes on the warpath against any attempt to "moralise" trust in his "Trustworthiness" (in the *Ethics* symposium) pp. 28, 42. If "moralising trust" means that one always ought to trust, then, of course, this is nonsense. But if "moralising trust" means only some version of holding that "trust is a (morally) good thing", then it is hard to imagine someone not doing so.

not trusting, in general, is devastating.[28] Nevertheless, trust, that is, trust-**ing**, is a neglected human virtue, indeed, a "non-relative" virtue, one that is essential to all forms of society regardless (more or less) of the particular culture. Thus Fukuyama distinguishes between "high trust" and "low trust" societies as a matter of degree, not kind. Without some degree of trust, there would be no society at all.[29]

Trustworthiness is a virtue for all of the usual utilitarian, social stability, and predictability, sorts of reasons. But trust(ing), too, is a basic human virtue, indeed, a basic human need, and its absence is not only lamentable but disastrous. I would also suggest that it may be blameworthy. A person incapable of trust is a person who is something less than fully human, less than fully socialised, less than fully a member of society.

In business ethics, the specificity of trust and the asymmetry of trust and trustworthiness are more obvious than it is in many less well-defined relationships. It is a mistake, however, to move immediately into talk about implicit contracts and agreements. Business relationships may well follow trusting or partially trusting relationships, and, in rare cases, they may replace trusting relationships, but by all means we should not reduce trusting relationships to contractual relationships, no matter how loosely or "implicitly" we understand the nature of contracts. In business, it is pretty obvious that trust is always specified, we trust a person or a corporation to do X at or by time T. But, again, all such specificities imply a more general trust. A shop-owner trusts a sales assistant to take care of customers, watch the cash register and take care of sales transactions, but virtually no list (and no employment contract) could include all of the possibilities such trust encompasses. (In return, the employee trusts the shop owner to pay him on time, to not "set him up," to not expect more than is reasonable, and so on.) One can list any number of possible actions encompassed by the trust (including such small probabilities as acting sensibly in case of an armed robbery or protecting fragile goods near-at-hand in an earthquake), and, no doubt, one could manufacture any number of "principles" which apply, most of them either impossibly broad and vague or casuistic and ad hoc. But

---

28   For example, see SISELA BOK: *Lying: Moral Choice in Public and Private Life*,
      New York (Random House) 1978.
29   Thus Hobbes explicitly invokes trust, along with justice, as features of society
      that result from the social compact rather than precede it. [THOMAS HOBBES:
      Leviathan, New York (Datton) 1950.]

what is really going on is **a certain kind of relationship** between the shop-owner and the assistant, and its viability depends on the character of both of them. On the shop-owner's part, he must be trusting, if not in general (and who can or should be trusting in general, these days?) then in the specific context of his business and his employee. Inability to trust, in addition to being terribly inefficient and time-consuming (enforcement costs, keeping a watchful eye, re-doing what one has already paid another to do, not to mention thereby provoking resentment and possibly rebellion, even sabotage) thus suggests a managerial as well as a moral defect.

VI. Conclusion: A Different Kind of Conception of Business?

Any defence of the "caring corporation" should expect and deserves to be greeted with patronising smiles and scowls of scepticism. After all, we have all been raised to believe that "business is business", and even if it isn't "dog-eat-dog" it is pretty rough stuff and no place for the kinder, gentler sentiments. But although the corporate world has its share of brutality (as does Academia, I might add), the difference between the old images and the new are far more matters of perception than practice, and what I find so odd is the extent to which the undeniably humane aspects of corporate life are ignored or denied while the more brutal features are highlighted and even celebrated. But between word and deed, attention and policy there is easy slippage, and as executives talk in Darwinian terms, not surprising, their thinking becomes Darwinian as well. But when we think in terms of care and compassion, and of corporations of communities in which we all share, the slippage is called "humanity", and the "dog-eat-dog" world of business becomes - as relationships between real dogs make obvious - a warm and mutually rewarding experience.

It takes no leap of faith to move from the actual cultures of most corporations to the recognition that these are co-operative communities, not military installations or mere legal fictions, and that mutual respect, caring and compassion is what we all in fact expect and demand in our various jobs and positions. To be sure, it is unfortunate that so many managers and employees and even executives do not get that respect, do not care or show compassion as they should, in part because of the brutally competitive and chauvinist images in which they conceive of what they do. But once we start insisting that the ethics of business is not simply confined to "business" but begin by examining the very nature of the good life and living well in a business society, those conceptions are bound to change.[30]

---

30 FREEMAN AND LIEDTKA: *op. cit.* and R. C. SOLOMON: *Ethics and Excellence,* op. cit.

148- 92

M14

Chapter 7

Corporate Ethics and Management Theory[1]

HORST STEINMANN AND ANDREAS GEORG SCHERER

---

1   We would like to thank Stanley Deetz and Brigitte Kustermann for helpful
    comments on the earlier drafts of this paper.

I. Introduction

In what follows we try to develop a concise line of reasoning concerning a conceptual clarification of the relationship between corporate ethics and management. Our proposal will draw from philosophical considerations developed by philosophers of the methodical constructivism of the so-called Erlangen-School (Lorenzen 1968, 1981, 1982, 1987a, 1987b, Kambartel 1989). We use the term "corporate ethics" instead of (the more fuzzy term) "business ethics" to stress that the focus of our paper is the firm and not the economy as a whole. The word "management" denotes all *actions* which are directed towards the (purposeful) *co-ordination* of corporate activities by which the transformation of goods and services is accomplished (i.e., procurement, operations, logistics, marketing etc.). These actions are traditionally grouped in five "managerial functions" under the headings of (1) planning, (2) organising, (3) staffing, (4) leading (directing), and (5) control (Koontz/O'Donnell 1964). Management theory then is the body of knowledge about managerial functions developed to describe, understand (or explain) and improve management practice. Note that this definition implies an approach to the field of management which is guided by the theory of action (instead, e.g., by systems theory). The arguments of this paper are thus developed within the framework of a means-end-relationship: Managerial functions are regarded as *means* to the *end* of fulfilling the firm's objectives.

From this perspective, two questions arise and prove relevant to clarify the conceptual relationship between corporate ethics and management (theory):

(1) The first question is concerned with the *ends* of a company: How is the traditional objective function of the firm affected by the integration of corporate ethics? Our answer to this question will be: the objective function should no longer be regarded as an *unconditional* request to maximise profits (within the limits of the law). It should rather be put under the *proviso of peace*, i.e., the moral obligation of management is to strive for a peaceful settlement of conflicts with the stakeholders of the company in so far as these conflicts are caused by its strategy (Steinmann/Löhr 1994, 1996, Steinmann/Zerfaβ 1993). This general statement needs, of course, further elaboration. But the intention of incorporating this proviso in the objective function of the firm should already be clear by now: it is intended to estab-

lish a *moral relationship* (beyond legal requirements) between the responsibility of *private* business and the *public* interest of which we propose to regard "peace" as its highest value.

(2) The second question is concerned with the achievement of ends through appropriate *means*: Is it possible to design a management system which can serve economic and ethical requirements simultaneously? We will try to defend the thesis that providing for the fulfilment of the new objective function of the firm will require a re-structuring of the management system (i.e., the role of and the relationship between managerial functions) which is (to a large extent) *compatible* with the economic requirements of modern management (cf. Deetz 1995, Steinmann/Kustermann 1996, 1998). In other words: We assert that pursuing the *economic* goals of efficiency and effectiveness to make profits on the one hand and satisfying the *ethical* side condition to contribute to a peaceful co-ordination of strategy-related interests and actions in society on the other hand, will each require similar management structures which are equifinal towards both ends. Note that we refer in this second proposition to the *co-ordination of management actions* to steer the corporation. This should not be confused with the co-ordination of the physical transformation process mentioned above (i.e., procurement, operations, logistics, marketing etc.) as the task of management. Conflicts and dilemmas between economic and ethical requirements are today, of course, rather the rule than the exception in businesses and constitute a critical problem area for management (otherwise there would be no need for corporate ethics). This is even true under a *purely economic* perspective: Under conditions of ambique environments and a bounded rationality of economic actors problems of conflict, truth-seeking and interpretation have to be treated when formulating and implementing strategy. Thus we have similar *historical side conditions* for re-structuring the management system. To be more concrete, we assert that with the classical *taylorist* management model becoming increasingly obsolete (Schreyögg/Steinmann 1987, Simons 1995), the conditions for effectively integrating corporate ethics into the *modern* (re-designed) management process will improve considerably.

II. Corporate Ethics and the Objective Function of the Firm

Before we start to defend our first proposition we should point out that the proposal to regard all profit-oriented corporate actions as being subject to the proviso of societal peace is not of a purely theoretical character. Rather, it can be regarded as an extension of the basic idea of the "U.S.-Sentencing-Guidelines for Organisations" of 1991 (Dalton/Metzger/Hill 1994, Ferrell/Leclair/Ferrell 1998, Nagel/Swenson 1993), namely to rely on a close co-operation of *public* authorities and *private* companies to combat criminal behaviour in industry. In case of an offence, these guidelines offer substantial reductions in penalty fine to companies who have taken certain organisational steps, well-defined by law, to prevent criminal actions of their employees, thereby supporting the state in its task to keep up peace and order in society. Our proposal extends this idea in a double sense: (1) it is not restricted to criminal offences but comprises *all corporate activities* in so far as they may cause conflicts with stakeholders and – more important – (2) it is not restricted to regulations by *law* but relates to the meta-level of *moral* obligations in general.

Now, to develop and defend our answer to the first question we have to delineate, first, what we propose as a meaningful notion of *"peace"* and why it should be regarded as the highest expression of public interest (1.). Then we have to argue why making peace *more stable* cannot and should no longer be regarded in modern societies as the exclusive task of the law, resp. the law-making bodies, but must be considered as an *essential* part of the responsibility of the modern corporation and, of course, many other institutions of society like labour unions or federations of industry (2.). Finally, the relationship between "profit" and "peace" has to be clarified in order to come to an adequate notion of corporate ethics (3.).

1. The Notion of Peace

We know from many epistemological contributions that there is no way to prove validity claims for values via *deductive* reasoning. This would lead either into an infinite regress (regressus ad infinitum), a logical circle or to arbitrarily breaking off giving reasons (Albert 1980). So, whether or not it is possible to *begin* our line of reasoning about peace as the highest value of society in a *non-arbitrary* way depends on whether or not one can produce a rationally acceptable alternative to deductive reasoning. Such an alternative has recently been presented by Lueken (1992). According to him, the notion of reasoning as deductive reasoning is based on two premises, namely (1) that reasoning is a *method* (of logical operations) and (2) that this method is *standardised by a certain set of rules*. Reasoning (as a deductive operation) is then the *application of predefined rules*. When one questions this notion of reasoning on a philosophical level one has to reconsider both these preceding decisions. In order to do this, however, one needs already a *distinct beginning* with a methodical structure of argumentation which does not use this standardised set of rules in order to avoid the impending circular argument or regressum ad infinitum (for the following see also Scherer /Steimann 1997).

With respect to the first of these two premises Lueken (1992) therefore suggests a concept of argumentation which avoids any preliminary decision about the method. Argumentation should be understood – he proposes – as a *practical concept* which precedes all methods. With regard to the second premise, he suggests disposing of a link of a concept of argumentation to the preliminary decision about the rules and orientating argumentation only towards the purpose of *consensus*. Consequently, Lueken (1991, p. 246) proposes the following definition: "Argumentation is a symbolic action performed to overcome a controversy and aiming at consensus". Firstly, understood as a *symbolic action* argumentation is here not bound to a specific method of reasoning. Secondly, focusing on *consensus* as the final aim of argumentation avoids any reference to a predefined set of rules of argumentation and, thus, gives room to adopt the process of argumentation to the specific problem which has to be clarified.

Lueken (1992, p. 208, translation by the authors) asserts that argumentative action in this sense

> is already rational in so far as it is an outstanding way to overcome conflicts and to solve problems peacefully. Whenever the rationality of actions is called into question, besides our practical wisdom ['Ur-teilskraft'] we only have the possibility of argumentative action through which the rationality of actions and decisions must unfold itself and is shown. The rationality of means for the pursuit of ends must be shown in argumentation about technical knowledge. The rationality of purposes and good intentions must be shown through moral-practical ['moralisch-praktische'] argumentation. An argumentative action can be considered as rational in so far as it is – as a

symbolic action – comprehensive ['verständlich'] or appropriate to bring about comprehensibility and, furthermore, in so far as it aims at agreement (consensus) to the validity claims of technical and political knowledge.

Obviously, if this assertion could be made comprehensible as a non-arbitrary form, we would have found already a meaningful notion of peace and would have qualified its status as the highest value to strive for. Peace could then be regarded as the result of argumentative action and could be defined as *"general free consensus"* (see also Lorenzen 1987b, pp. 228 ff.) based on the *insight* of all concerned in the *good reasons* put forward in the process of argumentation. As an *"outstanding* way to overcome conflicts" (Lueken) it could at the same time justifiably be regarded as the dominant form of conflict resolution.[2]

Now, if deductive reasoning is ruled out from the outset, there is, obviously, no longer an *external* (exogenous) "vantage point" (from an observer perspective) from which to judge Lueken's assertion correctly. This concept of argumentation can thus only be made comprehensible as a non-arbitrary form from "the inside" (participator perspective) by showing that the notion of argumentation proposed here makes sense indeed. From "the inside" means that one has to *re-construct* the introduction of the notion (concept) of argumentation: How is it constructed? At what point does the introduction of the notion begin? – By unfolding the answers to such questions it can be shown that what is at stake here is the correct understanding of the *relationship between theory and praxis*, respectively knowledge and action.[3] With the background of a deductive concept of reasoning, praxis is always the application of explicit or implicit theories. Theory methodologically

---

2   We do not neglect the productive character of "meaningful controversy" (Stanley Deetz). However, in case of conflict there is an inherent need for a peaceful solution. Here the concepts of argumentation and consensus apply in order to *make* the controversy meaningful and useful. In contrast to this, there is no principal need for dissens nor is a controversy by itself productive (LUEKEN 1991, 1992).

3   When we use the word "praxis" here we refer to actions or systems of actions. In so far the theory-praxis-relationship refers to the distinction between knowledge and action. By contrast, the word "practice" is used here to distinguish between scientific insitutions, such as universities or research institutes, and, e.g., management practice.

precedes praxis and has an axiomatic and thus unjustified beginning. This relationship is turned around in Lueken's (1992) concept, who follows here the constructivist conception of the Erlangen school of philosophy (Mittelstrass 1977, 1985, Lorenzen 1968, 1987b).

He unfolds his concept by differentiating between pre-theoretical praxis and theoretical praxis (Fig. 1) and thus on the basis of whether validity claims (for means and ends) are raised and treated (theoretical praxis) or not (pre-theoretical praxis) (for an overview see also Scherer/Dowling 1995, pp. 219 ff.).

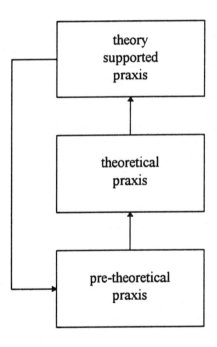

Figure 1: The theory-praxis-relationship in the constructive philosophy of the Erlangen-School (from Steinmann/Scherer 1994, p. 269, modified).
Reproduced by permission of Gabler (Wiesbaden).

CORPORATE ETHICS AND MANAGEMENT THEORY

Pre-theoretical praxis forms a part of everyday life in which people are engaged in and familiar with the control over activities and occurrences without consciously activating knowledge (Mittelstrass 1977, Lueken 1992). Here people are able to solve technical and political problems, their ability is simply based on practical *know-how* ("Können") acquired in the past. However, people know from experience that they cannot always accomplish their purposes. Instead life is a mixture of success and failure. During action, people experience whether they are successful by registering whether their technical aims are achieved or conflicts about means and/or ends arise which are not solvable with the know-how available at present. If this is the case, validity claims about questions of truth and justice have to be treated and people have to turn to *theoretical praxis*. Theoretical praxis, thus, needs only to be put in use when the pre-theoretical practical know-how is no longer sufficient to cope with the problems of everyday life and new knowledge has to be created or validity claims have to be considered in order to improve the actions at stake. So, here "praxis" methodically precedes "theory": praxis is the *reason* and the *systematic starting point* of every attempt to create knowledge: "Theory arises out of practice, and the first theoretical steps must be rooted in practice" (Sagal 1987, p. 176). The results of theoretical praxis are then given back to the praxis as theoretical instructions *(theory-supported praxis)*. When these results are successfully accomplished again and again, they will in time emerge into a habit and become an unproblematic part of the pre-theoretical know-how until new problems appear at this *advanced* development stage of pre-theoretical praxis – problems whose solutions demand the creation of new knowledge in theoretical praxis. From this feed-back loop between theory-supported praxis and pre-theoretical praxis it is obvious that Lueken's concept is a *dynamic* one which incorporates the *historical* perspective of the development of knowledge in society.

To understand the meaning of the relationship between theory and praxis, two points seem especially important to mention (Steinmann/Scherer 1994):

(1) Theoretical praxis is not identical with science. Theoretical praxis only appears where a distance from the daily practical know-how is necessary because this has become problematic and validity claims must be considered. Thus theoretical praxis is present *everywhere* where validity claims are made and their solution is attempted. This can even be so in daily actions, this can also be the case, among others, in companies or in scientific

155

institutions (management practice or scientific practice). And by the same token it is true that for theoretical praxis – that means for the verification of validity claims – a pre-theoretical practical know-how is always to be required also. As far as the manual creation of objects is concerned, for example within the execution of scientific experiments, this happens through craftsmanship and the *ability to create* as we learn it in everyday life (Christenson 1976, Mittelstrass 1977). And as far as elementary social actions, e.g., the choice of purposes and appropriate means or the use of language in day-to-day human social interactions are concerned, people can rely on *social routines* practised in every day life (Giddens 1984). They need not and finally cannot construct entirely new solutions for every little step they take, rather they have learned routines which can be applied as *implicit* know-how in order really to focus on problematical issues and concentrate on the development of particular solutions in theoretical practice where necessary. In this matter, the pre-theoretical praxis forms *the reason and the methodical underpinning* (Steinmann/Scherer 1994, Scherer /Dowling 1995) of theoretical considerations in theoretical praxis with regard to the problem of the correct beginning of the argument that was mentioned above. In this sense, science is therefore only a special institutionalised form of theoretical praxis which was established in our culture in order that scientists can think methodically about problems and solutions with general concern (which then could be taught to others). In their role as scientists they are excused from directly solving immediate practical problems of everyday life.

(2) With regard to the common objection of the adherents of an axiomatic-deductive paradigm, namely, that the pre-theoretical praxis has always been guided by theories and that a clear beginning in pre-theoretical praxis is not at all possible, it is necessary to point out the following according to Lueken (1992): it cannot be denied that actions are guided at least partly by knowledge. The aim of theoretical praxis is of course to improve the practical know-how through theoretical knowledge. However, what is important is the *role* this knowledge plays in the particular situation.

> The crucial point is that for this situative actualisation of practical know-how no previous actualisation of knowledge is needed. It is not necessary that the actor understands his/her practical know-how as the following of a rule or the using of a theory and can explicitly formulate this rule or theory. It is also crucial that know-how does not enter into the situation as knowledge with a claim for validity. As

long as we are in the area of pre-theoretical praxis, claims for validity are not discussed. The success of a pre-theoretical situation can neither be seen as confirmation nor can a failure as such be seen as its refutation. Success and failure are simply contingent features of the historical situation. (Lueken 1992, p. 177, translation by the authors).

In the light of this reconstruction of the relationship between praxis and theory it becomes clear that the concept of *argumentation* proposed by Lueken has its *origin* in pre-theoretical praxis, and this only in so far as argumentation has already become part of everyday life of people. It must have become a part of their "culture" to engage in attempts to overcome controversies peacefully by argumentation (Kambartel 1989). For argumentation on the level of theoretical praxis the word "reasoning" is reserved, and – as Lueken (1992) shows – reasoning can be reconstructed meaningfully as a (speech-)acting. This means that the operation of *deductive* reasoning is indeed only a category among others within this conception of reasoning.

Lueken's definition of argumentation as given above is thus to be understood as the attempt to comprehensively re-construct what is *already experienced successfully* in the pre-theoretical culture of argumentative action and to bring this in a precise notion. This notion only makes sense at all in so far as the proposed re-construction of the theory-praxis-relationship makes sense itself. And this question can only be answered from a participator perspective: one must experience again and again in everyday life that the proposed concept can be regarded as a fruitful means for orientation of practical action. And this obviously requires a *practical* judgement and can by no means be derived theoretically.

The *consequences* of this re-construction of the theory-praxis-relationship are far-reaching. Some important ones are mentioned below:

(1) The notion of "peace" as defined above is available only to societies which have already developed a *"culture of argumentation"* (Kambartel 1989, 1998). The "consensus" referred to above in the notion of peace is thus *"general"* only in as much *as all* subjects of the (relevant) culture are concerned. Moreover, all words we use to define peace (and argumentation) can get their "strict" sense (Kambartel 1992) only in so far as we can refer to a *praxis* of peace-making-routines. This strict sense is based on a difference we must have already learned and experienced in practical life. It is the difference between a "peaceful" resolution of conflicts based on the

insight in good arguments on the one hand and the application of "power", i.e., using the other only as means for one's own ends, on the other hand. This is, of course, the difference between *"consensus"* and *"compromise"* as modi of conflict resolution well-known in literature. Without such a practical experience, one cannot understand the strict sense of the word "peace" either. The central pre-condition of peace is that everybody strives to *transcend his/her own subjectivity*, i.e., that he/she does not insist on the realisation of his/her interests simply because they are his/her own (Lorenzen 1987). The "attitude of transsubjectivity" is not a natural disposition of human beings but must be learned during the process of socialisation. Thus peace (or reason) is *culture bound* and not apriori universal! (In a review of discussions in recent German philosophy we consider this point more closely, cf. Steinmann/Scherer 1998, 1998).

(2) Obviously, this position runs counter to all *transcendental* reasoning (see, e.g., Apel 1973). Kambartel (1989) has clarified the epistemological status of statements by which we normally elucidate the word "argumentation", e.g., by referring to "unprejudiceness" or "non-persuasiveness" or similar words. These are not to be understood as "conditions of the possibility" of argumentation derived at by a "presuppositional analysis" (Habermas 1991), as within the context of transcendental reasoning and the discourse ethics of the Frankfurt School (see e.g. Apel 1973, Habermas 1983, 1991), but are *explanations ("Erläuterungen") of an experience made in ordinary life* (Kambartel 1989). The constructivist philosophy from which our paper draws rejects apriorism. There are only two "a prioris" which are required of the ability of individuals (Mittelstrass 1977): the ability to *construct* ('Herstellungs-vermögen') and the ability to *differentiate* ('Unterscheidungsvermögen').

(3) Against *post-modernism* (see e.g., Lyotard 1984) we hold that the difference between conflict resolution by argumentation and use of power has been proven useful in our culture in the sense that argumentative conflict resolution makes peace *more stable* than power. Giddens comes close to our position when he argues (1992, p. 20, translation by the authors):

> If arguments were (in a final analysis) solely the imposition of power it would make no sense to develop them, or to try to respond to them. Validity claims, then, would only be a manifestation of demagogy if put forward without efforts of justification which could be critically scrutinised and rejected. There are many versions about the world possible (included here is the social as well as the natural

world), but aiming at the creation of valid propositions as a legiti-mising principle of argumentation does mean to try to differentiate between them.

So, against post-modernism one must insist that the usage of language in speech-acts is not only and always a manifestation of power. Otherwise, and ironically, protagonists of post-modernism would be unable to defend their own validity claim, that language is solely a manifestation of power.

(4) Our position is based on *reflexivity* in a twofold way: (1) It relies on the *re-construction* of a preceding praxis (of technical or political problem resolution), and re-construction (contrary to construction anew) needs self-reflection on one's own practical actions; and (2) it relies on practical judgement as a self-reflexive activity for detecting (differentiating) what is good (or better) practice: It was also Giddens (1992) who stressed in his "Critical Theory of Late Modernism" the reflexive character of this devel-opment stage of society. In our context, reflexivity is a necessary part of the participator perspective.

From what has been said so far, it follows that the distinction between "peace" and "power" is a categorical one and is at the basis of a successful solution of societal conflicts and thus the successful co-ordination of ac-tions[4]. It is in pre-theoretical praxis that we learn that argumentation (as opposed to the use of power) makes peace more *stable*. Argumentation relies on the "forceless force of the better argument" (Habermas) and – if successful – brings about the *insight* of all concerned in the truth (of a proposition) and the *fairness* or justification (of an assertion). And insight is something that befalls someone (*"Widerfahrnis"*) and is as such *no longer at his/her arbitrary disposal* (Kambartel 1997): one cannot change one's in-sight like a shirt. Thus, in a lifeworld which is governed by a "culture of reason" (Kambartel 1989, 1998) co-ordination of actions achieved by argu-mentation is stable as long as the good reasons underlying it are still valid.

---

4   See also recently JANICH (1996) who stresses the point that questions of truth and justice are instrumental relative to pre-theoretical praxis to successfully co-ordinate actions.

2. Ethics, Law and Administration as Measures to Make Peace More Stable

Having shown that "peace" can be identified as the highest value of public interest, at least in societies which have already developed a "culture of reason", we have now to argue why making peace more stable cannot and should not longer be regarded as the exclusive task of legislation and administration of justice, respectively, law-making and law-applying bodies. In modern societies, law has undoubtedly become an essential instrument for social integration (Summers et al. 1986). Its function can neither be relinquished nor entirely substituted. While law is therefore a *necessary* part of society, it is at the same time not *sufficient* to guarantee justice, stability and peace. Instead, it has to be complemented and accompanied by ethics and by a common concept of the good life, this is well acknowledged today (e.g., Stone 1975, Paine 1994a, 1994b, Dunfee 1996). The reasons are manifold. First, law must be based on ethics, in order to direct law-making and law-applying activities towards a common purpose. Secondly, the efficiency of law to control everyday actions cannot be guaranteed solely and primarily by extrinsic motivation and punishment but requires as its basis the insight and good will of the large majority of the citizens. Thirdly, ethics has to amend law in all cases which are not (yet) covered by formal rules. This is especially true within modern societies which have become so complex and dynamic that law cannot control every aspect of life. As societies grow, law and administration itself are becoming more and more complex and inflexible and somehow detached from the functions they have to fulfil (Eisenberg 1992). As a result, the ability of law and administration to regulate social actions towards a common good is limited in principle (Eisenberg 1992, Stone 1975, Yaeger 1991). These issues have been covered by several authors for a long time:

In his well-known book "*Where the Law Ends*", Stone (1975) points out the principle reasons why the law and the market are not sufficient to direct the conduct of companies toward a common good. It is necessary, he holds, to complement these institutions by a *corporate social responsibility*. The reasons for market failures are extensively covered elsewhere (e.g., Deetz 1995); so we summarise only the main reasons for *law failure*. Stone (1975, pp. 93 ff.) mentions three problems: (1) the time-lag problem, (2) limitations connected with the making of the law, and (3) default mechanisms for implementing the law.

CORPORATE ETHICS AND MANAGEMENT THEORY

(1) It is commonly accepted that law-makers respond to emerging problems in society. However, whenever new issues arise, it takes time for proposals for new laws or modifications of old laws to be made, negotiated, and eventually passed. This results in a *systematic time lag* between the emergence of new issues and the availability of rules to regulate them. In the meantime people have to find other ways to handle conflicts.

(2) Stone argues that legislation often formally acknowledges what is already the case in business. Law-makers frequently adopt standards which are worked out and applied in industry, e.g., industry codes of conduct or good business practice. Therefore, *legislation cannot count as principally independent of business* in order to set guidelines for business conduct. Moreover, policymakers are often systematically influenced by corporate lobbying and even manipulation, so that their contribution towards the common good can be questioned.

(3) The third category is concerned with *problems of implementing the law*. Stone here mentions the costs of implementing the law and the unsuitability of legal forums to resolve complex issues.

Paine (1994a) adds to these aspects the fundamental concern, that as issues are becoming more complex and dynamic, rules tend to become complex as well. This results in thicker and more and more complex law-books and guidelines of corporate conduct, which can finally only be handled by experts. "Overregulation" is a characteristic of modern societies which points to the problem that people are not able to identify and apply appropriate regulations to deal with problems anymore. Furthermore, as conditions are changing, it is at stake whether rules are appropriate at all. Therefore, people must not simply trust the rules, but have to reconsider whether they are appropriate to the situation or have to be modified or even abandoned. Therefore, as Paine (1994a) argues, a simple *compliance to the law*, i.e., a conformity with externally imposed standards, is not enough. Instead, it has to be complemented by self-governance actions ("self-regulation") which enable people to consciously act where rules are not available or where rules have to be modified *("integrity approach")*.

As is well-known, law-making bodies have to promote many, often conflicting, purposes. Therefore, it is a very difficult and complex task to define a legal system of rules which serves all of the conflicting purposes at the same time. Moreover, as various stakeholder groups may be affected by the rules of law in different ways, law making is an essentially political process which powerful stakeholders try to influence in order to take ad-

161

vantage. Finally, legal rules often have side effects which cannot be anticipated (Eisenberg 1992, Yaeger 1991).

Today, the limits of law are particularly obvious in *international business*. The reduction of trade barriers, the tremendous advances in information technologies, the decline of transportation costs and the growing infrastructure and better educational systems in many developing and emerging countries enable multinational enterprises (MNEs) to operate on a worldwide basis. Companies shift activities to those areas in the world where supply of resources, work and know-how is cheapest. "Global sourcing" and "global supply" are on the top of the agenda of multinational corporations (Kogut 1985). At the same time the ability of national state law to direct the efforts of global firms toward a common good is declining (Ohmae 1995, Thurow 1996). On a transnational level, organisations like U.N., I.L.O. or W.T.O. have not reached very far to define global standards of business conduct (Orts 1996, Thurow 1996). And even in cases where common standards are negotiated and principally available many countries do not enforce them in order to lure or hold businesses (Deetz 1995, Greider 1997). In such a situation, companies which operate world-wide are called to behave as moral actors in order to stop the threatening downward spiral of social and environmental standards. This role for the multinational corporation was recently emphasised by U.S. president Bill Clinton. In 1995 the U.S. Department of Commerce passed the so-called "Model Business Principles" which call on global firms to promote human rights world wide in their business activities (U.S. Department of Commerce 1995, U.S. Department of State 1997). As the efforts of transnational organisations have not reached far enough, the power of the multinational enterprises should be used to set global social and environmental standards. It has been known for a long time that multinational corporations politically influence their host countries (e.g., Boddewyn 1995). This was one of the reasons why multinationals have been extensively criticised in the past (cf., e.g., Hood/Young 1979, pp. 325 ff., Warren 1980, pp. 125 ff.). However, MNEs are now called to use their political influence in an ethically sound way in order to promote global peace and justice. As political efforts and international law are insufficient to guarantee for the common good, corporate ethics of multinational firms should accompany law and administration.

3. Relationship Between "Profit" and "Peace" and the Notion of Corporate Ethics

a) The Notion of Corporate Ethics: Basic Considerations

Up to now we have argued *that* and *why* it is in the *public interest* that *private* corporations should be held responsible to contribute to peace as the highest ethical principle of modern societies in so far as conflicts with corporate stakeholders are – or may be – caused by corporate strategy. Methodologically speaking, this is a *necessary* but not at the same time also a *sufficient* condition for arriving at a suitable notion of corporate ethics. This is so because any *principle*, understood as a "universalised" rule for action in a given culture (or as a "regulative idea" in the sense of Kant), does by definition not relate to specific historical side conditions relevant for the problem at hand. Neglecting these side conditions by demanding, for instance, that all institutions in our society should be strictly organised on the basis of consensus alone, would lead to "*utopian*" solutions. So, to construct a "*realistic*" notion of corporate ethics we have to consider as the dominant historical side condition that corporate ethics has to be implemented in a *capitalist market economy*, with competition (instead of consensus) and individual freedom to make profit, respectively, utility (instead of transsubjectivity), as its central elements. The next question therefore arises: How is the relationship between "peace" and "profit" to be conceptualised in the notion of corporate ethics?

Our *answer* to this question has already been given at the outset. We suggest to look at corporate profit making as being subject to the moral proviso for peace in society: the licence to operate a company is principally regarded to be granted by law under the proviso of private business to contribute to peace in society. Our argument concerns two levels: the level of the economic order (1) and the level of the firm (2):

(1) Corporate ethics – as we propose the term – is not intended to fundamentally change the *objective function* of the firm in the sense of replacing the request for profits by any other objective. Such a demand would imply the transformation of the economic system as a whole, since in market economies making profits is a precondition for the survival of the firm

163

(in the long run).[5] Contrary to such a demand, corporate ethics is understood here as a device to modify our understanding of corporate responsibility *within* the capitalist market economy by tying business more closely to the public interest of peace. In this sense corporate ethics does *not regulate* the objective function of the capitalist firm. In other words: There are no other formal or substantial societal objectives added to the profit principle via corporate ethics. This excludes, for instance, all forms of corporate philantrophy as *primary* part of managerial responsibility. However, to avoid misunderstandings here, we add, that corporate philantrophy is, of course, not morally forbidden, it is discretionary. What we want to stress is, rather, that according to the very purpose of the firm in a market economy, it is *constructed* as an *economic* institution. To function properly as such, the firm should not in principle be (over-)loaded with an unspecified general responsibility to solve any societal problems. Instead, the firm has to resolve those problems which occur as a result of it's profit seeking. In as much as these problems cannot be foreseen and successfully resolved through general rules on the level of the economic order (or maybe as "soft law" on the level of the federation of industry, see Steinmann/Zerfaß 1993, Steinmann/Löhr 1996), they have to be resolved on the level of the firm.

(2) Therefore, corporate ethics has to take up at the level of the firm where it is to be understood as a *restriction*: it reduces the set of feasible *means* (the set of feasible solutions), available to management for making profits. In this respect one can say that corporate ethics demands that ethical reflections *dominate* the profit motive in *all* management decision processes and in all situations. At the same time, when we use the word "restriction" here, this does not mean that corporate ethics should be understood as merely a set of rational principles which could be applied in a somewhat technical way. Instead, proper ethical management requires a great deal of personal virtue and judgement which even enables actors to make ethically sound decisions without having a general principle at their disposal (Solomon 1992, Kambartel 1989). In this sense one can also say that corporate ethics "motivates" to take both efficient and responsible actions.[6]

---

5   The existance of a firm as part of the economic system is linked to this precondition. This does not imply, of course, that any particular firm is expected to survive.

6   In economic theories trust, loyalty, commitment, altruism, etc. are often totally neglected. Instead, economists focus on the self-interest of actors as the *only*

These two clarifying remarks run up to a *double role* of management in modern societies[7]:

(1) Management is held responsible for the *survival of the firm* with sufficient profits as an indicator of whether this role has been fulfilled successfully; and

(2) in striving for profits, management is held responsible for corporate strategies being designed and implemented in such a way that they contribute to a *peaceful relationship with corporate stakeholders*. In this sense one can say that corporate ethics has to do with those means for making profits which are ethically acceptable (Schneider 1990, in contrast to Ulrich 1997, p. 408) so that they lead to what one may call *"reasonable profit"* (Stanley Deetz).

Now, to *defend* this understanding of corporate ethics we have, first, to show how the objective of making profits can be justified. Then we have to show why managers can justifiably be held responsible to self-impose ethical restrictions on strategic choices.

b) How to Justify the Profit Maximisation Principle

As to the first problem, it becomes immediately clear from what we have said above about the philosophical foundation of corporate ethics that the market itself cannot be regarded as an *original* source of legitimacy. According to our distinction between "consensus" and "compromise" the market has to be classified as an instrument of *compromising* and not of consensus, with money and purchasing power as the means to satisfy one's own private interests (Habermas 1981). So, for the legitimation of the market and the profit motive we must, in order to avoid circular reasoning, draw on the procedure of consensual conflict resolution by argumentation, as the only procedure, by which *unity* of society and individual *freedom* can be reconciled and peace assured or made more stable.

Now, if this is so, why – one could argue – don't we simply use consensual procedures everywhere to co-ordinate all economic plans of individuals: Would this not be an immediate and direct way of legitimation? Putting

---

source of motivation which is not only contra the experience of practising managers (KUHN 1992), but undermines the potential for economic success (HOSMER 1994, PAINE 1996).

7   Obviously, this double role of management is incompatible with a pure shareholder-value concept; instead, it comes close to what one calls today the stakeholder theory of the firm (FREEMAN 1984).

the question in such a radical manner already paves the way for an answer: Because consensual procedures are unable to cope with the entire *complexity* of the economic co-ordination problem in highly developed societies as the historical side condition[8]. This we know at least since we have convincing empirical evidence of the failure of all centrally planned economies in Eastern Europe and elsewhere. These economies – without, of course, being based on consensus – nevertheless neglected the complexity problem. The market and the price system have empirically been proven to be more *efficient* in solving the economic co-ordination problem (Steinmann/Löhr 1994).

The reason for this superiority is, of course, that in market economies individual actions are no longer co-ordinated via the *intentions* of the actors but via the *consequences* of their acts (Habermas 1981). Individuals are free to follow their own objectives and interests in setting up and carrying out their economic plans; and it is left to the market to co-ordinate the individual plans and to figure out ex post facto the economic consequences (profit or loss) for each actor. In our language, this change of the co-ordination mechanism from "intentions" to "consequences" can be paralleled to the transition from "consensus" to "compromise". We would propose legitimating this *transition* by pointing to the overwhelming *empirical evidence* of higher efficiency of market economies co-ordinated by consequences as compared to centrally planned economies which are co-ordinated by the intentions of political planners. Starting from this point we can, then, connect "efficiency" with "peace" by two other *empirical* arguments, namely:

(1) Economic efficiency helps to remove scarcity of goods and poverty, and

(2) scarcities and poverty are a permanent source of conflict in society, as we also know from empirical evidence in East European countries.

Thus the market is – according to all that we know from experience – generally speaking a *better means* for securing peace in society than central planning.

---

8   ULRICH (1997) seems to acknowledge this complexity argument (p. 333). However, in his proposals for what he calls an "integrative corporate ethics" he defines consensual procedures principally as the primary source for co-ordination of actions. This could be misunderstood and needs clarification of how he conceives of the relationship between both co-ordination principles.

Two remarks may be helpful at this point to understand properly the "process of legitimation" as it is proposed here:

(1) Because we refer to the status of the market as a *means* to an end (and not as an end in itself), our proposal is only a *weak* legitimation in the sense that whenever better means are found in the future it may be necessary to replace the market by more efficient co-ordination mechanisms. But at the moment no such better means are in sight.

(2) Our proposal to legitimate the market rests on *empirical* and *comparative* reasoning using a (testable) hypothesis about the relative efficiency of economic systems and about the effect of efficiency on peace; this approach contrasts with any *axiomatic-theoretical* reasoning about Pareto-optimal solutions in welfare economics (see, e.g., Arrow/Debreu 1954, Arrow/Hahn 1971). The important consequence is that the argument of "universal external effects", put forward sometimes to question the legitimation of market co-ordination in toto (Ulrich 1997), does not have the disastrous consequences of destroying the legitimation of the profit principle. This is so for two reasons. *First*, in our comparative argument we do not refer to an *optimal* solution of the problem of allocation of resources in an *absolute* sense. We simply do not know what such an allocation would look like in reality; but what we know is that market economies because of decentralisation of economic decisions are in principle more efficient in removing scarcities and poverty than centrally planned economies. We do not overlook here, of course, questions of income distribution and the severe problems of poverty in western societies (Thurow 1996). But these problems, which have to be solved *within* market economies (and under conditions of globalisation), are inappropriate to undermine the legitimation of market economies.[9] This, together with the *second* point, namely that the principle to make profits is an indispensable part of decentralisation of decisions in market economies and is as such a *precondition to increase (relative*

---

9   It is, of course, a matter of degree of how much state intervention (respectively, how much central planning) is desired under the conditions of a market economy. E.g., the "*Soziale Marktwirtschaft*" in Germany or the economic system in Sweden differ from the somewhat more capitalist economy in the United States. However, these considerations do not concern our argument for a market economy to be more efficient to co-ordinate the economic system and therefore to be the frame of reference *within* which suitable political interventions into market processes takes place. The examples from Germany and Sweden seem to acknowledge this as a precondition.

to centrally planned economies) economic efficiency, makes for the argument of "external effects" becoming irrelevant in our line of reasoning for the principal legitimation of the corporate objective function to make profits. Each firm – regardless of its specific governance structure (capitalist or not) – must in a decentralised market economy satisfy profit requirements as a precondition for survival.

The argument of "external effects" becomes, of course, extremely relevant when we turn from the level of corporate objectives to the level of corporate *means* with which to generate profits. It is on this level that "external effects" may arise and cause conflicts with the stakeholders of the corporation. This is so, because it is on this level that the mere *formal* principle of profit making is turned into concrete means by *substantial* strategic choices. It is the strategy of the firm which may, then, affect stakeholder interests in concrete terms. This leads us to the second question raised above, namely why, in a market economy, it may be reasonable for management to self-impose restrictions on their strategic choices.

c) Why Is it Reasonable to Self-Impose Ethical Restrictions on Corporate Management?

Now, following our line of reasoning developed thus far, to argue in favour of corporate ethics would require to show that it is a *necessary* means for the end of a peaceful co-ordination of economic activities and thus for societal peace in general. If this can be proved successfully it will have, of course, repercussions for our understanding of the profit principle and its legitimacy. It would imply that the profit principle cannot be understood as an *unconditional* request to pursue one's own private interests in business; instead, it must be understood from the very beginning as conditioned by a *proviso for peace* and the concrete rules following from it. The objective function of the corporation would than read as follows:

"Make profits as far as this is in accordance with peace in society!"[10]

Seen this way, the profit principle would then have to be regarded as a *necessary* but not at the same time as a *sufficient* condition for peace. It

---

10 This formula implies that intelligent managers will choose the best economic alternative among those which are available and ethically justifiable. Nevertheless, we do not use the term "maximisation of profits" here because it is often used in economic theories under the assumption of comprehensive rationality as a call for the (ethically) unconditional quest for profits.

would become a necessary *and* sufficient condition only in conjunction with ethical provisos for peace concerning corporate strategy.

There are two steps to prove this assertion:

(1) one has to show that the proviso is indeed necessary; and

(2) one has to show that peace cannot be provided for fully and sufficiently at the political level of the state, the legislator and the law. Otherwise there would be no need for ethical reasoning on the corporate level.

The first part of the proof runs as follows. Contrary to all *liberal positions,* we hold here that not the *freedom* of the individual per se can be regarded as the highest value of society and the starting point of any argument, but only "freedom *and* unity", combined together in the notion of peace as "general free consensus" and as an expression of the public interest. The principle of peace, thus, implies by definition that *freedom* must be seen as inseparably intertwined with the *responsibility* for unity. And responsibility for unity is to be understood as the responsibility to contribute to consensual conflict resolutions wherever necessary in society. Thus, the principle, often cited by managers or politicians: "No freedom without responsibility!" makes sense as a direct consequence of the notion of peace. It is *universally* valid in all societies which are based on the principle of peace and as such applicable, wherever necessary, to the design of *all* institutions in society, including economic institutions as, for instance, the private corporation. And that it is in principal necessary with respect to the private corporation to add a proviso to the profit objective in order to provide for consensual resolutions of conflicts, this does follow directly from the argument of *universal external effects.*

Of course, nothing has been said as yet about how the proviso for peace should be imposed on managerial action: Should it be imposed by law at the political level? Or should it be self-imposed by management? Or both? These questions relate to the second part of the proof.

Our assertion is here that *legal provisions* for peaceful resolutions of conflicts at the company level are necessary but not sufficient; such provisions may concern all stakeholders, the shareholders as well as customers, workers or suppliers, just to mention a few. To support the argument that such legal provisions are not sufficient, one normally points – as we have done at length above (II, 2) – to the limited capacity of the law. We would like to enrich this argument by introducing an important distinction, namely the distinction between what one may call "structural" or "general conflicts" and "ad-hoc-" or "specific conflicts".

Structural conflicts arise where there are structural, not accidental, inequalities in the power distribution between the parties of the market, as, for instance, between capital and labour. For such conflicts, because they can generally be foreseen and analysed ex ante, general legal provisions for a peaceful conflict resolution are possible and make sense. Indeed, these are well-known problems of *corporate governance* (e.g. Monks/Minow 1995).

Additional questions for *corporate ethics* arise when there are "*ad-hoc-conflicts*", i.e., conflicts which are caused by *specific features* of the individual corporate strategy, as, for instance, in the well-known Nestlé-case (cf. Dobbing 1988, Löhr 1991). Such conflicts cannot be anticipated since they arise as a consequence of creative acts to renew corporate strategy or as unintended side-effects of it. It is with respect to such ad-hoc-conflicts that an ethical proviso seems to be necessary to assure that corporate strategy is not only profitable but contributes at the same time to a peaceful coordination of economic activities. And such a proviso can only be *self-imposed* and must necessarily be of a procedural nature, because only management and those stakeholders who are concerned by a specific strategy, can and must together find out a peaceful solution to the specific conflict by dialogue (Deetz 1995). It follows that corporate ethics must be regarded as an integral, indispensable and important part of all endeavours to provide for peace in society. And what is important here: to act ethically is, of course, not at the *discretion* of corporate managers at all. This follows from the principle stated above, namely that managerial *freedom* does by necessity correspond to the *responsibility* to contribute to peace in society. In so far it is, indeed, correct to propose that the large corporation should no longer be understood as a private institution in its strict sense but as a *semi-public* institution (Ulrich 1976), even more so as society is more and more affected by the policy of large firms (Deetz 1992, Korten 1995).

We could now, to sum up our line of reasoning, propose an understanding of corporate ethics which comprises the following elements:

(1) Corporate ethics should be understood as *discoursive ethics*;

(2) directed towards a *consensus* on the basis of *good reasons*;

(3) for a *peaceful* solution of *conflicts* with the (internal and external) stakeholders of the corporation;

(4) conflicts, which are caused by striving for *profits* and profitable *corporate strategies*; and

(5) the results of a successful conflict resolution are *self-imposed* rules which supplement the existing law as a basis to *legitimate* corporate action.

170

III. Corporate Ethics and the Management Process

The notion of corporate ethics and its relationship to profit as developed in part II is the basis for dealing with the second problem of this paper mentioned at the beginning: What structure of the management process allows for an efficient *implementation* of corporate ethics under conditions of division of labour such that striving for corporate profits does not hurt the proviso for peace.

In general, corporate ethics as discourse ethics (or ethics of dialogue), i.e., its *argumentation-based* character, requires a structure of the management process which is itself open to and promotes argumentation between organisation members, be they managers or employees. Corporate ethics thus, points to the necessity for a paradigmatic change in management (theory) from a *monologue-oriented* to a *dialogue-oriented* rationality (cf. Steinmann/Kustermann 1996, Steinmann/Löhr 1994, see also Alvesson/Willmott 1996). It is our basic assertion here that this paradigmatic change is not contradictory in general to what is required today under the economic imperative to strive for corporate profits (see also Deetz 1995 and Quinn 1996 who sketch the same argument). In fact, this change from monologue to dialogue is already under way in practice if we look at modern devices for corporate re-organisation, which abandon the former "taylorist" model of management. These proposals are, e.g., *"decentralisation"*, *"empowerment"* or *"team based"* and *"learning organisations"* (e.g., Ford /Fottler 1995, Lawler 1992, Mohrman/Cohen/Mohrman 1995, Nonaka /Takeuchi 1995, Pfeffer 1994). New developments in *management theory* reflect this empirical tendency and try to explain it as a necessary requirement for the survival of the corporation operating under conditions of increasing environmental uncertainty and complexity in hyper-competitive technology-driven and (often) world-wide markets (see, e.g., Simons 1995).

Thus we hold that what emerges today in industry opens a better chance of incorporating corporate ethics into the management process than there has ever been under conditions of taylorism and the taylorist management model. And it is from this perspective that we are more in favour of the *"integrity approach"* as compared to the *"compliance approach"*, two models mentioned above and discussed today in the U.S. as organisational alternatives for implementing corporate ethics (Paine 1994a, Steinmann/Olbrich 1995).

1. The Problem of Management: Three Generic Strategic Operations

To describe and explain the paradigmatic change in management theory, a basic understanding of the management process itself is necessary. This understanding can serve as the background for a comparison of the "taylorist" and the modern management model.

Speaking very generally, management has the task of establishing and implementing an economically sound strategic course of action for the company. This general task can be specified further at a still relatively abstract level by focusing on three *generic strategic operations*, namely "selection", "concretisation" and "reflection" (Steinmann/Schreyögg 1997, Steinmann/Kustermann 1996, for the following see in particular Steinmann/Kustermann 1998). Note that this is a more abstract level to describe the task of management as compared to the level of management *functions* or concrete actions (mentioned in the introduction).

Establishing a strategic direction implies from the outset an act of *selection*, i.e., choosing an option from a basically unlimited range of possibilities (cf. Simons 1995, pp. 14 ff.), an option which is considered to be a good basis for (long-term) economic success in a competitive market. Once selected, this general strategic orientation must be made more *concrete* so that it can actually provide guidelines for action day by day. And, finally, it may be necessary to adjust the strategic direction to new conditions; there must, therefore, be a potential for critical *reflection* within management which, by taking up a critical stance towards the status quo, makes innovation possible.

All three generic operations are processes of gathering and handling (assimilating) information with the aim of continually preparing, authorising, implementing and controlling decisions about the strategic course and the operational programs of the company and their revision. At any one time, the process of gathering and handling information must be carried out such that potential problems can be identified and assessed, and that a definitive decision (authorisation) can be made about the most appropriate course of action binding for the whole organisation. Fig. 2 illustrates the three generic operations as processes of gathering and handling information.

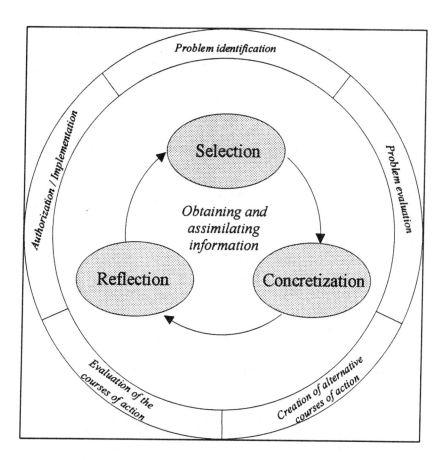

Figure 2: Management as a process of gaining and handling information (from Steinmann/Kustermann 1998).
Reproduced by permission of Gabler (Wiesbaden).

With the aid of these three generic operations it should be possible to re-construct different (theoretical) approaches to management at hand for pur-poses of comparison and critical analysis (see, e.g., Steinmann/Kustermann 1996, 1998 with respect to the theoretical framework proposed by Simons 1995).

2. The Three Generic Operations in the Taylorist Management Model and Implications for the Implementation of Corporate Ethics

In the taylorist management model, these three generic operations are viewed as being performed by one *central* authority, conceived as an actor who selects the strategic orientation, who makes operational plans and who will order a change in direction if necessary. *Unity* of management manifests itself here in the "idea" of *one* central actor operating at the top of the hierarchy and using hierarchy as a means to carry out the plans for action developed centrally. The taylorist management model assures rationality to the extent that the central actor itself *is* rational. Rationality is conceived of here monologically as a *feature* of the central authority (and not as a process of argumentation or dialogue the result of which can be claimed to be rational in so far as it is based on good reasons) (Schreyögg/Steinmann 1987, Steinmann/Kustermann 1998).

This top-centred steering model has two other important implications which further underpin our understanding of it as a manifestation of monological rationality: the model makes sense only when one can assume (1) that business plans developed at the top are (sufficiently) *correct* and (2) that people are *self-interested* and driven by *external* motivation so that *incentives* are a proper and effective means of implementing business plans (cf. Mintzberg/Waters 1985).

The first assumption makes corporate planning the central function of the management process (*"primacy of planning"*). The other four management functions (organising, staffing, directing, control) must by necessity be regarded as being instrumental for the execution of plans; any attempt to activate creativity and initiatives of organisation members would be dysfunctional and contra-productive to the correct execution of plans. The central actor (senior management) is the rational entity here; he/she thinks, forecasts, plans and controls (strategically and operationally). The employees come into the picture only in their capacity to *execute* plans. It is this separation of "thinking" and "executing" which justifies calling this management model – as is often done – "taylorist" or "machine-like" (Spender 1996).

The second assumption rules out – and this is consistent with the first assumption – any possibility of relying on the *intrinsic* motivation of employees (Ghoshal/Moran 1996, Osterloh/Frey 1997). The central actor, i.e. top management, is the sole locus and origin of rational action and he/she alone is regarded as acting in the interest of the corporation. The other members of the organisation are assumed to follow their own personal interests. Thus, to motivate employees to act according to corporate plans and in the interest of the corporation requires incentives, financial and others, which appeal to the *specific* motives of organisation members (or homogeneous subgroups of them). They will act in the interest of the corporation, as laid down in corporate plans, only *in order to* gain the rewards promised. If corporate policy fails to grant the necessary rewards actions of employees will stop or become at least less and less efficient.

Against the background of relatively constant environmental conditions which are to a great extent amenable to analytic penetration and good forecasting, this traditional "one-actor-model" proved successful for quite a long time until up into the seventies. Corporate planning could then proceed under the assumption of certainty; basic tasks of planning such as environmental analyses and the choice of means and ends did not have to be radically reconsidered all the time. And plans could be worked out in sufficient detail such that *concrete* and *conflict free* instructions could be given to employees, instructions which had only to be changed (eventually) when a new planning cycle started.

The monologic rationality behind this management model manifested itself in the form of invariant criteria. Under the given environmental conditions especially the criterion of *efficiency* ("doing the things right"), i.e., minimising the costs of the management process by routinising managerial functions, held sway, while the criterion of *effectiveness* ("doing the right things") was relatively unimportant since the environmental setting made continuous revisions of the strategy, and thus strategic awareness, unnecessary (Schreyögg/Steinmann 1987).

Now, what consequences does this management model have for the implementation of corporate ethics? It was already mentioned that the so called "compliance-approach" as practised in some U.S.-companies (Paine 1994a, Steinmann/Olbrich 1995, 1998) comes close to the basic philosophy of the taylorist model. The basic features of this model are quite similar to the taylorist model. By explicating and confronting them with our understanding of corporate ethics, the limited usefulness of taylorist approaches to sensitise corporations for ethical requirements will become obvious.

Figure 3 gives an overview of the two ideal-types of ethics management as proposed by Paine (1994a).

175

	Characteristics of Compliance Strategy	Characteristics of Integrity Strategy
Ethos	conformity with externally imposed standards	self-governance according to chosen standards
Objective	prevent criminal conduct	enable responsible conduct
Leadership	lawyer driven	management driven with aid of lawyers, HR and others
Methods	education, reduced discretion, auditing and controls, penalties	education, leadership, accountability, organisational systems and decision processes, auditing and controls, penalties
Behavioural Assumptions	autonomous beings guided by material self-interest	social beings guided by material self-interest, values, ideals, peers

	Implementation of Compliance Strategy	Implementation of Integrity Strategy
Standards	criminal and regulatory law	company values and aspirations, social obligations, including law
Staffing	lawyers	executives and managers with lawyers, others
Activities	develop compliance standards, train and communicate, handle reports of misconduct, conduct investigations, oversee compliance audits, enforce standards	lead development of company values and standards, train and communicate, integrate into company systems, provide guidance and consultation, assess values performance, identify and resolve problems, oversee compliance activities
Education	compliance standards and system	decision making and values, compliance standards and system

Figure 3: Strategies for Ethics Management.
Reproduced by permission of Harvard Business Review. From "Managing for Organisational Integrity" by L. S. Paine, March/April 1994, p. 113, modified.
Copyright © 1994 by the President and Fellows of Harvard College; all rights reserved.

From Figure 3 it becomes clear that the compliance approach focuses explicitly on measures to prevent criminal *misconduct*, centring on standards that are *external* to and *imposed* on the corporation by law. "Designed by corporate counsel the goal of these programs is to prevent, detect, and punish legal violations. ... Such programs tend to emphasise the prevention of unlawful conduct, primarily by increasing surveillance and control and by imposing penalties for wrongdoers." (Paine 1994a, p. 106/109). The whole philosophy of this approach is geared towards the proper execution of the law by breaking down legal norms into (numerous) specific rules of behaviour via compliance standards and their enforcement, standards, which are adjusted to the different corporate activities (marketing, finance etc.) or even to specific jobs. Going further through the characteristics and implementation measures of Fig. 3 it becomes convincingly clear that the compliance approach comes close to the *three features* of the taylorist management model, mentioned above, namely: focusing on a central actor, planning oriented and relying on external motivation and incentives to provide for self-interested employees to give due regard to legal norms.

The compliance strategy is dominated by a monologue-oriented rationality. The three generic operations of ethics management are carried out at the top. Top management (with support of the legal department or lawyers) is expected definitely to *select* and enumerate legal norms (and, maybe, further values) regarded as relevant for keeping the activities of the corporation within the limits of law; it is expected to *concretise* these norms and values in such a way that they can form part of the *role* of each employee, and it *reflects* which and when revisions of the internal norms are due because law has changed.

From this characterisation it becomes clear that both the taylorist management model and its manifestation in form of the compliance approach, are totally unable to take account of the *dialogic* nature of corporate ethics.

This is different if one turns to the integrity approach (Fig. 3). It seems to come somewhat closer to what is required by discourse ethics but also to the modern management model outlined in more detail below. This characterisation comes to mind, at least, when one looks at the different dimensions Paine (1994a, p. 112) uses to describe this approach. She speaks of the necessity that "guiding values and commitments make sense and are clearly communicated", that "company leaders are personally committed, credible, and willing to take action on the values they espouse", that "the espoused values are integrated into the normal channels of decision making", that "managers throughout the company have the decision making skills, knowledge, and competence needed to make ethically sound decisions on a day-to day basis". The whole approach is more directed towards facilitating *responsible conduct* than to assure compliance to the law. As such it is more *active* (than reactive), more *open* (than definitely closed in its requirements) and *less selective* than the compliance approach. But, from what Paine says, it remains unclear whether a paradigmatic change from monologue-oriented to a dialogue-oriented rationality is really intended. It seems – and this would be in accordance with the general orientation of U.S.-management literature (see, e.g., Simons 1995) – that top-management alone is still regarded here as the only source and origin of corporate values (see also our critical analyses of Simons' [1995] concept in Steinmann/Kustermann 1996, 1998). To switch to a dialogic rationality is the aim of the modern management model to which we turn now. This switch would then increase the probability to reconcile management theory and management praxis with corporate ethics.

3. The Modern Concept of Management and its Relevance for the Implementation of Corporate Ethics

a) Basic Theoretical Considerations

It was the crisis of the taylorist approach in management practice which gradually brought about new concepts in management theory in the last ten years or so. All these concepts have in common that they re-interpret the role and the relationship between the five managerial functions for steering the corporation, and, i.e., for performing the three generic strategic operations. The basic features of the modern management framework are inter alia "decentralisation" and "empowerment" in the sense of integrating managers of all levels and – in the final analysis – even all employees into the process of gathering and handling information for (re-)evaluating, authorising, implementing and controlling decisions about the strategic course and the operational programs of the company (see also Daft/Lewin 1993, Simons 1995). It is these structural features which open the chance for dialogical oriented rationality in management and thus for successfully integrating corporate ethics into the management process (Quinn 1996). To argue for this assertion we have to unfold the new management model in more detail.

The crisis of the taylorist management model is the crisis of planning (Mintzberg 1994, Alvesson/Willmott 1996, pp. 129 ff.). The prominent role which this management function played in the taylorist approach up to the seventies, proved to the more and more dysfunctional in order to cope with the increasing turbulence, the discontinuities and the ambiguities of the (external and internal) environment of the company. Thus, the decisive assumption that the central authority alone is able to perform all three generic operations of management (i.e., selection, reflection, concretisation) had to be given up. Under conditions of ambiguity the results of the (central) planning process, i.e., the (strategic) plans, can no longer be considered as (sufficiently) correct and resistant to surprise (Schreyögg /Steinmann 1987). As a consequence the four other managerial functions (organising, staffing, leading, control) had to be released from their mere *instrumental* role of executing plans. Instead of contributing to the fulfilment of the three generic operations of strategic management only *indirectly* via planning, the question arose now what *direct* contribution these functions had to make to have a good chance of successfully steering the corporation under conditions of environmental turbulence. The result was a concept of management which can be summarised as follows by referring to the three generic operations (Steinmann/Schreyögg 1997, Steinmann /Kustermann 1996, 1998):

(1) *Selection*: Here the assumption is that although (strategic) planning cannot guarantee the correctness of plans, it does nevertheless not become totally superfluous. It is presupposed that compared to simply "muddling-through", planning can still contribute to rational action, namely by arguing ex ante for orientations of corporate action which have – for good reasons – a better chance of being successful than others. But, what follows from the precondition of environmental turbulence and ambiguity is that the degree of selectivity of planning, and thus the degree of fine tuning of plans, had to be drastically reduced in order to allow for the necessary latitude to adopt corporate actions to the specific circumstances of the present and the near future. In the taylorist model synoptical planning results in detailed strategic and operational plans for all operational areas of the company. In contrast to this, only broad strategies and general orientations could now reasonably be expected of planning in view of the extremely limited predictability of the future. One could thus speak of a "*weak* selection" performed by planning. Moreover and secondly, one has to take into account that even this weak selection may prove to be wrong at every future point in time; planning provides the company only with a *tentative* orientation for action (Schreyögg/Steinmann 1987). These two aspects of planning have direct repercussions for the other two generic operations of management, namely

"reflection" and "concretisation". They are now open for broad dialogic processes.

(2) *Reflection*: The selective character of planning and the tentative status of plans involves a high risk of having chosen a wrong orientation. Things may happen different by than anticipated because of events which were undetected or undetectable during the planning process. For this reason management has to take measures which can compensate for the risk inherent in the selectivity of planning (Schreyögg/Steinmann 1987, Preble 1992). To fulfil this compensatory function these measures must (of course) be non-selective (as far as possible) and must have their own independent information base in order to be able *continually* to question the process and the results of planning. We call this device "strategic control" (Schreyögg /Steinmann 1987). To fulfil these requirements – and this is decisive for our argument – strategic control must by necessity be organised as a dialogical and company wide activity of information gathering and information handling involving all employees – managerial or not – in a process of argumentation and reflection about the status quo of corporate strategy, its underlying explicit or implicit assumptions, be they value judgements or answers to truth questions about the world. What is required here is thus a broad strategic *awareness* and a *critical* attitude of organisational members in order to question the intended strategy and to stimulate innovative thinking about new courses of action in the sense of emerging strategies (Mintzberg 1994, Simons 1995). This perspective obviously, has repercussions for all management functions from decentralising organisational activities to a more consensual leadership style and to the development of human resource capabilities, which are relevant for contributing to dialogical processes in management.

(3) *Concretisation*: As a consequence of the merely "weak" selection brought about by planning a third device is necessary to provide for successful corporate management under conditions of environmental turbulence and ambiguity: the rather general orientation derived from planning must be made sufficiently concrete so that employees can perform their everyday activities. This is the task of *operational* planning and control. In light of the situational conditions of the overseeable future and in view of the strategic orientations given, both functions have actively to create and monitor an action programme which is not only effective but also sufficiently *efficient* ("doing the things right"). The other management functions (organising, staffing, directing) serve the implementation of the operational plans.

Now, looking at these three generic operations in toto, it becomes immediately clear, that conflicts and tensions between these operations are basic characteristics of the modern management process. Concretisation and implementation of corporate strategy requires bridging the gap between the *abstract* and the *concrete* by argumentative procedures, which is a creative and conflict loaden process. Moreover, reflecting requires distancing from the status quo whereas concretisation and implementation demands rather unconditional commitment to it. Therefore, conflicts and dilemmas are endemic. And the same is true of the tensions between selection and reflection: selection asks for decisions about future orientations to make action possible at all, whereas reflection is prone to keep future options open as long as possible. Here again, conflicts and dilemmas prove to be central features of the modern management process as opposed to the taylorist view where dilemmas and conflicts are ruled out ex ante through planning via a strict ordering of means-end-relationships.

All these conflicts and dilemmas cannot be solved definitely ex ante in a generalised way through planning because their solution depends on still unknown or merely probable circumstances of the specific situation. What is thus necessary, instead, to resolve dilemmas and conflicts are "practical judgements" in view of the concrete historical side conditions under which a decision has to be made (Spender 1992). And such judgements, in order to be reasonable, require *argumentative processes* between members of the organisation who are competent for the problems in all stages of the process of information gathering and handling. This is what we mean by the turn from a monological to a dialogue-oriented management philosophy. And it is at this point where the fundamental requirements of modern management match with the dialogical character of corporate ethics.

b) A Practical Case: Levi Strauss & Co.

This conclusion from our theoretical considerations is supported by the practical experience made at Levi Strauss in implementing corporate ethics. Levi Strauss is one of the rare companies from which we have a rather concrete and well reflected report about the process of ethics management, and this from the CEO and chairman of the Board, Robert Haas, himself, delivered at the well-known "Conference Board" in New York City in 1994 (Haas 1994). Haas summarises the experience gained in a number of years in pointing to the severe deficiencies of the "compliance approach" and the strength and preferability of the "integrity approach" (see Paine 1994a). In re-constructing the actual procedure of ethics management at Levi Strauss on the basis of the three generic operations it is possible to show its structural equivalence with the model of modern management outlined above (Steinmann/Olbrich 1998).

But before we do so it might be useful to quote Robert Haas on the experience gained with the compliance approach:

> Until recently, we were among the companies that took this approach. The centrepiece of our efforts was comprehensive collection of regulations that spelled out our world-wide code of business ethics. In it, we laid out rules for hiring practices, travel and entertainment expenses, political contributions, compliance with local laws, improper payments, gifts and favours. We addressed topics ranging from accounting practices to potential conflicts of interest. As you might guess, it was a long and weighty list of do's and don'ts for our people to follow.

> This approach didn't serve us well. First, rules beget rules. And regulations beget regulations. We became buried in paperwork, and any time we faced a unique ethical issue, another rule or regulation was born. Second, our compliance-based program sent a disturbing message to our people – WE DON'T RESPECT YOUR INTELLIGENCE OR TRUST YOU! Finally, and one of the most compelling reasons for shedding this approach, was that it didn't keep managers or employees from exercising poor judgement and making questionable decisions (Haas 1994, p. 507 f., emphasis in the original).

So, one quickly learned at Levi Strauss that the compliance approach tended to destroy the intrinsic motivation and the positive attitude of the employees towards the company (Osterloh/Frey 1997). Moreover, the ability of managers and employees to successfully treat ethical dilemmas was not developed. Haas summarises the experience in one sentence: "We learned that you can't force ethical conduct into an organisation" (Haas 1994, p. 508). For this reason ethics management at Levi Strauss was re-oriented towards the integrity approach but enriched by dialogical processes as a means to help clarifying basic dilemma situations. The measures taken and the structure developed can be outlined by referring to the three generic operations:

(1) *Selection*: Drawing on the insight that a complete enumeration of all ethical issues which were ever experienced in the company or which could

be imagined for the future was not only unpracticable but impossible and the ethics management of Levi Strauss was shifted to six rather abstract ethical principles. These were regarded to be binding for the whole organisation. These principles are: honesty, promise-keeping, fairness, respect for others, compassion and integrity. They can be regarded as a "code of ethics" in a rather general form. The abstractness of these principles give room and latitude for developing more concrete rules of conduct which are in accordance with specific (types of) situations, e.g., in procurement, production, finance or marketing. This freedom to act is in the final analysis due to the shift in organisational devices from *role-structures* to (less selective) organisational culture.

(2) *Concretisation*: These six principles are then made concrete so that they can guide departmental and individual action. This is done by a dialogue procedure described by Haas (1994, p. 508) as follows:

> Today, at Levi Strauss & Co., we base our approach to ethics upon six ethical principles – honesty, promise-keeping, fairness, respect for others, compassion and integrity. Using this approach, we address ethical issues by first identifying which of these ethical principles applies to the particular business decision. Then, we determine which internal and which external stakeholders' ethical concerns should influence our business decisions. Information on stakeholder issues is gathered and possible recommendations are discussed with "high influence" stakeholder groups, such as shareholders, employees, customers, members of local communities, public interest groups, our business partners and so forth.

The discourse mentioned here serves two purposes. First, it is intended to clarify the *interests* of those groups or individuals who are affected by concrete plans or actions. Secondly, it is meant to help scanning the situational conditions relevant for successful action:

> This principle-based approach balances the ethical concerns of these various stakeholders with the values of our organisation. It is a process that extends trust to an individual's knowledge of the situation. It examines the complexity of issues that must be considered in each decision, and it defines the role each person's judgement plays in carrying out his or her responsibilities in an ethical manner.

The result of this concretisation process are e.g. policies for functional areas of the company. Haas (1994, p. 508) gives a concrete example:

Our guidelines describe the business conduct we require of our contractors. For instance, the guidelines ban the use of child or prison labour. They stipulate certain environmental requirements. They limit working hours and mandate regularly scheduled days off. Workers must have the right of free association and not be exploited. At a minimum, wages must comply with the law and match prevailing local practice and working conditions must be safe and healthy. We also expect our business partners to be law abiding and to conduct all of their business affairs in an ethical way.

In developing our guidelines, we also recognised that there are certain issues beyond the control of our contractors, so we produced a list of "country selection" criteria. For example, we will not source in countries where conditions, such as the human rights climate, would run counter to our values and have an adverse effect on our global brand image or damage our corporate reputation. Similarly, we will not source in countries where circumstances threaten our employees while travelling, where the legal climate makes it difficult or jeopardise our trademarks, and where political or social turmoil threatens our commercial interest.

(3) *Reflection*: The necessity continuously to stay at a critical distance from the status quo of ethical principles, policies and rules is well acknowledged by Levi Strauss. It is recognised that one needs an organisational climate which is based on trust and organisational rules which reinforce ethical reflection on all levels of the corporation. Haas (1994, p. 508), again, clearly hints to these points when he argues:

Ethics is a function of the collective attitudes of our people. And these attitudes are cultivated and supported by at least seven factors:

1) commitment to responsible business conduct;
2) management's leadership;
3) trust in employees;
4) programs and policies that provide people with clarity about the organisation's ethical expectations;
5) open, honest and timely communications;
6) tools to help employees resolve ethical problems; and
7) reward and recognition systems that reinforce the importance of ethics.

Ultimately, high ethical standards can be maintained only if they are modelled by management and woven into the fabric of the company.

> Knowing this, your challenge and mine is to cultivate the kind of environment where people do the right thing.

What Haas describes here as a central part of ethics management at Levi Strauss runs counter to an organisation which is mainly based on distrust, surveillance and monitoring, punishment and the assumption that people are exclusively motivated extrinsically. What is essential, instead, is enabling employees to "do the right thing", and this would mean two things: to develop the ethical sensitivity and intrinsic ethical motivation on all levels of the organisation and, secondly, to support ethical behaviour of people by adequate structural measures concerning information and communication, reward and recognition systems, leadership etc. So, instead of a central actor who alone determines the course of ethical conduct we have here, at least as a regulative idea, a concept, which bases ethics management on *decentralisation* and *empowerment*.

4. Conclusion

If one looks back now at all these three generic operations in ethics management as performed at Levi Strauss, its similarity with the structural requirements of modern management as outlined above becomes obvious. Both start with weak selections (management principles resp. codes of ethics) to allow for enough freedom and flexibility for concretisation of corporate strategy and plans according to situational requirements. And both rely on organisation-wide participative processes to provide for critical reflection as a compensating device for the risk inherent in the selectivity of strategies and moral principles, policies and rules. Thus, the answer to our second question raised at the beginning runs as follows: It is possible to design a system of ethics management which is compatible with the economic requirements of modern management. This answer relates, of course, as was also pointed out at the beginning, merely to the level of managerial functions designed to steer the company and to handle and resolve conflicts and dilemmas inherent in this task. And here Haas (1994, p. 509) is rather optimistic that in the *long run* the conflict between striving for profits and ethical requirements for business will vanish ("ethics pays"). But at the moment, this is, of course, only a *hope* which may or may not prove valid. Recently, Hosmer (1994, 1997) proposed that being right, just, and fair "*is absolutely essential to the long-term competitive success of the firm*" (1994,

p. 192, emphasis in the original; see also Paine 1996). He argued that today companies become more and more dependent on the contributions of various stakeholder groups to achieve success. Only in as much as a company is able to generate trust and commitment stakeholders will show effort, improvisation, creativity, innovation and the willingness to share their ideas with the company, which are preconditions for long-term economic success. However, Hosmer (1994, pp. 201 f.) rightly suggested that his proposals still have to be empirically shown.

A more realistic perspective would rather in the short run be for management to reckon with conflicts between ethics and economics ("ethics costs"). And then it becomes a hard decision for management whether or not and under what competitive conditions one could stick to the principle set up by Levi Strauss: "Ethics must trump all other considerations" (Haas 1994, p. 509).[11]

References

ALBERT, H.: *Treatise on Critical Reason*, Princeton (University Press) 1985. Original: *Traktat über kritische Vernunft*, Tübingen (J.C.B. Mohr [P. Siebeck]) 1980.

ALVESSON, M., WILLMOTT, H.: *Making Sense of Management. A Critical Introduction*, London (Sage) 1996.

APEL, K.-O.: *Towards a Transformation of Philosophy*, London (Routledge & Kegan Paul) 1980. Original: *Transformation der Philosophie*, Frankfurt a. M. (Suhrkamp) 1973.

ARROW, K. J., DEBREU, G.: "Existence of an Equilibrium for a Competitive Economy", *Econometrica*, 22 (1954), pp. 265-290.

ARROW, K. J., HAHN, F.: *General Competitive Analysis*, San Francisco (Holden-Day) 1971.

BODDEWYN, J. J.: "The Legitimacy of International-Business Political Behaviour", *The International Trade Journal*, IX, No. 1 (1995), pp. 143-161.

---

11 In 1997 it was reported that Levi Strauss & Co. announced a mass lay-off of employees, particularly in the U.S. Whether or not this decision has been trumped by ethical consideration is open to scrutiny.

CHRISTENSON, Ch.: "Proposal for a Program of Empirical Research into the Properties of Triangles", *Decision Sciences*, 4 (1976), pp. 631-648.

DAFT, R. L., LEWIN, A. J.: "Where Are the Theories of the 'New' Organisational Forms? An Editorial Essay", *Organisational Science*, 4 (1993), pp. i-vi.

DALTON, D. R., METZGER, M. B., HILL, J. W.: "The "New" U.S. Sentencing Commission Guidelines: A Wake-Up Call for Corporate America", *Academy of Management Executive*, 8 (1994), pp. 7-13

DEETZ, ST.: *Democracy in an Age of Corporate Colonization: Developments in Communication and the Politics of Everyday Life*, Albany (State University of New York Press) 1992.

DEETZ, ST.: *Transforming Communication, Transforming Business*, Cresskill, N.J. (Hampton Press) 1995.

DOBBING, J. (Ed.): *Infant Feeding. Anatomy of a Controversy 1973-1984*, London 1988.

DUNFEE, TH. W.: "On the Synergistic, Interdependent Relationship of Business Ethics and Law", *American Business Law Journal*, 34 (Winter 1996) 2, pp. 318-326.

EISENBERG, J. A.: *The Limits of Reason. Indeterminacy in Law, Education, and Morality*, New Brunswick (Transaction Publishers) 1992.

FERRELL, O. C., LECLAIR, D. T., FERRELL, L.: "The Federal Sentencing Guidelines for Organizations: A Framework for Ethical Comliance", *Journal of Business Ethics*, 17 (1998), pp. 353-363.

FORD, R. C., FOTTLER, M. D.: "Empowerment: A Matter of Degree", *Academy of Management Review*, 9 (1995), pp. 21-31.

FOUCAULT, M.: *Power/Knowledge*, Brighton (Harvester Press) 1980.

FREEMAN, R. E.: *Strategic Management. A Stakeholder Approach*, Boston (Pitman) 1984.

GHOSHAL, S., MORAN, P.: "Bad for Practice: A Critique of the Transaction Cost Theory", *Academy of Management Review*, 21 (1996), pp. 13-47.

GIDDENS, A.: *The Constitution of Society. Outline of the Theory of Structuration*, Cambridge, Mass. (Polity Press), 1984.

GIDDENS, A.: *Kritische Theoie der Spätmoderne*, Wien (Passagen Verlag) 1992.

GREIDER, W.: *One World, Ready or Not. The Manic Logic of Global Capitalism*, New York (Simon & Schuster) 1997.

HAAS, R. D.: "Ethics – A Global Business Challenge", *Vital Speeches of the Day*, 60, No. 16 (1994), pp. 506-509.

HABERMAS, J.: *The Theory of Communicative Action. Volume 2*, Cambridge (Polity Press) 1987. Original: *Theorie des kommunikativen Handelns, Band 2*, Frankfurt a. M. (Suhrkamp) 1981.

HABERMAS, J.: "Discourse Ethics: Notes on a Program of Philosophical Justification", in: J. HABERMAS: *Moral Consciousness and Communicative Action*, Cambridge, Mass. (The MIT Press) 1990, pp. 43-115. Original: "Diskursethik. Notizen zu einem Begründungsprogramm", in: J. HABERMAS: *Moralbewußtsein und kommunikatives Handeln*, Frankfurt a. M. (Suhrkamp) 1983, pp. 53-125.

HABERMAS, J.: "Remarks on Discourse Ethics", in: J. HABERMAS: *Justification and Application. Remarks on Discourse Ethics*, Cambridge, Mass. (The MIT Press) 1993, pp. 19-112. Original: "Erläuterungen zur Diskursethik", in: J. HABERMAS: *Erläuterungen zur Diskursethik*, Frankfurt a. M. (Suhrkamp) 1991, p. 119-226.

HOOD, N., YOUNG, ST.: *The Economics of Multinational Enterprise*, London (Longman) 1979.

HOSMER, L. T.: "Why be Moral? A Different Rationale for Managers", *Business Ethics Quarterly*, 4 (1994), pp. 191-204.

HOSMER, L. T.: "Why be Moral? A Reply to Shaw and Corvino", *Business Ethics Quarterly*, 7 (1997), pp. 137-143.

JANICH, P.: *Was ist Wahrheit?*, München (Beck) 1996.

KAMBARTEL, F.: "Vernunft: Kriterium oder Kultur?", in: F. KAMBARTEL: *Philosophie der humanen Welt*, Frankfurt a. M. (Suhrkamp) 1989, pp. 27-43.

KAMBARTEL, F.: "Die Vernunft und das Allgemeine. Zum Verständnis rationaler Sprache und Praxis", in: V. GERHARD, N. HEROLD (Eds.): *Perspektiven des Perspektivismus. Gedenkschrift zum Tode Friedrich Kaulbachs,* Würzburg (Königshausen und Neumann) 1992, pp. 265-277.

KAMBARTEL, F.: *Wahrheit und Begründung*, Erlangen/Jena (Palm & Enke) 1997.

KAMBARTEL, F.: "Vernunftkultur und Kulturrelativismus. Bemerkungen zu verschiedenen Problemen des Verstehens und Begründens", in: H. STEINMANN, A. G. SCHERER (Eds.): *Zwischen Universalismus und Relativismus. Philosophische Grundlagenprobleme des Interkulturellen Managements*, Frankfurt a. M. (Suhrkamp) 1999, pp. 212-220.

KOONTZ, H., O'DONNELL, C.: *Principles of Management*, New York (Mc Graw-Hill) 3rd ed. 1964.

KOGUT, B.: "Designing Global Strategies. Profiting from Operational Flexibility", *Sloan Management Review*, 27 (1985), pp. 27-38.

KORTEN, D. C.: *When Corporations Rule the World*, West Hartford (Kumarian)

KUHN, J. W.: "Ethics in Business: What Managers Practice that Economists Ignore", *Business Ethics Quarterly*, 2 (1992), pp. 305-315.

LAWLER, E. E.: *The Ultimate Advantage. Creating the High-Involvement Organisation*, San Francisco (Jossey-Bass) 1992.

LÖHR, A.: *Unternehmensethik und Betriebswirtschaftslehre. Untersuchungen zur theoretischen Stützung der Unternehmenspraxis*, Stuttgart (M&P) 1991.

LORENZEN, P.: "Methodical Thinking", in: P. LORENZEN: *Constructive Philosophy*, Amherst, Mass. (The University of Massachusetts Press) 1987, pp. 3-29. Original: "Methodisches Denken", in: P. LORENZEN: *Methodisches Denken*, Frankfurt a. M. (Suhrkamp) 1968, pp. 24-59.

LORENZEN, P.: "Political Anthropology", in: P. LORENZEN: *Constructive Philosophy*, Amherst, Mass. (The University of Massachusetts Press) 1987, pp. 42-55. Original: "Politische Anthropologie", in: O. SCHWEMMER (Ed.): *Vernunft, Handlung und Erfahrung*, München (Beck) 1981, pp. 104-116.

LORENZEN, P.: "Ethics and the Philosophy of Science", in: D. E. CHRISTENSEN et al. (Eds.): *Contemporary German Philosophy*, Volume 1, University Park (The Pennsylvania State University Press) 1982, pp. 1-14.

LORENZEN, P. (1987a): *Constructive Philosophy*, Amherst (The University of Massachusetts Press) 1987.

LORENZEN, P. (1987b): *Lehrbuch der konstruktiven Wissenschaftstheorie*, Mannheim (BI-Wissenschaftsverlag) 1987.

LORENZEN, P.: "Philosophische Fundierungsprobleme einer Wirtschafts- und Unternehmensethik", in: H. STEINMANN, A. LÖHR (Eds.): *Unternehmensethik*, Stuttgart (Poeschel) 1989, pp. 25-58.

LUEKEN, G.-L.: "Incommensurability, Rules of Argumentation, and Anticipation", in: F. H. VAN EEMEREN et al. (Eds.): *Proceedings of the Second International Conference on Argumentation*, Amsterdam (SicSat) 1991, pp. 244-252.

LUEKEN, G.-L.: *Inkommensurabilität als Problem rationalen Argumentierens*, Stuttgart-Bad-Cannstatt (Frommann-Holzboog) 1992.

LYOTARD, J.-F.: *The Postmodern Condition*, Manchester (Manchester University Press) 1984.

MARTIN, H.-P., SCHUMANN, H.: *Die Globalisierungsfalle. Der Angriff auf Demokratie und Wohlstand*, Reinbek bei Hamburg (Rowohlt) 1996.

MINTZBERG, H.: *The Rise and Fall of Strategic Planning*, New York (Free Press) 1994.

MINTZBERG, H., WATERS, J. A.: "Of Strategies, Deliberate and Emergent", *Strategic Management Journal*, 6 (1985), pp. 257-272.

MITTELSTRASS, J.: "Changing Concepts of the A Priori", in: R. E. BUTTS, J. HINTIKKA (Eds.): *Historical and Philosophical Dimensions of Logic. Methodology and Philosophy of Science*, Dordrecht, (D. Reidel), 1977 pp. 3-128.

MITTELSTRASS, J.: "Scientific Rationality and Its Reconstruction", in: N. RESCHER (Ed.): *Reason and Rationality in Natural Science*, Lanham, MD (University Press of America) 1985, pp. 83-102.

MOHRMAN, S. A., COHEN, S. G., MOHRMAN, A. M. JR.: *Designing Team-Based Organisations. New Forms for Knowledge Work*. San Francisco (Jossey-Bass) 1995.

MONKS, R. A. G., MINOW, N.: *Corporate Governance*, Cambridge, Mass. (Basil Blackwell) 1995.

NAGEL, I., SWENSON, W. M.: "The Federal Sentencing Guidelines for Corporations: Their Development, Theoretical Underpinnings, and Some Thoughts About Their Future", *Washington University Law Quarterly*, 71, 2 (1993) pp. 205-259.

NONAKA, I., TAKEUCHI, H.: *The Knowledge-Creating Company: How Japanese Companies Create the Dynamics of Innovation*, New York (Oxford University Press) 1995.

OHMAE, K.: *The End of the Nation State. The Rise of Regional Economics*, New York (Free Press) 1995.

ORTS, E. W.: "The Legitimacy of Multinational Corporations", in: L. E. MITCHELL (Ed.): *Progressive Corporate Law*, Boulder (Westview Press) 1995, pp. 247-279.

OSTERLOH, M., FREY, B.: "Managing Innovation: Crowding Effects in the Theory of the Firm", in: INSTITUT FÜR BETRIEBSWIRTSCHAFTLICHE FORSCHUNG: *Diskussionsbeitrag Nr. 31*, Zürich (Universität Zürich) 1997.

PAINE, L. S. (1994a): "Organising with Integrity", *Harvard Business Review*, 72 (March-April 1994), pp. 106-117.

PAINE, L. S. (1994b): "Law, Ethics, and Managerial Judgement", *The Journal of Legal Studies Education*, 12 (Summer/Fall 1994) 2, pp. 153-169.

PAINE, L. S.: "Moral Thinking in Management: An Essential Capability", *Business Ethics Quarterly*, 6 (1996), pp. 477-492.

PFEFFER, J.: *Competitive Advantage Through People: Unleashing the Power of the Work Force*, Boston (Harvard Business School Press) 1994.

PREBLE, J. F.: "Towards a Comprehensive System of Strategic Control", *Journal of Management Studies*, 29 (1992), pp. 391-409.

QUINN, J. J.: "The Role of 'Good Conversation' in Strategic Control", *Journal of Management Studies*, 33 (1996), pp. 381-394.

SAGAL, P. T.: "Paul Lorenzen's Constructivism and the Recovery of Philosophy", *Synthesis Philosophica*, 3 (1987), pp. 173-178.

SCHERER, A. G., DOWLING, M. J.: "Towards a Reconciliation of the Theory-Pluralism in Strategic Management – Incommensurability and the Constructivist Approach of the Erlangen-School", *Advances in Strategic Management*, 12A (1995), pp. 195-247.

SCHERER, A. G., STEINMANN, H.: "Some Remarks on the Problem of Incommensurability in Organisation Studies", paper presented at the Academy of Management annual meeting, Boston, Mass., Aug. 1997.

SCHNEIDER, D.: "Unternehmensethik und Gewinnprinzip in der Betriebswirtschaftslehre", *Zeitschrift für Betriebswirtschaftliche Forschung*, 42 (1990), pp. 869-891.

SCHREYÖGG, G., STEINMANN, H.: "Strategic Control. A New Perspective", *Academy of Management Review*, 12 (1987), pp. 91-103.

CORPORATE ETHICS AND MANAGEMENT THEORY

SIMONS, R.: *Levers of Control – How Managers Use Innovative Control Systems to Drive Strategic Renewal*, Boston, Mass. (Harvard Business School Press) 1995.

SOLOMON, R. C.: "Corporate Roles, Personal Virtues: An Aristotelian Approach to Business Ethics", *Business Ethics Quarterly*, 2 (1992), pp. 317-339.

SPENDER, J.-C.: "Strategic Theorizing: Expanding the Agenda", *Advances in Strategic Management*, 8 (1992), pp. 3-32.

SPENDER, J.-C.: "Villain, Victim or Visionary?: The Insights and Flaws in F. W. Taylor's Ideas", in: J.-C. SPENDER, H. J. KIJNE (Eds.): *Scientific Management. Frederick Winslow Taylor's Gift to the World?* Boston/Dordrecht/London (Kluwer) 1996, pp. 1-31.

STEINMANN, H., KUSTERMANN, B.: "Die Managementlehre auf dem Weg zu einem neuen Steuerungsparadigma", *Journal für Betriebswirtschaft*, 46, No. 5-6 (1996), pp. 265-281.

STEINMANN, H., KUSTERMANN, B.: "Management Theory on the Way to a New Paradigm? Critical Reflections on the Concept of Robert Simons", in: S. URBAN (Ed.): *Europe's Economic Future*, Wiesbaden (Gabler) (in print).

STEINMANN, H., LÖHR, A.: *Grundlagen der Unternehmensethik*, Stuttgart (Poeschel) 2nd ed. 1994.

STEINMANN, H., LÖHR, A.: "A Republican Concept of Corporate Ethics", in S. URBAN (Ed.): *Europe's Challenges. Economic Efficiency and Social Solidarity*, Wiesbaden (Gabler) 1996, pp. 21-60.

STEINMANN, H., OLBRICH, TH.: "Business Ethics in U.S.-Corporations. Some Preliminary Results from an Interview Series", *Journal für Betriebswirtschaft*, 45 (1995), pp. 317-334.

STEINMANN, H., OLBRICH, TH.: "Ethik-Management: Integrierte Steuerung ethischer und ökonomischer Prozesse", in: G. BLICKLE (Ed.): *Ethik in Organisationen*, Göttingen (Verlag für angewandte Phsychologie) 1998, pp. 95-115.

STEINMANN, H., SCHERER, A. G.: "Lernen durch Argumentieren: Theoretische Probleme konsensorientierten Handelns", in: ALBACH, H. (Ed.). *Globale Soziale Marktwirtschaft. Ziele – Wege – Akteure. Festschrift für Santiago Garcia Echevaria*, Wiesbaden (Gabler) 1994, pp. 263-285.

STEINMANN, H., SCHERER, A. G.: "Corporate Ethics and Global Business. Philosophical Considerations on Intercultural Management", in: B. N. KUMAR, H. STEINMANN (Eds.): *Ethics in International Business*, Berlin/New York (De Gruyter) 1998, pp. 13-46.

STEINMANN, H., SCHERER, A. G.: "Interkulturelles Management zwischen Universalismus und Relativismus. Kritische Anfragen der Betriebswirtschaftslehre an die Philosophie", in: H. STEINMANN, A. G. SCHERER (Eds.): *Zwischen Universalismus und Relativismus. Philosophische Grundlagenprobleme des Interkulturellen Managements*, Frankfurt a. M. (Suhrkamp) 1999, pp. 23-87.

191

HORST STEINMANN AND ANDREAS GEORG SCHERER

STEINMANN, H., SCHREYÖGG, G.: *Management. Grundlagen der Unternehmensführung*, Wiesbaden (Gabler) 4th ed. 1997.
STEINMANN, H., ZERFAβ, A.: "Privates Unternehmertum und öffentliches Interesse", in: G. R. WAGNER (Ed.): *Betriebswirtschaft und Umweltschutz*, Stuttgart (Schäffer-Poeschel) 1993, pp. 3-26.
STONE, CH. D.: *Where the Law Ends*, New York (Harper and Row) 1975.
SUMMERS, R. S., CLERMONT, K. M., HILLMAN, R. A., JOHNSON, S. L., BARCELO, J. J. III, PROVONE, D. M.: *Law: Its Nature, Functions, and Limits*, St. Paul (West Publishing) 3rd ed. 1986.
THUROW, L. C.: *The Future of Capitalism. How Today's Economic Forces Shape Tomorrow's World*, New York (William Morrow & Co) 1996.
ULRICH, P.: *Transformation der ökonomischen Vernunft. Fortschrittsperspektiven der modernen Industriegesellschaft*, Bern/Stuttgart (Haupt) 1976.
ULRICH, P.: *Integrative Wirtschaftsethik. Grundlagen einer lebensdienlichen Ökonomie*, Stuttgart/Wien (Haupt) 1997.
U.S. DEPARTMENT OF COMMERCE: Model Business Principles, *New York Times*, May 27, 1995, p. 17, http://www.depaul.edu/ethics/principles.html
U.S. DEPARTMENT OF STATE: Promoting the Model Business Principles, *Publication 10486*, Released June 1997, Bureau of Democracy, Human Rights and Labour, http://www.state.gov/www/global/human rights/business principles.html
WARREN, B.: *Imperialism: Pioneer of Capitalism*, London (NLB) 1980.
YAEGER, P. C.: *The Limits of Law. Public Regulation of Private Pollution*, Cambridge (Cambridge University Press) 1991.

M14 A13

Chapter 8

Business Ethics and Discourse Ethics: Germanic Roots with Intercultural Applications

WARREN FRENCH AND STEFAN KIMMELL

Business conflicts are not always centred on the quest for market share, competitive growth or return on investment. As we increasingly globalise our transactions, personal values and, especially, cultural values will be at the core of business conflict (Huntington 1993). Is there a viable way to resolve moral conflicts resulting from business transactions which span nation state borders? Three options come to mind. The first is to adopt the adage: "When in Rome do as the Romans do." But, this does not always sit well with social critics at home. The second option is a type of moral imperialism which centres on persuading the other party to succumb to your values. This option appears to underpin the US's Foreign Corrupt Practices Act. Even when supported by an economic power base, moral imperialism, as pointed out by Claud Levi-Strauss (1988), has its pitfalls. The third option is grounded on rational argumentation and embodied in the theory on discourse ethics. Discourse ethics as proposed by Lorenzen (1987) and (Habermas 1990) has possibilities, but does the theory travel well when it leaves the Frankfurt-Erlangen region of Germany?

This paper examines discourse ethics in order to evaluate its potential application in cross cultural business transactions. Emphasis will be placed on the results of empirical tests to determine if and under what conditions discourse ethics can attain its objectives as a procedure for conflict resolution. If the results prove positive, a more business basic question can be answered: "Where does business ethics belong?"

I. Business Ethics as a Social Science

Over the centuries the focus of ethics has been on moral principles which enhance societal well-being. That focus, though, has continually evoked one question. Which moral principles should hold sway? At times it has appeared that each moral philosopher of stature had posited a set of moral principles that were somewhat different from those presented by his predecessors.

Given this history, the study of business ethics has been viewed by some scholars with scepticism. Social scientists, including those in the business disciplines, note that ethics as a subject of study has been traditionally housed in the "humanities" or "arts" departments within a university. Just because the descriptive adjective, business, has been applied as a modifier to the word, ethics, it does not bestow legitimacy on the subject for inclusion as part of a social science curriculum.

Cultural anthropologists question whether the pursuit of universal cultural values, upon which traditional business ethics are based, is feasible. Economists, in turn, claim that market forces and the invisible hand of free competition serve as regulators to ensure that societal well-being is enhanced. If the invisible hand appears to have arthritis, to the point that business practices harm societal well-being, economists explain that "in the long run" these practices will be eliminated.

A benchmark treatise in moral philosophy, which changed the existing paradigm for business ethics, was offered by Kurt Baier (1965). Baier proposed that a meaningful treatment of morality should focus on conflict resolution. Baier viewed ethics as a system of guidelines for conduct which is conducive to societal well-being. The study of such guidelines changes the focus of ethics from an art obsessed with principles to that of a social science centred on applying guidelines. Baier's proposition has been adopted by psychologists such as James Rest who claims "the function of morality is to provide basic guidelines for determining how conflicts in human interests are to be settled and for optimising mutual benefits of people living together in groups" (Rest 1986).

Giving support, as well as grounding for Baier's proposition, a group of theoreticians from Germanic speaking countries have offered a framework for resolving moral conflicts, including those occurring in a business setting. What Habermas and other proponents of discourse ethics, such as Apel, Lorenzen and Kambartel have given business ethics is a basis for legitimacy among social scientists.

Thomas Kuhn's (1962) work paved the way for the Erlangen school to claim that science could be grounded on reasoning (the consensus theory of truth) rather than on empirical, objective phenomena (the correspondence theory of truth) (Lorenzen 1968). Their constructivist approach may prove especially appropriate for applying ethical norms across cultures.

This approach, though, does not preclude the traditional steps of the scientific method, i.e., problem statement and hypothesis testing. Rather, the constructivist approach calls attention to the context in which problems occur and to the influences which affect hypothesis testing. Whether the standards of argumentation toward successful resolution of ethical issues in business are culture invariant is still subject to debate.

This debate influences the structure of the research to be reported in the following sections. Before that, it should first be established if discourse ethics leads to conflict resolution and under what conditions. To address this point, the results of natural versus guided discussion - an argumentation process in which there is an overt attempt to uncover the presuppositions (Apel 1986) of parties involved in a conflict over an ethical issue - are reported. Guided discussion, given the admonition by Steinmann (1996) that final values should not be the starting point for argumentation, relies on revealed shared values only as a validation for the soundness of a resolution to conflict arrived at through discourse/argumentation. Only then can second question be dealt with: "Are shared values necessary to resolve moral conflicts through discourse?" The following three studies provide partial answers to the concerns about discourse ethics.

II. Tests of Discourse Ethics

Habermas (1976) claimed that an individual's level of moral reasoning parallels the type of communication which that individual uses in attempts to resolve conflict. We tested that claim by comparing the style of communication (Kurtines and Pollard 1989) which discussants used to resolve a moral dilemma regarding workplace safety to the level of moral reasoning (Rest 1979) attributed to the discussants. Propositions were advanced predicting a greater use of discursive communication by those gauged to be capable of post conventional moral reasoning, and a greater use of strategic communication by those gauged to operate at the conventional level of moral reasoning.

Neither of these propositions could be supported by the tests (French and Allbright 1998). It appeared that those gauged to be capable of higher moral reasoning viewed changes to their positions as prostitution of their original values rather than as part of a constructivist effort to establish common norms. In turn, those gauged to be operating at the conventional level of moral reasoning appeared to sense no competitive advantage or leverage to be gained by strategic communication while discussing a moral issue with individuals whom they judged as equal peers.

When conflict resolution was attained by the discussants, as it was in about 50% of the cases, it was based on expediency, not on shared norms, let alone the construction of new norms. Ironically, in two-thirds of the discussions, the parties in conflict shared at least one common value, but made no overt effort to base a resolution on that value. As a mitigating factor, though, it should be mentioned that each of the discussants came from a culture in which pragmatic results are prized while theoretical justifications are, at best, an afterthought. A secondary conclusion drawn from this research was that Habermas' theory of discourse ethics requires a more detailed instruction manual for proactive implementation if it is to be of use to business - especially with respect to intercultural operations.

We then conducted a second study using a guided discourse protocol based on Habermas' theory (Kurtines and Pollard 1989). Taking into consideration Lorenzen's (1987) and Kambartel's (1987) concerns about culture's effects on norms, our study contrasted the efforts to resolve moral conflicts between individuals within the same culture versus individuals from different cultures. Propositions were advanced predicting a greater probability of resolving moral conflicts when using guided discourse procedures and when discussing the issue with an individual from the same culture rather than with an individual from a different culture. Two moral issues were the subject of argumentation, one related to stealing in order to help another person in need, and the second related to appropriate punishment for the theft.

The results of this second study lend strong support to the viability of discourse ethics (French and Mülfriedel 1996). Guided discourse, based on Habermas' structure, resulted in successful conflict resolution in 19 of 20 discussions. The one failure was between parties from different cultures. More important to the theory of discourse ethics, 80% of guided discussions resulted in new positions which were grounded upon mutually constructed values that were different from those which underpinned the parties' original positions. Three of the four failures to ground the new position on constructed, mutually shared norms resulted from discussions in which the parties came from different cultures.

It was interesting to note, while acknowledging the dangers of stereotyping, that some of the cultures represented by the discussants seem to prize norms of obligation while other cultures prized utilitarian calculations. This may be the *caveat* that Lorenzen and Kambartel warned about in the conduct of discourse ethics. This puts more stress on two of Habermas' preconditions for successful discourse - that all data relevant to moral issue be presented by the parties in conflict as well as the necessity for mutual comprehension of not only terms but the values behind those terms.

Given Lorenzen's and Kambartel's previously mentioned concerns, a third study was conducted using a different analytical procedure. The genesis of the research came from the work of Ferdinand Tönnies (1957) who wrote about the ethical dimensions of the relationship between individual and society. Both Hall (1981) and Hofstede (1991) report that how people discuss problems is strongly influenced by whether they come from individualist or collectivist cultures.

Propositions were advanced predicting that individuals from low communication context cultures would use more ego centred and confrontational discussion tactics than would individuals from high communication context cultures when they argued about a moral issue. The issue discussed was lying so as to prevent mental anguish in the listener (Kurtines and Pollard 1989). This issue relates to Habermas' precondition of truthfulness in moral discourse. The classification system for "verbal transacts" used in moral

197

discussions was created by Berkowitz and Gibbs (1983) with a grant funded by Kohlberg.

Neither of the propositions bore up under scrutiny (French and Kimmell 1997). These results, though, should not be viewed as evidence that there are no intercultural obstacles to the use of discourse ethics. In 90% of the discussions, no resolution was reached when arguing the moral issue. The low context subjects, using linear deductive logic, showed little appreciation for the holistic, intuitive thinking (Piagaet 1965) that appeared to underlie the arguments of the high context subjects. In a matched sample with individuals from the same culture arguing the same issue, 50% of the discussions ended with a resolution, but not as the result of constructing a mutually shared norm. What also proved interesting was that in each discussion pairing, involving individuals from low and high communication context cultures, the high context culture subjects chose not to tell the truth. They did not dismiss the value of honesty out of hand but relegated truthfulness to a secondary position behind the norm of not harming a friend. This prioritising of values was consistent across high context subjects from China, Korea, Turkey and India.

What the three aforementioned studies reveal is that discourse can lead to perceived resolution of moral conflict, that guided discourse is more successful than unguided discourse and that intercultural discourse does have its problems. If Habermas' four preconditions for successful discourse are viewed as vital for successful discourse, were the irreconciliations in those studies due to problems of comprehension, truth and/or truthfulness? In hindsight, it is easy to say "yes," but perhaps a slightly different perspective of the standards for discourse ethics than that of Habermas should be investigated.

III. Culture and Sociomoral Discourse

What has been labelled discourse ethics as an approach to resolving business problems with moral implications is termed sociomoral discussion by developmental psychologists (Keller and Reuss 1985). Fritz Oser (1981) in his study of sociomoral argumentation, found that sociomoral discussions could be classified on two dimensions - levels of interaction and levels of communication compactness. This taxonomy bears some resemblance to the one used by Habermas (1976), which matches stages of moral reasoning to communication acts.

Based on the works of Oser, Keller and Reuss as well as on other studies in developmental psychology, Berkowitz, Oser and Althof (1987) have outlined a framework for sociomoral discussion which comprises six stages. We integrated (Exhibit 1) Kurtines' application of Habermas' levels of communicative action into those six stages to analyse the components of successful discourse. Then using Kambartel's (1984) conditions for rationality and Keller and Reuss' (1985) rules for moral discourse we gathered data to investigate the question posed earlier: "Are the standards of argumentation toward successful resolution of ethical issues in business culture invariant?"

IV. A Pilot Study

To bring evidence to the dispute about culture invariant standards for successful discourse ethics two propositions were advanced:

P1. Resolution of a moral conflict in business through discourse requires apparent transsubjectivity on the part of both parties.

P2. Resolution of a moral conflict in business requires the same standards for intercultural discourse as for intracultural discourse.

The sample for the investigation included 40 subjects, half of whom were paired with individuals from their own country. The remaining subjects were paired with individuals from other countries (Table 1). All subjects possessed university degrees and had returned to a university setting for advanced business training. None of the subjects had knowledge of writings on discourse ethics.

The subjects were paired according to opposite views on an issue regarding a fair day's pay, presented so as to encourage moral discourse (Kurtines and Pollard 1989). The issue entailed paying two friends who had done some voluntary work an equal amount or an unequal amount based on one friend's family needs. Each pair in the intercultural group mirrored a matching pair, according to gender and moral reasoning as measured by Rest's (1979) DIT, in the intracultural group.

The subjects were given a tape recorder and audio tape to record their discussions on the issue. They were then instructed to seclude themselves sometime in the next two weeks and attempt to reconcile their positions. They were also told that a "no resolution" result was acceptable as long as a good faith effort was made to reconcile positions.

Two judges from different cultures analysed the taped negotiations. Discussion statements were classified according to the taxonomy outlined in Exhibit 1. All differences in classification were reconciled by jointly reviewing the tapes. The results as summarised in Table 1 were as follows.

The judges determined from the taped dialogues that three of Friedrich Kambartel's (1984) conditions for satisfying the discourse principle of rationality had been met. That is: 1) the parties were "sincere and mutually transparent in their orientations and arguments", 2) there was "absence of external sanctioning", and 3) there was a "symmetry of positions" in the discourse situation as to the rules accepted by the participants. Likewise, the judges believed that Monika Keller's and Siegfried Reuss' (1985) rules for moral discourse had been abided by. That is, the parties were free to express personal corrections as well as criticise the moral arguments of each other. The degree to which each party respected the orientations and arguments of the other negotiator is another matter. The empathy that Kambartel, Keller and Reuss believe is necessary for discursive moral decision making was not always apparent when listening to the discussions. Nor did the parties distance themselves from their personal biases.

Ninety percent of both the intercultural and intracultural discussions resulted in what the parties believed was a resolution. Fifty percent of the discussions resulted in resolutions that made limited use of the stages of sociomoral discussion. Those results showed one party accepting the reasoning of the other party and reordering the personal value of equity into a secondary position. In each of these cases, the levels of discourse showed minimal transsubjectivity. The mutual acceptance of applied values, let alone abstract values, appeared non-existent. But, efficacy of those resolutions is suspect. If the conceding parties had to report as a representative to a larger group who also were motivated by the value of equity, would the larger group have made the same concessions? The lack of reasoned argumentation in the discussions would cause doubts about such an acceptance.

More disturbing are the results of the 40% of both intercultural and intracultural discussions that resulted in a new position. A majority of those discussions embodied shared facts but not shared values. In no case was

200

Stage 5, Ideal Discourse, reached. While there was some transsubjectivity of values in those discussions, it was quite limited. Yet, those resolutions stood a good chance of being accepted as both feasible and ethical by third parties.

In brief, the standards for successful discourse about and ethical issue in business, as applied by the parties in conflict, appeared limited, situational and pragmatic both within and between cultures. This observation brings to the surface a variation of the issue at hand. Perhaps, the focus should be less on the culture invariance of standards of argumentation and more on just what standards are necessary (*sine qua non*).

V. Preliminary Conclusions

In his desire to posit universal prescriptions with respect to discourse ethics, Habermas seems to have overestimated the strength of the relationship between his communicative interaction process and Kohlberg's stages of moral development. The parallel which Habermas posits follows from the descriptions which both he and Kohlberg ascribe to their respective levels of communication and moral development (meeting the definition of the coherence theory of truth). The problems with this parallel reside in Kohlberg's taxonomy. In a majority of the world's cultures, apart from the northern parts of North America and Europe, Kohlberg's Stage 3 is considered just as advanced a stage of moral reasoning as is Stage 5 (Vine 1985). Also, while businesspeople may be capable of and show signs of postconventional moral development/judgement they can and do revert back to conventional and even preconventional moral reasoning in times of stress (Krebs 1991).

In fact, Rest (1979) has found that most people normally make decisions at the conventional level of moral reasoning. Perhaps, that explains why the subjects in the four tests reported earlier in this paper shied away from Stage 5 of sociomoral discussion (Ideal Discourse). However, even those whose test scores indicated a capacity to reason at the postconventional level seem to operate at the conventional level.

A more important issue is the degree to which ethical discourse depends on the standards of reasoned argumentation that have been suggested by authors such as Kambartel, Habermas and Keller and Reuss. Perhaps, not as much as originally hypothesised. One of the conditions for rational argumentation, in particular, may be absent from many business discussions over ethical conflicts - that of freedom from external sanctions and coercive power.

The presence of such power does not necessarily squash moral discourse. That power can be counterbalanced by the "weaker" party taking the lead in guiding moral discourse. This is in line with Luhmann's (1979) concept that power simply serves to guide the selection of actions by the other person. Power, according to Luhmann, can be used constructively, and why not within a constructed world of meaning in which the parties jointly create and limit the possibilities of different actions. The use of guided discourse in such a manner can be successful, as evidenced in the study by French and Mühlfriedel (1996). The use of guided discourse also goes farther in meeting the goals of Ideal Discourse than does nonguided discourse. Discourse ethics can and does work.

One result from the pilot study conducted for this paper was that ethical decisions could be arrived at (in the eyes of the conflicting parties) with limited transsubjectivity by a new shared position that did not entail a new emerging shared value. This result coincides with the theory recently offered by Robert van Es (1996) under the guidance of Henk van Luijk. Van Es diagrams a minimal threshold that must be met when evaluating options for action so that the action can be deemed ethical. Above that threshold are other options which approach the ultimate level of consensus which he equates to Habermas' Ideal Discourse. His threshold level approximates Stage 4C in Exhibit 1.

Is the practical course of action then to abandon Ideal Discourse and satisfy minimum conditions? Not necessarily! The closer we move toward Ideal Discourse and the conditions that depict it, the better we can defend ourselves from critics who claim that we have compromised our values or have not maximised the potential for enhancing societal well-being. In some situations, given the natures of the parties in conflict and their lack of awareness of the procedures for and standards of discourse ethics, the minimum threshold may be the best that can be attained. For those who are aware of not only the possibilities of discourse ethics but also the limits of human nature in the pursuit of Ideal Discourse, the words attributed to the observer of Chinese culture, Pearl Buck, should be kept in mind: "ideals are like the stars; we can never hope to reach them but like a good mariner we plot our course by them".

VI. The Future

Philosophers such as Apel and Habermas have proposed a communication ethics theory which we could label a grand scale theory. Like all grand scale theories, it has received its share of both constructive and destructive criticism (Benhabib 1990). But, the use of discourse ethics to resolve moral conflicts in business does not depend on how grand the scale is but on its applicability to individual ethical issues. We should not ask for a theory that enables us to leap over rivers of moral turbulence when what business needs is a theory which helps them step around ethical mud puddles. We must keep in mind that discourse ethics is a proceduralist theory. It is strongest when it focuses on the resolution of individual conflicts. It is weakest when it delves into universal norms. Its premises have been laid. Now it is time for empirical testing to test, articulate and perhaps modify the theory.

Van Es (1996) has suggested that the success of the discursive resolution of ethical conflicts can be predicated on four negotiation styles which, suspiciously, mirror Kohlberg's stages of moral development. He further states that compromises, based on reciprocity, can produce ethical results. If Apel and Habermas demand too much from the theory, perhaps, Van Es asks too little from it. Inductive testing of discourse ethics has shown that more than compromise and reciprocity is possible (French and Mühlfriedel 1996). The procedure for guided argumentation outlined in Exhibit 2 has been able to lead to consensus rather than just to compromise. That procedure, in turn, is by no means definitive.

Since discourse ethics is a proceduralist theory, time can be well spent articulating that procedure. What is the next step? The discourse ethics processes suggested independently by Berkowitz, Oser and Althof (1987) Noam (1985) and Kurtines and Pollard (1989) merit particular attention. A melding of their processes may not only provide us with a discursive procedure that leads to a consensual resolution based on shared values, but also provide evidence as to the existence of frequently shared values which transcend national borders. From that evidence we may draw sounder conclusions about the possibility of evolved universal norms.

Exhibit 1
Stages of Sociomoral Discussion*

Stage 0 Pre-argumentation	State own position. Resolutions grounded on power. Justify only when asked; Justifications idiosyncratic/irrelevant. Manipulation, intimidation, deception, personal attacks.
Stage 1 Single Reason Argumentation	Personal, experiential, pragmatic justification. State facts/observations/assumptions. Nongeneralizable value; no abstract values. Inadequate consideration of Alter's perspective.
Stage 2A Maintaining Connections	Generalizable values. Identify weakness in own position/values. Identify similarities between positions/values. No solution based on shared positions/values. Seek/Acknowledge Alter's Position/vales. Ego must attempt to generalise values.
Stage 2B Reflection on Facts	Ego shows understanding of Alter's factual justification of Alter's position.
Stage 2C Reflection on Values	Ego shows understanding of Alter's principles or the value. Justification which underlies Alter's position.
Stage 3 Counter-Evidence	Ego attempts to find faults with Alter's argumentation. Ego defends against Alter's critiques. Differentiate "is" versus "ought." Adversarial but based on logic. Stress differences over similarities.

* Modification of a model proposed by BERKOWITZ, OSER & ALTHOF (1987, pp. 337-347).

Stage 4A Shared Analysis	Establish a new shared mutual understanding of the facts through integration of old facts or construction of new facts.
Stage 4B Shared Analysis	Establish a new shared mutual understanding of principles underlying the facts through the integration of old principles or the construction of mutually acceptable new principles.
Stage 4C Shared Analysis	Establish a new shared position based on a new mutual understanding of the facts while holding original principles.
Stage 4D Shared Analysis	Establish a new shared position. This position has to be mutually accepted as both true (matching shared facts) and right (matching shared principles).
Stage 5 Ideal Discourse	Establish the most just solution by testing for reason, objectivity, generalisability, consistency while recognising personal fallibility.

Exhibit 2
Negotiating Moral Conflicts

Sequential Steps	Major Obstacles
1. Each party states a personal position on the issue	Miscomprehension Complexity of the issue
2. Each party presents reasoning as well as the underlying principles that validate the personal position	Held-back information Less than complete honesty
3. Each party paraphrases the other party's position, principles, and the reasoning that links them	Failure to empathise Organisational pressures/expectations
4. Each party explains why the other party's position conflicts with one's own personal principles	Adversarial rather than critical explanations Failure to look for similarities as well as differences
5. Each party explores: • Alternative positions which do not violate the other party's stated personal principles, or • Each party explores for unstated principles that are mutually held. Then alternative positions are derived from the previously unstated principle(s)	Failure to abandon original position Transformation of principles into ordered rules
6. Alternative positions are tested against four normative guidelines to resolve conflict so as to enhance societal well-being	Weighing cost vs. Benefits Defining universalizability from narrow perspective
7. Implementation of appropriate alternative agreed-upon position	Failure to inform and/or implement

WARREN FRENCH AND STEFAN KIMMELL

Table 1
Discussion over Fair Day's Pay

Country	esult	esolutio	Highest Discussion Stage Used	Values		ountry	esult	Resolution	Values
El Salvador	CP	Gift	2C	Equity		USA	JR	Loan	Equity
USA	PP		2C	Friendship		USA	JR		Golden Rule
Japan	CP	Gift	2C	Equity		USA	JR	Advance	Equity
Denmark	PP		2C	Compassion		USA	JR	Pay	Altruism
France	CP	Gift	2B	Equity		USA	PP	Gift	Friendship
USA	PP		1	Compassion		USA	CP		Equity
France	JR	Loan	4D	Equity		USA	JR	Loan	Beneficence
USA	JR		4C	Compassion		USA	JR		Equity
France	JR	Loan	4C	Equity		USA	JR	Owner	Equity
USA	JR		4C	Utilitarianis		USA	JR	Pays	(no value)
France	JR	Loan	4C	Friendship		USA	PP	Gift	Compassion
USA	JR		4C	Equity		USA	CP		Equity
France	CP	Gift	2B	Equity		USA	NR	None	Equity
USA	PP		1	Compassion		USA	NR		Golden Rule
France	NR	None	2A	Friendship		USA	PP	Gift	Compassion
USA	NR		2A	Equity		USA	CP		Equity
France	CP	Equal	2C	Utilitarian		USA	PP	Gift	Friendship
USA	PP	Pay	2A	Equity		USA	CP		Equity
Argentina	JR	Loan	4C	Compassion		USA	PP	Gift	Beneficence
USA	JR		4C	Equity		USA	CP		Equity

*No resolution = NR, Prevailing Party = PP, Conceding Party = CP, Joint Resolution = JR

References

APEL, K-O.: "Grenzen der Diskwisethik? Versuch einer Zwischenbilanz", *Zeitschrift für philosophische Forschung*, 40 (1986), pp. 3-31.
BAIER, K.: *The Moral Point of View: A Rational Basis of Ethics*, New York (Random House) 1965.

207

BENHABIB, S.: "Communicative Ethics and Current Controversies in Philosophy", in: S. BENHABIB and F. DALLYMAR (Eds.): *The Communicative Ethics Controversy*, Cambridge (MIT Press) 1990.

BERKOWITZ, M., GIBBS, J.: "Measuring the Developmental Features of Moral Discussion", *Merrill-Palmer Quarterly*, 29 (1983), pp. 399-410.

BERKOWITZ, M., OSER, F., ALTHOF, W.: "The Development of Sociomoral Discourse", in: W. M. KURTINES, J. GEWIRTZ (Eds.): *Moral Development Through Social Interaction*, New York (John Wiley & Sons) 1987.

FRENCH, W., ALLBRIGHT, D.: "Resolving a Moral Conflict Though Discourse", *Journal of Business Ethics*, forthcoming 1998.

FRENCH, W., KIMMEL, S.: "Intercultural Discourse Ethics: Value and Communication Problems", in: M. BOHATÀ (Ed.): *Proceedings of the 10th Annual EBEN Conference*, Prague 1997.

FRENCH, W., MÜHFRIEDEL, B.: "Discourse Instead of Recourse", in: A. LÖHR (Ed.): *Proceedings of the 9th Annual EBEN Conference*, Seeheim, 1996.

HABERMAS, J.: *Communication and the Evolution of Society*, Boston (Beacon Press) 1976.

HABERMAS, J.: *Moral Consciousness and Communicative Action*, Cambridge (MIT Press) 1990.

HALL, E. T.: *Beyond Culture*, New York (Anchor Books - Doubleday) 1981.

HOFSTEDE, G.: *Culture and Organizations: Software of the Mind*, London (McGraw-Hill) 1991.

HUNTINGTON, S.: "The Clash of Civilizations", *Foreign Affairs*, 72 (1993), pp. 22-49.

KAMBARTEL, F.: "The Grammatical Culture of Reason", *Working Paper*, May 1984.

KAMBARTEL, F.: "Vernunft: Kriterium oder Kultur? - Zur Definierbarkeit des Vernünftigen," in: F. KAMBARTEL (Ed.): *Philosophic der humanen Welt*, Frankfurt/M (Surkamp) 1987.

KELLER, M., REUSS, S.: "The Process of Moral Decision Making: Normative and Empirical Conditions of Participation in Moral Discourse", in: M. BERKOWITZ, F. OSER (Eds.): *Moral Education: Theory and Application*, Hillsdale, NJ (Erlbaum) 1985.

KREBS, D., VERMEULEN, S., CARPENDALE, J., DENTON, K.: "Structural and Situational Influences on Moral Judgement: The Interaction Between Stage and Dilemma", in: W. KURTINES, J. GEWIRTZ (Eds.): *Handbook of Moral Behavior and Development V.2*, Hillsdale, NJ (Lawrence Erlbaum Associates) 1991.

KUHN, T.: *The Structure of Scientific Revolution*, Chicago (University of Chicago Press) 1962.

Kurtines, W. M., Pollard, S. R.: "The Communicative Functioning Scale - Critical Discussion Manual", *Working Paper*, Miami (Florida International University Department of Psychology) 1989.

LEVI-STRAUSS, C., ERIBON, D.: *De pres et de loin*, Paris (Editions Odile Jacob) 1988.

LORENZEN, P.: "Methodical Thinking", in: P. LORENZEN: *Constructive Philosophy*, Amherst, MA (University of Massachusetts Press) 1968.

LORENZEN, P.: *Lehrbuch der konstructiven Wissenschaftstheorie*, Mannheim (Bibliographisches Insitute) 1987.

LUHMANN, N.: *Trust and Power*, New York (John Wiley & Sons) 1979.

NOAM, G.: "Stage, Phase and Style: The Developmental Dynamics of Self", in: M. BERKOWITZ, F. OSER, F. (Eds.): *Moral Education: Theory and Application*, Hillsdale, NJ (Lawrence Erlbaum) 1985.

OSER, F.: *Moralisches Urteil in Gruppen*, Frankfurt/M (Surkamp) 1981.

PIAGAET, J.: *The Moral Judgement of the Child*, New York (Free Press) 1965. (First published in 1932.)

REST, J. R.: *Developments in Judging Moral Issues*, Minneapolis (University of Minnesota Press) 1979.

STEINMANN, H., LÖHR, A.: "A Republican Concept of Corporate Ethics", in: S. URBAN (Ed.): *Europe's Challenges. Economic Efficiency and Social Solidarity*, Wiesbaden (Gabler) 1996.

TÖNNIES, F.: *Community and Society*, New York (Harper & Row) 1957. (First published in 1887.)

VAN ES, R.: *Negotiating Ethics*, Delft (Eburon) 1996.

VINE, I.: "Moral Maturity in Socio-Cultural Perspective", in: S. MODGIL, C. MODGIL (Eds.): *Lawrence Kohlberg: Consensus and Controversy*, London (Falmer Press) 1985.

210- 28

M14

Chapter 9

Business Ethics and Management

HARTMUT KREIKEBAUM

I. Introduction

In its best tradition historism has always focused on the whole set of cultural, institutional, and economic constraints on decision-making. A second basic issue has been the development of a pragmatic attitude towards the theory of the firm. Entrepreneurial decisions undergo a basic learning process regarding the development of a company in the past with a future-oriented viewpoint. It is this pragmatic attitude which integrates an intelligent analysis of past failures and achievements into an overall picture of the future. The main task of management is thinking ahead, which includes basic missions, long-term strategies, and well-defined actions. To survive in the long run, managers must serve the present needs of the market.

The art of entrepreneurial decision-making is constantly undergoing change and requires the continuous development of new responsibilities. Empirical studies reveal that young businessmen are looking for new concepts of meaning and try to justify their day-to-day decisions. This would mean that they emphasise the moral and ethical ramifications of business. Young adults, e.g., tend to have a strong sense of interpersonal accountability and trustworthiness regarding face-to-face situations with colleagues and superiors (Daloz Parks 1993).

Therefore, management education must be more than the transfer of professional skills. It should also pass on the wisdom about responsible moral commitment in complex organisational decisions from one generation to the next. The educational trilogy of values, knowledge and skills has to be rebalanced by placing leadership, ethics, and corporate responsibility at the centre of teaching.

This article deals with the integration of ethical principles in managerial decisions. It considers the necessity to link ethical attitudes with the specific conditions (personnel, organisation, culture) in a company. Ethical attitudes are not only a question of assessing the consequences of decisions and actions, it also means to assume personal responsibility. It is necessary to implement ethical standards which can be applied to problems and critical incidents. This includes the discussion of the inherent reasons, the possibilities of solving conflicts and their evaluation. It also means to develop a more efficient decision-making process considering the economic as well as the ethical point of view.

II. Moral Aspects of Managerial Decision-Making

1. Terms and Definitions

The core of business ethics rests on the analysis of the values of company members and their reflection within the wide spectrum of possible decisions. In general, values derive from the interdependency between the firm, politics and society. This description of business ethics implies that corporate decisions are always aligned with certain criteria and influenced by a specific moral. The moral element is considered to be an integral part of the decision process itself (*Vernunftethik*) and not just a supplement to rational decision-making. Consequently, business ethics includes three significant aspects:

1. Basic attitudes and norms of company members are fundamental for ethical reflection. These attitudes and norms must be reflected in a critical manner. In this context it is important to realise that the norms and values of the top-management are of central significance for the decision-making processes of the firm. Nevertheless, ethical reflection has a binding character for all organisation members, thus including all employees.

2. Institutionalised values of a company are regarded to be a matter of business ethics. Apart from the moral attitudes of individuals, the company as an entity can provide an ethical code of conduct which determines the decisions of business units and individual decision makers. Obviously interdependent links between individual values and institutionalised corporate norms are existent.

3. In an open society as the present a company is permanently in contact with numerous external institutions and persons that are considered to be stakeholders. This heterogeneous group includes governments and communities, customers, suppliers, agents of the industrial relations system as well as citizen initiatives. Responding to the values of these stakeholders is regarded as an imperative task for any firm.

2. The Need for and Possibility of Ethical Action

Life in a pluralistic society is characterised by the existence of a diversity of fundamental moral principles, which are no longer valid for all its members, as well as by numerous conflicts. Naturally, these conflicts influence not only the relationships of decision makers within a firm but also the corporate decisions affecting external institutions. The resulting ethical dilemma often requires "tough decisions" (Toffler 1986). The situation in which an individual is forced to decide whether to act on the basis of egoistical opportunism or altruism, is defined as an intrapersonal conflict. Disputes between superiors and their subordinates can be regarded as a typical expression of intrapersonal conflicts. They result either from differences in the role understanding or from the opportunistic desire to extend the personal power. Situations, in which the values of individuals or groups collide with the values of their organisation or with those of external institutions, are defined as intraorganisational or interorganisational conflicts.

BUSINESS ETHICS AND MANAGEMENT

Business ethics as a discipline reflects critical decisions of a firm and its members. The focus lies on the normative elements of corporate decisions. Per definition every framework of regulations is incomplete and unable to regulate all possible events. Business ethics fulfils here a supplementing function in which the existent deficits of a framework are absorbed and possibly changed (Homann 1992). The methodological framework of business ethics is visualised below (cf. Kreikebaum 1996, also for the following figures).

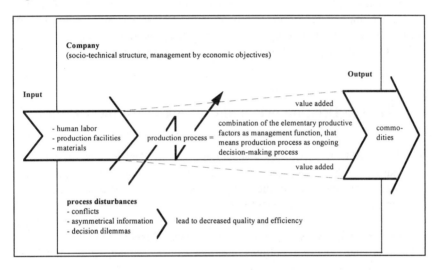

Figure 1: Methodological frame of business ethics.

According to the author's opinion business ethics must be directed towards the decision-making processes of corporate managers. This process will certainly be frictional and constantly interfered by conflicts, asymmetrically distributed information and decision dilemmas. The objectives of business ethics can therefore be summarised as follows:

- Solving conflicts resulting from differences between individual values and corporate objectives by intensifying the identification of organisation members with their corporation and integrating individual objectives into company actions as a reciprocal relationship.

- Increasing the efficiency of corporate decision-making processes by harmonising internal assent.

- Integrating all objectives in accordance with strategic imperatives into the corporate decision-making process in the sense of thinking towards ultimate objectives (*Denken vom Ende her*) (Kreikebaum 1988).

Analogous to "integrative economic ethics" (*integrative Wirtschafts-ethik*) (Ulrich 1997), business ethics also supports the critical analysis of all economic matters and provides proposals for ethical norms. Its subject is to critically accompany all corporate decisions with the aim of integrating their effects into the decision-making process from the very beginning.

III. The Decision-oriented Concept of Business Ethics

The ethical dimension of managerial strategic decisions is reflected in the nature of these decisions. In contrast to day-to-day routine decisions, strategic decisions relate to the company as an entirety. They are of significant importance for a successful market presence and cannot be delegated to other decision makers within company borders. Due to the widespread consequences it seems imperative for decision makers to act responsibly. The following diagram outlines the mechanism leading from individual ethical reflection to corporate success:

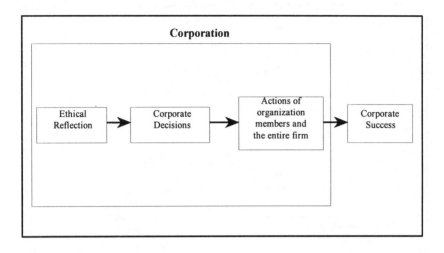

Figure 2: From individual ethical reflection to corporate success.

Material and immaterial values guide corporate decision makers during their decision-making processes. Norms of action can be designed as generally valid or individually obligatory in nature. Every economic action incorporates moral elements, since it is based on fundamental principles. The learning process of enculturation of such values originates during early childhood and adolescence and continues within the different socialisation stages of the decision makers. The interrelation between needs, values and objectives is summarised in the following figure:

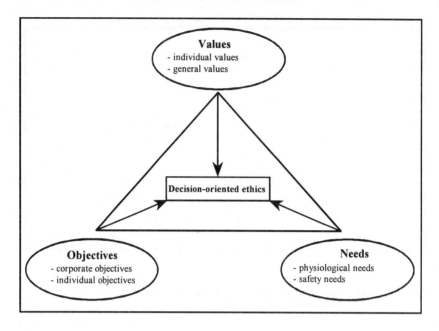

Figure 3: Interrelation between values, needs and objectives.

The concept of decision-oriented ethics is determined by three elements (Kreikebaum 1997, pp. 234-242):

1. Decision-oriented ethics analyses the interrelations between the norms and values of decision makers and the decision-making processes of the firm.

2. Decision-oriented ethics firmly rests on the concept of responsible ethics (*Verantwortungsethik*).

3. Decision-oriented ethics develops possible material norms from a norm-finding process.

BUSINESS ETHICS AND MANAGEMENT

1. The Decision-oriented Concept of Business Ethics in a Descriptive Perspective

Descriptive ethics records empirically the different forms of business moral and improbity. This important task is conducted by means of case studies, qualitative interviews, and statistically representative surveys.

One prominent example of such research is the work of Gellerman who has demonstrated that even "good" managers are liable to make ethically questionable decisions. These executives may deliberately conceal danger-ous effects of manufacturing processes on human safety and health (Geller-man 1986, pp. 85-90). In many instances, corporations are willing to com-pensate for damages rather than removing their underlying non-tolerable causes (*see the documentation of the* Manville Corporation *in* Paine 1995).

Through qualitative interviews it is possible to obtain the real motives of action and to analyse intraindividual conflicts. Representative empirical surveys of top-management representatives must be considered as develop-mental at this rather early stage. First examples of such research work per-formed in German-speaking countries can be found in the Federal Republic of Germany and Switzerland (Kaufmann/Kerber/Zulehner 1986; Ul-rich/Thielemann 1992).

In its descriptive nature, decision-oriented ethics directs itself alongside corporate decision-making processes. In particular, the genuine top-management decisions cannot be separated from the overall personality of the decision maker and from his or her individual norms which are embed-ded in the normative basic principles and the long-term objectives of top-management.

Furthermore, the concept of decision-oriented ethics regards responsi-bility as its fundamental ethical basis.

Responsibility is seen as a main focal point of corporate action. It en-compasses the responsibility for results, i.e., the consequences of corporate decisions, the moral responsibility as well as the responsibility for the tasks and roles accepted.

The term responsibility contains the noun "response", indicating a reac-tion to an order, a call or an inquiry. Therefore, managers are not merely responsible for guaranteeing the long-term market existence and market success, but are also responsible to external institutions or persons. Without this insight the expression "I will take responsibility" is meaningless. Re-sponsibility towards others can be legal or moral in nature. The legal aspect of responsibility is reflected in a framework of judicial laws and regulations and can be compelled and reinforced by sanction mechanisms. The moral aspect of responsibility on the other hand is determined by the conscience of the individual and allows for reparation by means of forgiveness. It should be stressed at this point, though, that the meaning of the word conscience can interpreted in intersubjectively different ways and can therefore be applied arbitrary. From this results the necessity to clarify to which superior authority, respectively, standard the conscience is attached to.

The differentiation of the ethics of responsibility (*Verantwortungsethik*) and the ethics of ultimate ends (*Gesinnungsethik*) originates in the work of Max Weber (Weber 1919, 1973). The following summary lists the contrasts between the two types of ethics:

Criterion	Ethics of ultimate ends	Ethics of responsibility
Concept	To execute an action is the direct fulfilment of an absolute moral command (conviction).	The legitimisation of an action includes the judgement of its possible consequences.
Responsibility for the consequences of actions	A calculation of the consequences of action can be neglected resp. is not admissible; responsible are others or the environment as a whole.	Delegating the responsibility for action to others resp. to the person acting represents actual origin and expresses guilt and credit.
Consideration of causal context between decisions	Refusal of accounting for consequences (denying the world).	Accepting the world, including its ethical irrationality; empirical assumptions concerning the consequences of action and their likelihood.
Individual motivation	Maintaining a "good conscience"; no tolerance of exceptions; legitimisation of measures is not questioned.	Willingness to discuss measures and objectives; realities and burdens of life are seen and endured.

Figure 4: Comparison of the ethics of ultimate ends and the ethics of responsibility.

Max Weber pointed out that both types of ethics are in fact complimentary. Therefore, actions which are not pragmatic and ethically responsible cannot be ethical under conviction aspects.

The ethics of responsibility is based on the concept idea of openness and faces new developments without prejudice. The prerequisite is a process of efficient search for information and a rational judgement of alternatives, but it does not provide a definite answer to what can actually be considered as "good" in a specific case. These normative questions are dealt with in the following chapter.

2. The Concept of Decision-oriented Ethics in a Normative Perspective

The specific elements of a normative perspective result from the figure shown below:

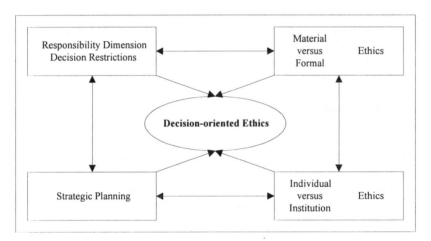

Figure 5: Elements and basic conditions of decision-oriented ethics.

The responsibility dimension represents the starting point of decision-oriented ethics together with decision restrictions. In addition, material norms, i.e., content norms, are necessary. They result from a norm-finding process which should preferably be conducted in a dialogues manner between top-management and all organisation members and possibly include the external interest representatives. Such a consensus-management prevents biased ethical guidelines, based merely on monologues, from coming into effect.

A corporation cannot act as a single moral person, but it is able to take morally relevant actions as a superordinate decision system. In the sense of decision-oriented ethics, the corporate institution must take responsibility for the effects of actions initiated by its individual decision makers.

The search process for content norms is concerned with measures for individual actions as well as measures for actions of the firm in its entirety. Especially institutionalised values play an important role in solving decision conflicts. For example, ethical guidelines can function as regulator in the event of differences of opinion between the headquarters of a multinational corporation and its decentralised foreign subsidiaries (*see the forth-coming results of our own empirical research pertaining to "Ethical Conflicts in Multinational Corporations"*).

The present empirical research shows that the focal point of ethical conflicts rests within the conflict between organisation and individual (intraorganisational conflict). This statement is supported by empirical research. If, for example, the company owner desires to donate a specific amount of money for non-profit purposes and the corresponding department head is exposed to heavy cost pressures, it may seem practical for him or her to shift these donation expenses to another cost centre (Toffler 1986).

In order to avoid such conflicts in the future, it is recommended to introduce ethical guidelines of action. It is necessary to distinguish between repeatedly occurring conflicts and novel conflict situations so far unknown. This differentiation influences the structural sequence of the norm-finding process. The following flow chart visualises a norm-finding process, depending on first-time or repeated conflict situations.

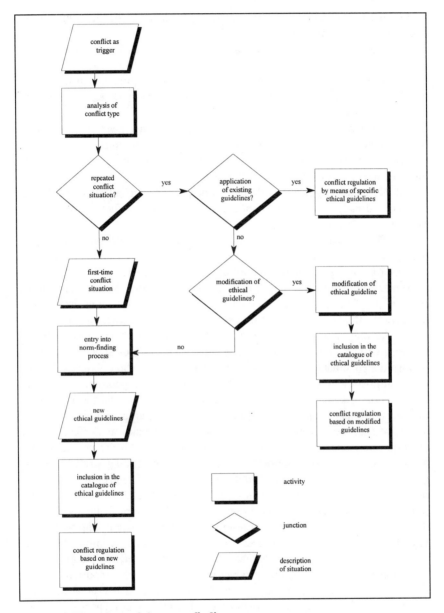

Figure 6: Flow chart of the norm-finding process.

For pragmatic reasons the formulation of ethical guidelines must consider six requirements (Kreikebaum 1997, p. 239):

(1) Harmonisation of new ethical guidelines with all interest groups affected in a dialogous manner.

(2) Written documentation to avoid asymmetrical information concerning the up-to-date status of the norm-finding process between participants and those persons affected.

(3) Clear and simple user-friendly formulations not necessitating additional explanations. This requires the application of operational standards.

(4) The creation of new guidelines should already consider the practical implementation in order to avoid future problems.

(5) New ethical guidelines should encompass known aspects of conflicts that have already occurred and should absorb future conflicts in a flexible manner.

(6) The formulation of new ethical guidelines should be aimed at insuring content consistency with existing guidelines. If this is not possible, a revision of existing guidelines should be performed accordingly.

Ethical guidelines are supportive in nature, e.g., they should promote a flexible and fast reaction to product damages and malfunctions in a non-bureaucratical way, even if recall costs are significantly high. It seems that this is the only way to extract ethical guidelines from their alibi-function, and to give them a real meaning. The different principles should therefore be formulated situation-specifically and be valid for a whole industry. Only then is it possible to eliminate free-rider positions of competitors.

Decision-oriented ethics deals with interrelations between the norms of the decision makers and the corporate decision-making processes. The objective of decision-oriented ethics is to improve efficiency and effectiveness of corporate decisions with regard to economic and ethical aspects. Thus, an addition to the above figure seems necessary, integrating strategic planning into the concept of decision-oriented ethics. Connecting decision-oriented ethics and strategic planning seems fundamental for the necessary integration of business and ethical elements. Starting point is the analysis of the values of top-management representatives as well as the empirical survey of ethical conflicts. The process of strategic planning is initiated by the formulation of long-term corporate intentions (corporate philosophy), an overall corporate purpose, and product/market objectives. Important issues for ethical reflection are already revealed at this stage. It is crucial for top-management to consider the consequences of decisions in respect to human capital (employees), the ecological environment, and technological developments. With respect to ecological guidelines, a corporation can manifest its responsibility for the health of humans, animals and plants in the following way: "We are obliged to preserve natural resources during the complete lifecycle of our products and to re-use materials. We develop and manufacture products that minimise negative effects on the ecology. We inform our customers about an ecologically responsible use of our products" (Adam Opel AG 1996, p. 5). A firm that is not aware of its moral responsibility and not willing to act accordingly may find itself confronted with decline. The management of the Manville Corporation deliberately misinformed its employees for decades regarding health hazards resulting from breathing in asbestos dust. When employee representatives expressed their concern about deadly lung diseases occurring as a result of the asbestos production, top- management simply prohibited the diffusion of any further information regarding the actual dangers.

Suggestions to solve conflict situations of this nature concentrate especially on the necessity for dialogous communication via the mechanisms of conflict regulation. To find the right solution in a specific situation is often a difficult task.

IV. Pragmatic Consequences

1. The Integration of Moral Aspects into Management

The integration of moral norms and values can proceed in three steps:
1. Analysis of the ethical dilemma.
2. Creation of a moral conscience.
3. Realisation of concrete measures.

The first step investigates if the conflict situation has occurred before, or if it is unprecedented. Seemingly harmless and minor conflicts should not be played down, since the public often reacts more sensitively than originally anticipated by top-management. For example, it is of utmost importance to immediately inform the neighbouring community as well as the interested public concerning the scope of damage and resulting consequences after a malfunction or accident in a chemistry plant has occurred.

If the instance reoccurs management is obliged to examine if there has been a violation of regulation norms. Especially corruption cases show evidence that regulations were not continuously monitored or that violations were not sanctioned. It is also possible that top-management failed to involve its internal inspection department in a timely manner, which then leads to irreversible damage. Internal corporate mechanisms that regulate corruption are of special importance in the Federal Republic of Germany, since a law such as the "Foreign Corrupt Act" implemented in the United States is still lacking.

Increasing international corruption negatively effects the educational and vocational system, confidence and trust in institutions decline and honesty and fairness loose their power. The German anti-corruption organisation "Transparency International" considers bringing corruption cases in developed and lesser developed countries to the public's attention as one of its main tasks.

The second step involves the creation of a moral conscience. The objective is to change individual patterns of thought and principles. The "defreezing" of habitualised behaviour patterns is an important condition for organisational change. Necessary is an overall alteration of personality in the sense of the Greek "metanoia" (personal turn around). The creation of conscience cannot merely encompass the individual, but must involve the complete corporate institution.

The third step contains the following measures to institutionalise business ethics (Wieland 1993).

- **Ethical guidelines/behavioural guidelines:**

According to a *Fortune* survey conducted in 1991/92 these guidelines are being applied by over 90% of the companies questioned, although only half of these firms have transferred the contents of their codes of conduct to all departments.

- **Ethics commission of the board of directors:**

This commission supports the ethical commitment of the Chief Executive Officer (moral leadership) by communicating ethical principles and values to stakeholders, by taking decisions in the event of ethical conflicts and by establishing a system of incentives and sanctions concerning moral and improbitious behaviour.

- **Ethics departments and officers:**

Ethics departments and ethics officers are responsible for the application of ethical guidelines throughout corporate hierarchy, for the education and training of employees, for the monitoring of ethically sensible issues, for the design and implementation of an "ethics alarm system", and for informing the public.

- **Ethical education and auditing:**

Apart from knowledge transfer the objective is to realise ethical measures in form of specific decisions.

- **Ethics hot line:**

All employees should be encouraged to convey their observations, impressions, suggestions and desires at any time and in an unconstrained manner to the ethics department. Topics of concern include the abuse of working time, of corporate and customer property, gifts and grants, pricing policy, quality control as well as product safety (Kreikebaum 1997, p. 245).

2. Implementation Problems

The management of American corporations is more strongly engaged in implementing ethical measures than their German counterparts. American firms react quickly and in a sensible way to information concerning insider trading, fraud in the savings and loan system, violations of product safety, illegal price agreements, the manufacture of hazardous materials, and dangerous environmental pollution. A research project conducted by the Centre of Business Ethics at Bentley College in Waltham, Mass. has shown that 93% of the companies questioned rank codes of conduct as the most important ethics measure. 52% of the corporations had established an ethical education programme and nearly one third had implemented ethics commissions and conducted ethical audits (Centre of Business Ethics 1992, pp. 863-868).

In comparison, the codes of conduct are rated as rather secondary ethics measure in a combined German and Swiss research project, with only 27% of the firms applying them (Ulrich/Lunau/Weber 1996). High-ranking ethics measures in German and Swiss firms are seminars pertaining to ethical aspects (35%) as well as drawing up social-ecological balance sheets (27%).

V. Conclusion

A responsible attitude of management is reflected in a behaviour which critically assesses the consequences of decisions and includes personal liability for these actions. The realities of daily life must be seriously considered as decision restrictions, but this does not imply merely accepting the pressures and surrendering to them. It is important to question them critically in the sense of rational ethics which opposes "economism" (*Ökonomismus*) (Ulrich 1997).

Ethical guidelines relate to a specific freedom of action. The more responsibility dimensions of the decision makers and the scope of corporate decisions expand, the more importance they gain. The figure below visualises this connection.

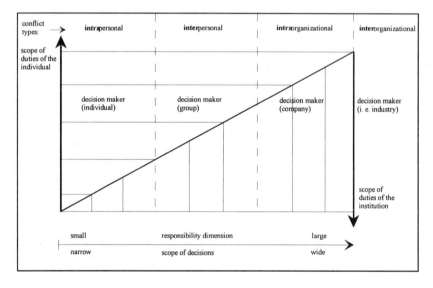

Figure 7: Connection of forms of conflict, responsibility dimensions and scope of decisions.

The significance of institution ethics increases with the number of decision makers involved in conflict regulation. Reaching an agreement by means of balancing between active and affected parties is especially important. The search for an appropriate consensus pertaining to difficult problems is often strenuous and time consuming. Conflict causes, possibilities of regulation, and the individual contribution of each decision maker to solving the conflict must be critically reflected. These may be "tragic choices" which can only be solved by way of compromise.

References

ADAM OPEL AG: *Initiativen für die Umwelt*, Rüsselsheim 1996.

CENTRE OF BUSINESS ETHICS: "Installing Ethical Values in Large Corporations", *Journal of Business Ethics*, Vol. 11 (1992), pp. 863-868.

DALOZ PARKS, SHARON: "Is It Too Late? Young Adults and the Formation of Professional Ethics", in: PIPER, THOMAS R., GENTILE, MARY C., DALOZ PARKS, SHARON (Eds.): *Can Ethics be Taught?: Perspectives, Challenges and Approaches at the Harvard Business School*, Boston, Mass. 1993, pp. 13-72.

GELLERMAN, SAUL W.: "Why "Good" Managers Make Bad Ethical Choices", *Harvard Business Review*, Vol. 64, No. 4 (1986), pp. 85-90.

HOMANN, KARL: "Marktwirtschaftliche Ordnung und Unternehmensethik", in: *Unternehmensethik: Konzepte - Grenzen - Perspektiven, ZfB-Ergänzungsheft 1*, Wiesbaden 1992, S. 75-90.

KAUFMANN, F.-X., KERBER, W., ZULEHNER, P. M.: *Ethos und Religion bei Führungskräften: eine Studie im Auftrag des Arbeitskreises für Führungskräfte in der Wirtschaft*, München 1986.

KREIKEBAUM, HARTMUT: *Kehrtwende zur Zukunft*, Neuhausen - Stuttgart 1988.

KREIKEBAUM, HARTMUT: *Grundlagen der Unternehmensethik*, Stuttgart 1996.

KREIKEBAUM, HARTMUT: "Die Integration moralischer Aspekte in die Unternehmensführung durch das Konzept der Entscheidungsethik", in: BRUHN, MANFRED/STEFFENHAGEN, HARTWIG (Eds.): *Marktorientierte Unternehmensführung: Reflexionen - Denkanstöße - Perspektiven. Festschrift für Heribert Meffert zum 60. Geburtstag*, Wiesbaden 1997, pp. 229-250.

PAINE, LYNN SHARP: *Manville Corporation Fiber Glass Group (A) - (D)*, Harvard Business School, April 24, 1995.

TOFFLER, BARBARA LEY: *Tough Choices - Managers Talk Ethics*, New York et al. 1986.

HARTMUT KREIKEBAUM

ULRICH, PETER: *Integrative Wirtschaftsethik. Grundlagen einer lebensdienlichen Ökonomie*, Bern - Stuttgart - Wien 1997.

ULRICH, P., LUNAU, Y., WEBER, T.: "Ethikmaßnahmen in der Unternehmenspraxis. Zum Stand der Wahrnehmung und Institutionalisierung von Unternehmensethik in schweizerischen und deutschen Firmen. Ergebnisse einer Befragung", in: *Institut für Wirtschaftsethik, Universität St. Gallen, Beiträge und Berichte*, Nr. 73, 1996

ULRICH, P., THIELEMANN, P.: *Ethik und Erfolg: unternehmensethische Denkmuster von Führungskräften - eine empirische Studie*, Bern - Stuttgart 1992.

WEBER, MAX: *Politik als Beruf*, München 1919.

WEBER, MAX: *Soziologie, Universalgeschichtliche Analysen, Politik*, 5th ed., Stuttgart 1973.

WIELAND, JOSEF: *Formen der Institutionalisierung von Moral in amerikanischen Unternehmen: die amerikanische Business-Ethics-Bewegung: Why and how they do it*, Bern - Stuttgart - Wien 1993.

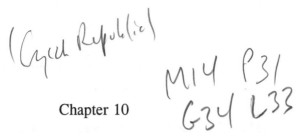

Chapter 10

Some Implications of Voucher Privatisation for Corporate Governance: A Business Ethics Perspective [1]

MARIE BOHATÀ

This paper is based on an empirical analysis of corporate governance in the Czech Republic (its model, its structures and the functioning of boards). Simultaneously, an effort is made to add a business/economic ethics perspective to this analytical view. The approach to ethics is primarily institutional: it refers less to actions than to institutions as sets of formal and informal rules.

In order to understand the present system of corporate governance, the essence of voucher privatisation, which led to a great number of publicly traded joint stock companies and dispersed ownership, is explained. Then, major players and issues in corporate governance, as well as the Czech model of how companies are governed and monitored, are described and some ethical aspects introduced.

---

1   This research was supported by Charles University, Czech Republic and by Egon Zehnder International.

MARIE BOHATÀ

I. Voucher Privatisation Programme and its Main Controversies

The economic transformation implemented in the CR after the "Velvet Revolution" was based on several pillars, such as macro-economic stabilisation, liberalisation of trade and prices and limited convertibility of currency. Privatisation of former state enterprises was considered the crucial pillar (under the previous regime, about 97 percent of assets was in state hands).

From the perspective of business (economic) ethics it should be stressed that several controversies arose from the Czech privatisation programme. These controversies led to different expectations of appropriate rules and patterns of behaviour. Internal rules may be viewed as the most problematic part of the whole privatisation process.

The most significant controversy was that between the designers and interpreters of privatisation (politicians and economists who were not involved in the privatisation design).

The philosophy of the designers of privatisation[2] can be summarised as follows:

1. Privatisation has extremely important economic consequences, but economics is not its primary goal. The object of the "privatisation attack" is the public sector: the state, its roles and behaviour.

2. Privatisation is primarily a costly process, not an income generating process. Its strategy should thus stress minimisation of cost, not maximisation of profit or returns.

3. The substance of privatisation and its secondary consequences are rooted in the following hypotheses:

* A privatised economy is a special case of a market economy.

* Privatisation is a way of increasing performance (efficiency) not of individual companies but of the economy as a whole.

* A purely socialist economy (not infected by any "perestroika" efforts) can be transformed more easily than a mixed economy.

4. The purpose of privatisation is not to find "optimal" (responsible) owners but some owners.

---

2   Expressed most comprehensively by Dusan Triska, one of the "fathers" of privatisation and the main designer of the software of voucher privatisation.

5. The most severe danger for privatisation is an ex ante regulation which is motivated by anticipated market failures. The preparedness of the government to politically sustain pressures and criticism resulting from privatisation and post-privatisation "accidents" is crucial.

6. Foreign investors should not be favoured, mainly because they are not serious enough until some credible, well functioning and strong domestic companies have emerged or have maintained their previous good reputation.

Without any attempt to criticise this philosophy of privatisation, I would like to make an important point: the philosophy was not clearly articulated and potential misunderstandings were not clarified. (I do not want to speculate whether this was by intention or by omission at the hectic time of reform.) According to this view, problems which emerged after the completion of voucher privatisation resulted from compromises which were made (only partial privatisation of banks and strategic companies, a 20 percent limit on investment privatisation funds and the establishment of the Fund of National Property, which was an organisation similar to the widely criticised German "Treuhand Anstalt").

The position of the interpreters of privatisation can be summarised as follows:

The Czech privatisation process aims at:

* improving economic efficiency at the micro-level, as well as in the broader macro-economic sense,

* building political support for the whole transformation process,

* creating a system of private property rights as a necessary, albeit not solely sufficient condition for achieving genuine democracy and ensuring personal liberties.

The best way to build a pro-market constituency is to create a broad class of owners (or a large middle class) who have an intrinsic interest in maintaining a stable system. Therefore, the idea of distribution of state assets (voucher privatisation) emerged.

Voucher privatisation was based on the free distribution of national wealth to the population on some equal but not egalitarian basis. The underlying ideology was social justice, providing equal chances for all. At the same time, it fit into the liberal/Hayekian concept of spontaneous order. This way of privatisation is economically rational because it safeguards that principally only the social elite (people with the best knowledge of markets and with the best ability to develop rational expectations about the uncertain future, and with this background capable of making correct decisions) can be successful in the course of privatisation. Put differently, thanks to the voucher method, national wealth will quickly and safely fall into the best hands existing in the society - the individuals with the greatest wisdom, ability and education.

In terms of ethics, what was lacking at this point was serious dialogue and efforts to resolve the main controversies.

Corporate governance (the way companies are governed and monitored) concerns the exercise of power over the most significant entities in modern society. A challenge for a decent society is to keep power under control. For this purpose, checks and balances, which the society surveys, are built in.

Another highly controversial idea in the Czech case was that of combining the German and Anglo-Saxon models of corporate governance. The motivation was to use advantages of both models; however, the role of the different business environments in which they operate was underestimated. Consequently, it was difficult to design appropriate structures to control power (assuming there was an intention to do so). The experience shows that such a hybrid does not work properly in practice.

Other controversies were those between legislators and economists and their understanding of the role of investment privatisation funds and the stock exchange. These issues will be discussed later.

In general, we may argue that the aforementioned controversies, the unwillingness of the government to moderate them and the inadequate enforcement of law (despite considerable criticism of the legal system, certain reasonable boundaries do exist) led to compromises which resulted in the relatively low performance of the economy and in the near discreditation of private ownership as such.

II. Why Is Corporate Governance on the Agenda in the Czech Republic?

1. In the CR, the transformation of former state enterprises is characterised by their privatisation, as well as their search for a place in the globalized world economy. The emphasis placed on privatisation in the CR was unique compared to other economies in transition. The voucher scheme,

which became a massive - although not an exclusive - privatisation method, led to the emergence of a large number of publicly traded joint stock companies. Thus, the exercise of newly acquired ownership rights and governance of incorporated companies became an important issue.

2. The globalization of markets requires that corporations be increasingly effective. Efficient and professional corporate governance is crucial for achieving this goal. For companies used to operating on highly protected Comecon markets, this process is even more problematic.

III. Players in Corporate Governance

Investment Privatisation Funds (IPFs)

IPFs were created within the framework of voucher privatisation. They became the major players in the game and also the major winners. The lawyers preparing the legislation for IPFs and investment companies were inspired by EU and US legislation and understood IPFs as tools of collective investment. IPFs were supposed to diversify their portfolios to minimise the risk but were not to be involved in active monitoring of companies. This was the reason why a fund's maximum stake in one company was limited to 20 percent of the shares, and simultaneously, the fund was not allowed to invest more than 10 percent of its assets in the equity of one issuer. The economists who designed the scheme, however, intended IPFs to be future active owners in privatised companies and to play an important role in corporate governance. Thus, a deep contradiction was built into the design of IPFs, a situation which lasted till 1996.

For the first wave of voucher privatisation, IPFs were created as joint stock companies with a minimal requirement of capitalisation. Shortly thereafter, some IPF managers experienced hostile take-overs of the IPFs. To avoid this danger, they pushed for a change of legislation. As a result, the second wave permitted the establishment of different types of mutual funds, closed or open-ended. The major difference between these funds and the IPFs from the first wave was the fact that individuals who committed their voucher points to these funds did not get voting rights. Nevertheless, the popularity of mutual funds was high (60 percent of voucher points in the second wave).

The Fund of National Property (FNP)

The FNP was designed to serve as a waiting ground for companies which were approved for privatisation and were waiting for its execution. There was an explicit attempt not to involve the FNP in corporate governance of the partially privatised companies. The philosophy was ultra-liberal: "State clerks are incompetent to run companies. The FNP has no capacity for corporate governance and since privatisation will be very quick, there is no need to develop corporate governance structures."

In fact, privatisation has taken longer than expected, and it was impossible to prevent the FNP from exercising ownership rights. In cases of partially privatised companies, the FNP allowed respective IPFs even with small ownership stakes to be represented on the boards. Surprisingly, these representatives were very passive and, thus, companies were under management control. To avoid this situation, the government decided in 1994 to pass the ownership rights of companies in question back to their founder, the Ministry of Industry and Trade, whose representatives would act on behalf of the state.

Czech Banks

Czech banks played *a crucial role in the process of voucher privatisation*. They established investment companies, which in turn established dozens of IPFs. These funds became the major players in both waves of voucher privatisation. At the same time, however, the major Czech banks were subjects of voucher privatisation: large blocks of their shares were given into public offer. Nevertheless, *the FNP retained over 40 percent of shares in major Czech banks*.

Obviously, there was a lot of speculation about this line of control. The FNP is the largest shareholder in major banks, which are the founders of investment companies (usually 100 percent owners), and those investment companies established dozens of IPFs, which control hundreds of companies. In other words, *privatisation was only nominal* in that the state could still influence a majority of "privatised" companies. In fact, however, the state can influence these companies, not so much because of the line of ownership, but more because of a high dependence of Czech companies on bank credits. The line of ownership is only secondary.

234

Some economists characterise this situation as "state capitalism" or "banking socialism". The main problem with this state of affairs, however, is that the state does not assume adequate responsibility. Roles and responsibilities of all parties involved are either unclear or conflicting and, thus, are not exercised properly.

It stands to reason that the complete privatisation of banks has become an important topic. However, it has also turned out to be a question of intense political controversy.

Individual Voucher Investors (Czech Citizens)

Individuals represented the largest but also the weakest interest group taking part in privatisation. Lacking access to relevant information and unable to take care of the acquired assets, they played the role of the first, passive owners who were not capable of exercising any ownership functions. However, it was they who, through collective investment approaches (e.g. IPFs, pooled investments, etc.), gave the impetus to create capital markets operating at a very low transaction cost. Only small and well-organised groups profited from this situation at the expense of small individual shareholders and also some weak IPFs.

In this way, the role of individuals in voucher privatisation has been marginalized. It is estimated that an overwhelming majority of participants have already sold their shares. It should be stressed that the individuals/small investors were not given adequate protection. Small investors were protected only by the law stipulating that IPFs are allowed to invest only in securities which are traded on:

a) the primary list of the stock exchange

b) the secondary list of the stock exchange

c) other securities markets where prices are disclosed

d) the primary or similar market of a foreign stock exchange which ensured that the choice of stock exchange has been approved by the Finance Ministry.

The insufficient protection of minority shareholders was one of the major failures of Czech economic legislation and the main ethical disaster of voucher privatisation. Neither shareholders of IPFs nor those of companies themselves were adequately protected. Not surprisingly, the strongest opponents of voucher privatisation refer to this as the greatest "cheat" of this century.

Foreign Investors

Foreign investors represented the strongest players in the privatisation process. Direct investors were well informed and were capable of acquiring the best quality assets for very good prices. Evidence suggests that they take care of the assets with the same efficiency.

A totally different case is represented by portfolio investors whose motives are only speculative and, thus, who are not interested in active governance of companies.

Managers

Managers represented a small but well organised group with established networks and strong individual relationships with banks. Another comparative advantage of this group was that they had access to the best available information about companies. In this respect, it should be mentioned that about 75 percent of approved privatisation projects were prepared by the management of the respective company. Managers wanted to acquire ownership rights for "their" companies. However, some used various unethical and borderline, if not criminal methods of "silent privatisation". Generally, we can state that this group had a common goal but different means of reaching that goal. Nevertheless, it may be assumed that in companies in which management has acquired a majority stake, the assets are taken care of properly.

IV. Czech Model of Corporate Governance

Corporate governance is a product of the environment in which companies in question operate. This environment is formed by several factors such as: the legal system, the culture, the ownership structure and the makeup of the financial sector.

Legal Framework

Czech legislation created *a hybrid* of corporate governance, with features of both the unitary and two-tier model. There are two bodies with separate governance and control functions: the Board of Directors (BoD) and the Supervisory Board (SB). Unlike in the typical two-tier model, members of the BoD are elected by the Annual Meeting of Shareholders (AMS) and are obliged to abide by AMS directions. Unfortunately, there is *no concrete concept* of how the model should work. Some elements are in accord with common world standards (setting up companies, increasing and decreasing companies' assets or protection of creditors). However, this is not true for organisational issues and the direction of companies.

The main weakness of the existing system is the unclear role of members of the BoD. The relationship between BoD members and the company is subject to a mandate contract. Members of the BoD are obliged to act in compliance with directions of the AMS (if these do not violate the law), with due diligence and reticence. Due diligence means implementing directions in accordance with the company's interests, with which the member of BoD is familiar or has exercised due diligence to familiarise himself (herself) with. Therefore, the member of the BoD is obliged to act in compliance with the interests of the company and not those of the particular owner who has, with his voting power, nominated or elected him.

Moreover, BoD members may be dismissed by the AMS without a stated reason. This means that they can be dismissed anytime even if they have fulfilled their duties.

Some critics of corporate governance demand improvements in legislation. The survey undertaken by Egon Zehnder International (EZI) indicates legal regulation as a possible problem area; however, the need for urgent action is not perceived. The main problem, in the opinion of the 77 board members responding to the questionnaire, is the prevailing conflict of duties and of interests.

Corporate Governance Structures at the Early Stages of Voucher Privatisation

Voucher privatisation resulted in dispersed ownership. Consequently, a very common picture was that a company was owned by a group of IPFs. Once voucher privatisation was completed, the idea that IPFs should be involved in corporate governance arose. During the "incorporation" of former state enterprises, boards had been established. At that time representatives of ministries and banks served on them. After the distribution of shares, general meetings of shareholders were called and new boards elected. Here we may observe a major difference compared to the German model: IPF representatives wanted to control management directly and, therefore, had to become board members. The main motivation for this behaviour was to stop a malignant "silent privatisation" and outflows in an unregulated environment after the demise of central planning.

Corporate governance in this situation was not an easy task. It was learning by doing. Usually, it was necessary to form a coalition. Empirical evidence shows that at least 4 IPFs used to organise tough preparatory meetings to reach a preliminary agreement so that general meetings of shareholders were merely formalities.

IPF representatives sat on boards, and they experienced *a conflict between loyalty to the IPF/investment company and to the company itself*. Managers realised very soon that they had to keep external board members happy and started to push for better remuneration and other benefits. IPFs found themselves in a rather uneasy position: They sent their representatives to the boards, but these people had to serve on the boards as private persons without any legal obligation to report to the owner.

Corporate Governance during Ownership Concentration

There were permanent discussions about the usefulness of the 20 percent ownership limit. For active owners it was too little, for passive owners too much. The OECD repeated its recommendation to decrease the limit to 10-15 percent. Some of the IPFs understood very quickly that the initial system of corporate governance was too costly and that something else had to be developed. This was the beginning of ownership concentration.

A radical solution that was developed by some IPFs at the beginning of 1996 was *the transformation of funds into joint stock companies (holdings)* with no restrictions. This "change of the rules" caused great dissatisfaction that was most visible among foreign investors. The immediate reaction was a fall in share prices. However, Czech citizens were also victims of this process. Many of these shareholders became real outsiders with no chance to sell their shares for a reasonable price or at all. Only then, did the government start preparing new legislation aimed at the protection of small shareholders, a better definition of board responsibilities and improved disclosure of information. This legislation was approved by the Parliament in May 1996 and put into practice in July 1996.

The economic rationality of ownership concentration is quite clear. The problem in the CR lies, however, in the motivation for this concentration. While foreign investors understand ownership as a means of doing business (power is a business tool), the prevailing motivation of Czech entrepreneurs for acquiring/concentrating ownership has been *to increase power*. Very often power has been understood as a tool of exploitation[3]. This fact together with illegal and unethical practices, implemented in acquiring ownership, and so far, tolerated by the Czech authorities, *may discredit the very concept of private ownership*. Under these circumstances, it is hard for an economist to argue that the present process of re-allocation of ownership rights can be justified on efficiency grounds.

As stressed above, with respect to globalisation, ownership concentration may be considered a prerequisite for Czech companies, mainly in the manufacturing sector, to work in the international arena. For this purpose, concentration should be a strategy aimed at creating partnership relations. In the Czech business environment, characterised by individualism, lack of responsibility and a distorted understanding of competition and co-operation, real partnership is difficult to achieve and maintain.

V. Some Ethical Issues in Corporate Governance

Capital Markets

Secondary markets have played a key role in the thinking of those proposing mass privatisation schemes. It was assumed that voucher privatisation would not produce an optimal distribution of ownership, and that afterwards, secondary markets enabling concentration and redistribution of shares would be needed. That was the main reason why smooth trading was considered to be crucial for further development. As a result of mechanisms

---

3 The most widespread form of exploitation has been the so-called tunnelling of companies (IPFs), i.e., the draining of money so that only a shell remains.

used for voucher privatisation, there are three markets for shares: one is a traditional bourse, the Prague Stock Exchange (PSE); the second is the "RM-SYSTEM", developed from a computerised system for electronic bidding used in voucher privatisation; and the third one is the central register for dematerialised shares (Centre for Securities).

Theoretically, all companies privatised through the voucher scheme could be traded on the PSE. In fact, only very few companies are really liquid, and thus, the main volume of trading was concentrated in the first 100 emissions.

Originally, the PSE was expected to develop into a conservative institution, trading only a few dozen of the best securities. However, after some hesitation the PSE, as the other two markets, traded all shares from voucher privatisation. By now it has become clear that this was a big mistake, breaking the ethics of stock exchanges where companies are allowed to be traded publicly on the condition of disclosure of information. The Czech companies are also supposed to deliver information, but the quality, reliability, and completeness of data provided are insufficient. In order to consolidate the PSE, it is expected that hundreds of shares be eliminated from trading. However, this will take a long time. Moreover, either the number of markets should be reduced or activities limited to the most suitable of the three markets.

Close Relationship Between Banks and Investment Companies

The close relationship between banks and investment entities leads to collusion or the imposition of improper objectives on controlled companies. There is a real conflict of interest between banks acting as owners of firms and as creditors to them. This situation has been widely discussed and there seems to be a consensus that these roles must be separated. What has been unclear so far is how to achieve this.

Orientation of Boards

At first, reformers and legislators in the area of corporate governance paid almost exclusive attention to the constitution of boards. We may observe (and the aforementioned survey suggests) that the situation in this sphere has already crystallised. According to the survey, the average size of

BoDs is 5 members. Large firms seem to favour the German model (BoD are composed entirely of managers). On average, the proportion of employees serving on supervisory boards is 37 percent while the law requires 33 percent. More than 60 percent of respondents serve on several boards, the average number of additional memberships being 2.79.

At present, problems of unclear board orientation and unclear roles and responsibilities of individual members, as well as institutional arrangement, represent the main concern. As the survey has shown, *the functioning of the BoD is characterised in different ways:*

- Setting strategy is the main job of the BoD, and it works on this in partnership with the CEO for the benefit of owners (29 percent of answers).
- The BoD is under managerial domination (26 percent of answers).
- Setting strategy is the main job of the BoD, and it works on this in partnership with the CEO for the benefit of owners and with respect to interests of other stakeholders (25 percent of answers).
- The BoD influences the decision of many strategic issues but does not influence the company's direction in a coherent manner (17 percent of answers).

Conflicts of Interest on the Board Level

Besides the above mentioned conflict stemming from a close relationship between banks and IPFs, there are many other potential conflicts. The core of the problem, however, may be seen in *the fuzzy definition of the role of boards and their responsibilities,* arising from a new concept of stewardship and fiduciary duties of board members. The survey has revealed substantial differences in characterising the importance of different board roles. One half of respondents give the highest priority to owners' representation, while the other half ranks much higher such functions as mission and vision setting, corporate strategy setting, supervising and appraising financial policy, operations and management performance.

Respondents stressed that it is extremely important to assure that board members properly understand their role and also be aware of the required efforts and the necessary due diligence. For this purpose, appropriate incentives are needed. The incentives favoured most by respondents are performance-related remuneration, limited contracts and share option schemes.

Education of Outside Board Members

A crucial problem is the need to educate a qualified forum of outside directors. It is the chicken and egg situation: an immature structure with an insufficient number of highly qualified people, people with professional and ethical competence, who can assist in developing the structure. Another problem resulting from the high number of joint-stock companies created by the voucher scheme of privatisation is an extremely high number of board members (about 10, 000).

The survey revealed the most serious inadequacies in international business experience, industry knowledge, general management, and functional experience. The most important personal skills and characteristics seem to be strategic skills and vision setting ability.

Long-term View

Short-term thinking in corporate decision making is not a viable option: it is impossible to base long-term strategy on such thinking (a short-term profit cannot be achieved permanently). Just like family businesses that take a long-term view (their tradition was interrupted in the previous regime), investment funds should consider the corporations' long range perspectives and lasting success. An essential first step is creating an awareness of the need for change. The second step is to decide who will take the lead. (There are some signals that this stage has just emerged). Finally, it may be assumed that, through international integration processes, standards common in the developed countries will also be adopted in the Czech Republic.

VI. Conclusions

The essence of governance is power. Corporate governance concerns the exercise of power over the most significant entities in modern society. "Power is a business tool and its effective use demands a continual assessment of both people and conditions. Power must rely on reason rather than habit or emotion."[4] Since the 19th century, when the concepts of joint stock and limited liability were conceived, ownership has been the ultimate basis of power, and in most jurisdictions it still is. However, due to the appearance of alternative power bases (labour, public interest and the stakeholder concept in general), reality may differ. In any case, in mature democracies and market economies, there are built in checks and balances which the society surveys. There are two elements which must be present in this process: existing checks and balances and the authorities surveying them.

Generally, the reform from a totalitarian regime and a centrally planned economy to a system of democracy and market stresses the technical and most visible part of the problem, i.e. formal institution building. In the transition and adjustment process which follows, appropriate attention should be paid to the cultivation of institutions and to the moral content of these institutions. This is where the main ethical deficiencies in the Czech case may be observed. Moreover, in many cases it is not just the structures that need to be changed but above all individual behaviour.

We may look at the problem of corporate governance from two ends: either *reactive and punitive* (what sanctions should be imposed for improper behaviour and how companies can be made competitive), or *proactive and educational* (how to develop a sense of vision, become global and create a business environment in which there is a reasonable return on share investment). This is an area where business ethics (self-regulation) is so important. Clearly, we need both, but the latter is crucial and its importance cannot be overstressed. In this respect, some suggestions from the above discussed survey should be mentioned:

- Build professional as well as public awareness, spread best practice (seminars, conferences, professional publications, extended media coverage, etc.).
- Develop and publish practical guides (for operation) for board members.
- Develop and offer tailored, focused training courses for board members.

---

4 FRENCH, W. A., GRANROSE, J. (1995).

References

CADBURY, A.: *The Report of the Committee on the Financial Aspects of Corporate Governance*, London (Gee and Co) 1992.

COCHRAN, P., WARTICK, S.: *Corporate Governance - a Review of the Literature*, Morristown, New Jersey (Financial Executives Research Foundation) 1988.

DEMB, A., NEUBAUER, F.: *The Corporate Board - Confronting the Paradoxes*, New York (Oxford University Press) 1992.

DESAI, M. R.: "Reformed Banks and Corporate Governance in the Czech Republic", *Post-Soviet Geography and Economics*, 1996.

FRENCH, W.A., GRANROSE, J.: *Practical Business Ethics*, (Prentice-Hall) 1995.

GREENBURY, R.: *The Report of the Committee on Directors' Remuneration*, London (Gee and Co) 1995.

KLVACOVA, E.: "Sedmero lecek", *Ekonom*, 28 (1997).

MEJSTRIK, M. (Ed.): *The Privatisation Process in East-Central Europe*, (Kluwer Academic Publishers) 1995.

M I 4
L 20

Chapter 11

An Institutional Approach to Business Ethics

JOSEF WIELAND

I. Organisational Form and Business Ethics
II. The Ethical Dimension of Contract and Organisation
III. A Proposal to Define Institutional Business Ethics

I. Organisational Form and Business Ethics

Whoever inquires about the ethics of a business, actually inquires about the ethics of an organisation. Technically speaking, the issue at stake is the moral characteristics of a governance structure for the performance of economic transactions. This statement leads to the possibly surprising consequence that the moral concepts and actions of an entrepreneur, his management team, and his employees cannot be the only or primary object of Business Ethics. The moral values guiding an entrepreneur, management and performance may even in this case still be important elements of Business Ethics. Virtues are important to start and continue Business Ethics in an organisation, but they do not constitute the entity of Business Ethics as such. They represent personal virtues attributed to agents but not to the normativeness of organisations. With respect to their normativeness, organisations are a system of institutionalised constraints.[1] In other words, Business Ethics

---

1   At this point it is important to note the theoretical distinction between 'institution' and 'organisation'. *Institutions* constitute a set of formal and informal rules defining the nature and the quantity of desired activities. Their aim is to impose constraints. *Organisations* are organisational systems relating to functional systems. They are constituted by a membership. They are institutions of society in

cannot be developed from a concept of action, rather from a concept of institution. Business Ethics constitutes no 'virtue' ethics, rather 'institutions' ethics.

This differentiation of virtue ethics and institutions ethics should be viewed as a distinction between two levels of Economic and Business Ethics. The following diagram is an attempt to systematise their relation.

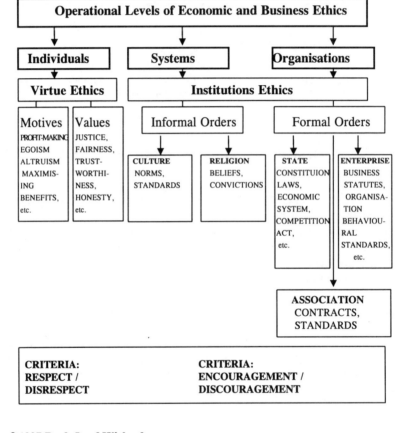

© 1997 Prof. Josef Wieland

as far as they represent normativeness, i.e. rules. Hence, from a certain point of view, organisations are also institutions but institutions are not organisations.

Clear statements can be made about the level of virtue ethics. Here we look at activities from the point-of-view of motives and values that lead to respect or disrespect for the agent as a result of his motives and activities. So in the context of virtue ethics we can make the following two statements:

"Some entrepreneurs in the construction industry give and take bribes because they strive for profit maximisation."

"Some entrepreneurs in the construction industry don't give and take bribes because the prefer honesty."

Profit maximisation and honesty are the motives or values and taking or not taking bribes are the resulting actions.

But it seems to be less clear what we mean, or rather could mean, by the term institutions ethics. One of the difficulties arises from the fact that we have to distinguish between formal orders and informal orders and come across different phenomena (culture, religion, social and private bodies) within these categories. Therefore this analysis of institutions ethics is restricted to the field of Business Ethics. Quite evidently, this restriction is of a purely theoretical nature. Above all, no statement is implied about the relative importance of virtue ethics or institutions ethics. However, a clarification of the relationship between these two kinds of ethics will be attempted in the conclusion.

Examination of those subsequent theoretical issues raised by our discussion so far may first begin with the term organisation itself. Organisation refers to the general *process* of organising as well as to the specific *form* within which the process takes place. Introducing this differentiation has far-reaching consequences which may be demonstrated realistically by the common distinction between market and hierarchy[2] in economic theory. Market and hierarchy represent distinctive patterns of governance controlling economic transactions. Seen as possible options for organising a transaction, market and hierarchy are equivalent. Understood as specific forms of governing the execution of the process, they are anything but equivalent. Since spot-markets and enterprises have differing characteristics and capabilities at their disposal for controlling economic processes, the economic problem which arises is to decide which particular transaction to assign to which efficient governance structure.

The difference between 'process and form' which is part and parcel of the concept of organisation may be employed for the theoretical construc-

---

2   WILLIAMSON (1975, 1985).

tion of Institutional Business Ethics. In as far as people act in the *process* of organising, their virtues and vices play a role. But the organisational *form*, the business within which this process takes place, lies beyond the conventional virtue ethics. Decoupling of form and process is derived from differing time references. The process of organising can only be established for an infinite period of time by means of the form of the business. This leads to the important consequence that this form is based on the exclusion of 'people', 'individuals' or 'parties' on which this form is based[3]. Business Ethics, if this term is meant to be taken seriously, must refer constitutively to this very form. It can only be developed as an institutions ethics.

The theoretical point in differentiating between process and form, however, can by no means be located where it is frequently expected, i.e. in the conditioning of processes by form or vice versa. What is actually meant by this is the restrictive effect economic facts have on moral aspirations, or the other way round. In both cases, nevertheless, the argument still maintains its orientation towards a theory of action. Termwise this line of thinking encounters 'discretion' offered within structures and 'responsibility' compelling one to make decisions. This is also true for the scarcely developed discussion of 'an enterprise as a moral agent'[4]. As a rule this discourse ends with analogising natural, legal, and moral parties 'responsible' for virtue ethics, as far as their 'scope of operating' or discretion will allow. The more leeway there is - says the inevitable conclusion - the greater is one's ethical responsibility.[5]

In this theoretical Bermuda triangle of 'responsibility, discretion, and an enterprise as a moral agent' the most decisive entity of our discussion so far has disappeared from sight: an enterprise as a distinctive form used (or not used) by economic agents in order to perform their transactions.

---

3 CHESTER BARNARD (1958) already elaborated this aspect of an enterprise as formal organisation in functionally differing societies. But for our topic it is even more important that he discriminates between the 'Principles' and the 'Elementary Conditions of Business Morals' and realises that only descriptive ethics will be able to outlive the strain.

4 For example DONALDSON (1982), ENDERLE (1989).

5 For example ENDERLE (1989, p. 173).

II. The Ethical Dimension of Contract and Organisation

The analysis of the issue of Business Ethics thus defined will be supported methodically by the New Economics of Organisation[6]. This particular research program of the New Economics of Institutions is on the one hand sensitive to the economic consequences of different forms of controlling economic transactions and, on the other hand, it is methodologically well equipped to deal with the topic of 'Business Ethics', due to its interdisciplinary orientation and its particular attention to 'soft facts' (informal contracts, atmosphere, morals etc.) of economic processes. There are two dimensions playing the central role here: first the contract, second the organisation.

First: from the point of view of the Economics of Organisation a economic team constitutes itself as the distinction of an collective agent from his individual agents by means of its company statutes.[7] These statutes will not only define the company goals and company policies but also the 'stakeholders' of the company. In the New Economics of Institutions and Organisations the process of constituting a team is ascribed to a 'nexus of contracts' between individual owners of resources.[8] The constitution of the company (or of the team) takes place because by co-operating with other owners of resources the rent for each individual owner of resources surpasses the level which would otherwise be obtainable to each of them alone. This rent through co-operation, however, assumes there is only the strictly individualistic and self-interest motive for team formation. The decisive question now is the following: How is it possible that agents, guided exclusively by their own interests, join up to form a lasting organisation to pursue a collective interest, i.e. of obtaining a rent through their co-operative efforts? The answer lies in intentionally long-term contractual arrangements in which all partners in the contract commit themselves to doing or not doing certain things. With this contractual agreement they at the same time agree to present and future constraints due to this co-operation. This is the purpose of contracts and only in this way team-work between agents who

---

6   See WILLIAMSON (1993).
7   This is the thesis of early German institutionalism. E.g., SOMBART (1902-1927/1987, pp. 101f.) and SCHMOLLER (1901, pp. 414, 438 f., 453, 457).
8   ALCHIAN/DEMSETZ (1972), JENSEN/MECKLING (1976), FAMA (1980), HART (1990), GIFFORD (1991), VANBERG (1992) as well as WIELAND (1996, part II).

act in their own self-interest is possible. Constituting a business as a network of explicit and implicit contracts therefore is an act of restricting operation. Formulated in a different way: the agreed upon constraints for the individual owners of resources constitute the collective agent called 'an enterprise'. This collective agent represents a restriction of Hobbes' 'right to do anything' for all team members and thereby distinguishes the difference of viewing the business organisation on the one hand as form and on the other hand as process.

With this interpretation of the form called 'a business' as a set of constitutional (e.g. business contracts, statues) and post-constitutional (e.g. employment contracts) contracts, a first starting point for an inquiry into Business Ethics has been marked out. Contracts in and between businesses are systematically incomplete and therefore always raise moral issues in the course of their fulfilment. Relevant literature[9] reminds us that contract-theoretical development of moral issues allows us to look at the ethics of a business in terms of its immanent problem of form.

Second: the co-operation of self-interested economic agents will only achieve stability if i) conflict, ii) interdependence, and iii) order within one organisation and between organisations can be balanced and iv) adequately communicated.[10]

i) At first *conflicts* inevitably arise in organisations due to the already developed self-interest of all team members. What makes these conflicts more difficult to avoid or overcome by technical or economic means is informal, personal, and situational uncertainty, bounded rationality and the ambiguity of facts and situations.

ii) *Interdependence* is a basic fact in co-operative relationships. It ensues because the success potential of agent A depends on the resources and the behaviour of agent B and vice versa. If there were dependence on resources but certainty with respect to expected behaviour, no moral problems would arise. This holds also true if there is uncertainty about behaviour but independence from resources.

---

9   For an overview see WIELAND (1996).
10   As already COMMONS (1934/1990, p. 58) pointed out.

iii) *Order* is documented in standard procedures, management principles, guidelines, organisational charts, codes of ethics, implicit expectation of performance etc., that means a set of formal and informal rules. Order is based on a decrease in the importance of individual identity, recognition, and status.

Economical and organisational problems resulting from conflict, interdependence and order have always a moral dimension. Therefore, morality might be a functional equivalent to deal with problems arising from conflict, interdependence and order in an economically efficient way. I shall explain the term "economically efficient" later on. But one should realise that this cannot mean profit maximisation but rent from co-operation.

iv) Businesses are *systems of communication*. Lately, the importance of formal and informal communication as a factor in production and co-operation has increasingly been the subject of research in the economics of organisations.[11] For our topic it is basically of interest that businesses are poly-lingual systems.

Unlike the market, which must encode every event into prices to be able to communicate it, businesses must be capable of simultaneously or selectively evaluating and processing relevant events in many specific languages or codes - economics, technology, law, procedures, morals.

Economic encoding has of course been given a leading function in the economy. It is superior for decision-making since the market system structures the environment of the business. Everything of relevance within the enterprises of an economy has its economic importance or consequence. But not everything actually *is* economy in the context of business organisations.

Formulated on the basis of the economics of institutions it is not profits that are a maximisation goal of enterprises but profit is the incontestable restriction of the relevancy of all specific codes and rules in the enterprise. In other words, profit is a constraint.

The moral communication of the business neither structures its environment nor is it a constraint constituted by the market system. Nevertheless, we have attributed to it the status of a constraint via the poly-lingual nature of the organisation. Evidently it is important, when analysing constraints to

---

11 PICOT/REICHWALD/WIGAND (1996).

concentrate on the specificity of their mode of operation and efficiency. Economic Analysis usually refers to the informal and societal nature of moral rules.[12] To put it differently: they are positive externalities. For the New Economics of Institutions the resulting ambiguity of informal rules and the corresponding problems of enforcement are of interest here. In this way morality becomes a internal aspect of the economic problem. If a firm formulates its own 'code of ethics', it is trying to turn moral ambiguity in the atmosphere of transactions into a credible commitment. Its goal is to economise on transaction costs. Whether or not all team members subscribe to this code of ethics is a different question. A code of ethics is a code of a organisation and a constraint to both the organisation and its members.

In this context I should like to introduce another characteristic feature of moral coding into the discussion. The philosophical theory of 'speech acts' has demonstrated that moral communication is distinguished by its performatory character.[13] Whoever talks about morals, also makes a promise of performance. A business therefore commits itself through its moral communication and creates justified expectations of action. In the case of deception the consequence will not only be moral contempt of the collective agent, but also ensuing costs due to loss of reputation and motivation or even political intervention.

III. A Proposal to Define Institutional Business Ethics

The differentiation of the form of an enterprise into contractual and organisational relationships allows for a development of Business Ethics based on the characteristics of this form. In this case Business Ethics is neither an positive external corrective to the negative external effects of economic activities, nor an external enlightenment for economic doggedness and blindness. Nor temporary assistance in the case of incomplete contractual relationships. It is rather a constitutive element of the form itself and thus in *every* respect a part of the economic problem. In 'every respect' means that

---

12 E.g. NORTH (1990).
13 SEARLE (1969, 1979).

the integration of the moral factor into the economic and organisational context corresponds to its economic and organisational relevance.

I think we are now in a position to draw the consequences of the theoretical outline I have just developed for determining the tasks of Business Ethics within the economics of institutions.

First of all, let us note that Business Ethics does not focus on the ethical freedom of action under economic conditions. Actually it deals with constraints resulting from formal and informal rules and their communication. Looking at Business Ethics in this manner, we switch from a term related to action to a term related to institutions. Institutions understood as communicated limitations of action constitute the collective agent and endow it with explicit and implicit rules of the game for contractual and organisational relationships. Formulated to provide a useful definition this change of focus results in the following:

Analytically, Business Ethics studies those formal and informal rules constituting and controlling the moral way of acting of individual and collective agents in an enterprise, between enterprises, and between enterprises and society. In this respect Business Ethics compares differing institutional arrangements under the aspect of whether they signalise moral or immoral preferences and, if they do, which preferences they signalise. It is also interested in the corresponding incentives. Business Ethics explains the relevancy and change of moral and immoral preferences as a result of the incentive structure of formal and informal institutional arrangements of a given organisation and its social environment. That is the analytical aspect of *Business Ethics as a comparative science.*

To demonstrate the consequences of this theoretical disposition we return to our two examples from the construction industry. If we realise that corruption is not a single case in a branch but nearly a dominant feature of behaviour virtue ethics explains next to nothing. Except one would presume that entrepreneurs and managers of the construction industry have a peculiar genetic defect which constantly leads to opportunistic behaviour. But if we do not accept this as a reasonable assumption the crucial question is: What are the incentives in a given governance structure which reward unethical behaviour?

Normatively, Business Ethics suggests the development and implementation of such institutional arrangements (Ethics Management Systems, Ethics Audit Systems etc.) promoting the morality of the individual and collective economic agents and which endow this morality with certainty of expectation. The means towards these ends are economical and organisational rewards and performatory communication. In this case, rewards are not defined as maximisation of profits or income but as rents from economising co-operation.

In conclusion, Institutional Business Ethics deals with the analysis and the construction of morally sensitive governance structures for economic transactions. By no means does this perspective diminish the importance of moral standards or the virtues of individual agents and their development, quite the opposite: it makes their importance effective. Only virtues that can be practised are protected from erosion. That is precisely what this approach to Business Ethics is aiming at. Virtue ethics is inevitable to start a ethics program in a company. It is also inevitable to make it a living program. But to analyse the problems which lead to such an ethics program in order to create organisational structures to promote and encourage ethical behaviour virtue ethics is of little help.

References

ALCHIAN, A. A., DEMSETZ, H.: "Production, Information Costs and Economic Organisation", *American Economic Review*, 62 (5) (1972), pp. 777-795.

BARNARD, CH. I.: "Elementary Conditions of Business Morals", *California Management Review*, 1(1) (1958), pp. 1-13.

COMMONS, J. R.: *Institutional Economics. Its Place in Political Economy*, New Brunswick - London (Transaction) 1934, 1990.

DONALDSON, TH.: *Corporations and Morality*, Englewood Cliffs, NY (Prentice Hall) 1982.

ENDERLE, G.: "Zum Zusammenhang von Wirtschaftsethik, Unternehmensethik und Führungsethik", in: H. STEINMANN, A. LÖHR (Eds.): *Unternehmensethik*, Stuttgart (Poeschel) 1989, pp. 163-178.

FAMA, E. F.: "Agency Problems and the Theory of the Firm", *Journal of Political Economy*, 26 (1980), pp. 301-325.

GIFFORD, A.: "A Constitutional Interpretation of the Firm", *Public Choice*, 68 (1991), pp. 91-106.

AN INSTITUTIONAL APPROACH TO BUSINESS ETHICS

HART, O.: "An Economist's Perspective on the Theory of the Firm", in: O. E.
WILLIAMSON (Ed.): *Organisation Theory: From Chester Barnard to the Present
and Beyond*, Oxford (Oxford University Press) 1990.

JENSEN, M. C., MECKLING, W. H.: "Theory of the Firm: Managerial Behaviour,
Agency Cost and Ownership Structure", *Journal of Financial Economics*, 3(4)
(1976), pp. 305-360.

NORTH, D. C.: *Institutions, Institutional Change and Economic Performance*, Cambridge (Cambridge University Press) 1990.

PICOT, A., REICHWALD, R., WIGAND, R. T.: *Die grenzenlose Unternehmung*,
Wiesbaden (Gabler) 1996.

SCHMOLLER, G.: *Grundriß der Allgemeinen Volkswirtschaftslehre*, Leipzig (Duncker
& Humboldt) 1901 (Vol. 1, 4th ed.).

SOMBART, W.: *Der moderne Kapitalismus*, München (dtv-reprint) 1902-1927/1987
(Vol. 2, 1st ed.).

SEARLE, J. R.: *Speech Acts*, Cambridge (Cambridge University Press) 1969.

SEARLE, J. R.: *Expression and Meaning. Studies in the Theory of Speech Acts*,
Cambridge (Cambridge University Press) 1979.

VANBERG, V.: "Organisations as Constitutional Systems", *Constitutional Political
Economy*, 3(2) (1992), pp. 223-253.

WIELAND, J.: *Ökonomische Organisation, Allokation und Status*, Tübingen (Mohr
[Siebeck]) 1996.

WILLIAMSON, O. E.: *Markets and Hierarchies. Analysis and Antitrust Implications*,
New York (Free Press) 1975.

WILLIAMSON, O. E.: *The Institutions of Capitalism. Firm, Markets, Relational
Contradicting*, New York (Free Press) 1985.

WILLIAMSON, O. E.: "The Evolving Science of Organisation", *Journal of Institutional and Theoretical Economics*, 1499 (1) (1993), pp. 36-63.

List of Authors and Discussants

MARIE BOHATÁ is Professor at the Centre for Ethics in Economics and Business at CERGE-EI, Charles University and Academy of Sciences of the Czech Republic, Prague.

WARREN A. FRENCH is I. W. Cousins Professor of Business Ethics at the Department of Marketing, University of Georgia, Athens, USA.

ALAN HAMLIN is Professor of Economics at the Department of Economics, the University of Southampton, United Kingdom.

MATTHIAS KETTNER is a lecturer at the Department of Philosophy of the Johann-Wolfgang-Goethe University in Frankfurt and a fellow at the Cultural Studies Center of Nordrhein-Westfalen (Kulturwissenschaftliches Institut NRW), University of Essen, Germany.

STEFAN KIMMELL is Business Management Graduate of the University of Erlangen-Nürnberg, Germany.

PETER KOSLOWSKI is Director of the Centre for Ethical Economy and Business Culture, The Hannover Institute of Philosophical Research, Hannover, and Professor of Philosophy and Political Economy at the University of Witten/Herdecke, Germany.

HARTMUT KREIKEBAUM is Professor of Industrial Management at the Johann Wolfgang Goethe-University Frankfurt am Main, Germany.

LORENZO SACCONI is Director of the Centre for Ethics, Law and Economics and Professor of Business Ethics at the Libero Instituto Universitario Carlo Cattaneo, Castellanza (Varese), Italy.

ANDREAS GEORG SCHERER is Senior Lecturer at the Department of Management, University of Erlangen-Nürnberg, Germany.

ROBERT C. SOLOMON is Quincy Lee Centennial Professor of Business Ethics, Distinguished Teaching Professor at the Department of Philosophy, the University of Texas at Austin, USA.

HORST STEINMANN is Professor at the Department of Business Management and Entrepreneurship, University of Erlangen-Nürnberg, Germany.

PETER ULRICH is Professor at the Institute for Business Ethics, University of St. Gallen, Switzerland.

LIST OF AUTHORS AND DISCUSSANTS

JOSEF WIELAND is Director of Constance Institute of Ethics Management, Professor at the Faculty of Business and Social Studies, Constance Polytechnic University, Constance, Germany.

Index of Names

Page numbers in italics refer to quotations in footnotes or references

INDEX OF NAMES

Studies in Economic Ethics and Philosophy

P. Koslowski (Ed.)
Ethics in Economics, Business,
and Economic Policy
X, 178 pages. 1992
ISBN 3-540-55359-2 (out of print)

P. Koslowski and Y. Shionoya (Eds.)
The Good and the Economical:
Ethical Choices in Economics and Management
X, 202 pages. 1993
ISBN 3-540-57339-9 (out of print)

H. De Geer (Ed.)
Business Ethics in Progress?
IX, 124 pages. 1994
ISBN 3-540-57758-0

P. Koslowski (Ed.)
The Theory of Ethical Economy
in the Historical School
XI, 343 pages. 1995
ISBN 3-540-59070-6

A. Argandoña (Ed.)
The Ethical Dimension of Financial Institutions
and Markets
XI, 263 pages. 1995
ISBN 3-540-59209-1 (out of print)

G. K. Becker (Ed.)
Ethics in Business and Society
Chinese and Western Perspectives
VIII, 233 pages. 1996
ISBN 3-540-60773-0

P. Koslowski (Ed.)
Ethics of Capitalism and Critique
of Sociobiology. Two Essays with
a Comment by James M. Buchanan
IX, 142 pages. 1996
ISBN 3-540-61035-9

F. Neil Brady (Ed.)
Ethical Universals in International Business
X, 246 pages. 1996
ISBN 3-540-61588-1

P. Koslowski and A. Føllesdal (Eds.)
Restructuring the Welfare State
Theory and Reform of Social Policy
VIII, 402 pages. 1997
ISBN 3-540-62035-4 (out of print)

G. Erreygers and T. Vandevelde
Is Inheritance Legitimate?
Ethical and Economic Aspects
of Wealth Transfers
X, 236 pages. 1997
ISBN 3-540-62725-1

P. Koslowski (Ed.)
Business Ethics in East Central Europe
XII, 151 pages. 1997
ISBN 3-540-63367-7

P. Koslowski (Ed.)
Methodology of the Social Sciences, Ethics,
and Economics in the Newer Historical School
From Max Weber and Rickert
to Sombart and Rothacker
XII, 565 pages. 1997
ISBN 3-540-63458-4

A. Føllesdal and P. Koslowski (Eds.)
Democracy and the European Union
X, 309 pages. 1998
ISBN 3-540-63457-6

P. Koslowski (Ed.)
The Social Market Economy Theory
and Ethics of the Economic Order
XII, 360 pages. 1998
ISBN 3-540-64043-6

Amitai Etzioni
Essays in Socio-Economics
XII, 182 pages. 1999
ISBN 3-540-64466-0

P. Koslowski (Ed.)
Sociobiology and Bioeconomics
The Theory of Evolution in Biological
and Economic Theory
X, 341 pages. 1999
ISBN 3-540-65380-5

J. Kuçuradi (Ed.)
The Ethics of the Professions:
Medicine, Business, Media, Law
X, 172 pages. 1999
ISBN 3-540-65726-6

S. K. Chakraborty and S. R. Chatterjee (Eds.)
Applied Ethics in Management
Towards New Perspectives
X, 298 pages. 1999
ISBN 3-540-65726-6

P. Koslowski (Ed.)
The Theory of Capitalism in the German
Economic Tradition
Historism, Ordo-Liberalism, Critical Theory,
Solidarism
XII, 577 pages. 2000
ISBN 3-540-66674-5

Printing: Weihert-Druck GmbH, Darmstadt
Binding: Buchbinderei Schäffer, Grünstadt